CAREY

GENESIS OF THE SONG

a memoir

CARY WINGFIELD RADITZ

Copyright © 2023 by Cary Wingfield Raditz

ISBN: 978-1-62429-481-5

All rights reserved. No part of this book may be used or reproduced in any manner whatsoever without written permission except in the case of brief quotations contained in critical articles or reviews.

Published through Opus Self-Publishing Services
Located at:
Politics and Prose Bookstore
5015 Connecticut Ave. NW
Washington, D.C. 20008
www.politics-prose.com // (202) 364-1919

To Joan: my sweet, faithful, indulgent friend,
artist genius & soulful inspiration.

ACKNOWLEDGMENTS

With gratitude to my loving wife, Annie, who has put up with me for three decades. To all my family, teachers & friends who have shown up in my life and endured listening to these tales. And to TBennett, patient alpha reader without whom this book would have remained forever a desultory pile of disorganized drafts.

CAREY

GENESIS OF THE SONG

by Cary W Raditz, 1978

PROLOGUE

Removing the lid from the cardboard banker's box, I spread decades of stuff across my desk. Out came reams of old postcards and letters, notebooks, and photographs marking family history, including a tattered, century-old King James family bible with births and deaths. I sorted the material by date, and flipped the stack face down, oldest on top. As I turned over each photo, faded letter, or postcard—it was like turning over cards in a Tarot deck.

Decades melted away. On top, the first photo dated 1909 showed my mother as a baby in her father's arms in the back of a new Model T Ford. The past raced ahead to the present, pooling memories in my mind as I examined each document. Among photographs from the nineteen-seventies appeared images of Joni and me.

One faded photograph from Easter 1970 showed us seated side by side in a garden in Iraklion, Crete, smiling. I could recall the faint aroma of her perfume mingling with thyme branches hanging on the wall of our cave in Matala. In another, taken seven years later at the Renaissance Faire in California, I lean over Joni's shoulder photographing our reflection in an antique mirror with my vintage Pentax. In one more, in 1982, at a party in his Waverly Place studio, Dick Duane photographed Joni holding a hammer in her hand, laughing.

I opened a pocket notebook from 1971 and read:

Chapel Hill, Autumn of 1967: I was in love with Dylan Thomas & in love with my new girlfriend & with my brand-new art gallery, The Other Ear. I felt blessed, in love with life. Could a crystal ball have foretold that in three years I would live in Greece sharing a cave by the sea with Joni Mitchell?

PART I

Vows of Poverty

*You can never get enough of what
you don't need to make you happy.*
—Eric Hoffer

CHAPTER 1

The Other Ear

Six years before meeting Joni in Crete I entered the University of North Carolina as a freshman in fall of 1964. Like many freshmen entering universities, I was trying to figure out who I was and what I believed in. This existential crisis spurred a quest for a true identity—a search for authenticity. It also meant I needed to find my peer group, my cohort of like-minded buddies. At Chapel Hill, I saw at least four prevailing cultures—academia, sports, fraternities, and nonconformists. Although I didn't actually sit down with a legal pad and draw up a list of pros and cons, this is what it came down to. First I had to cross-off academia and sports. My scholastic performance in high school had been lackluster at best. Aside from wrestling in the tenth grade, I played no sports, nor did I follow sports.

With a few exceptions my high school friends were bound for fraternities. Fraternity life had earned UNC Chapel Hill high status nationally as a party school. Opting for a fraternity was almost a given in my home. My mother had been a Pi Beta Phi at Hollins, and my brother, Bobby, a Kappa Sigma at University of Virginia. I was well-prepared for partying, having established a solid reputation as a drunk in high school.

What about the community of "Beats?" In the late 1940's, Jack Kerouac had coined the term, "The Beat Generation," the subject of his first major novel, *On the Road*, that I had read avidly in the eighth grade. It had made a huge impression on me. I could see myself traveling from town to town, drinking in lowlife bars and hipster jazz clubs, and having wild, sexual adventures. I could get into that. Therefore, I found myself juxtaposed between two opposing lifestyles—fraternity life and the nonconformist and Beat subcultures. Should I cast my lot with these cool hipsters and anti-establishment dropouts living on farms and in ramshackle, group houses around Chapel Hill, or should I pledge a fraternity and live in a Georgian mansion with Corinthian columns and party until I dropped?

When I arrived on campus as a freshman, students were holding free-speech protests amidst the ivy-covered dormitories and classroom buildings. Only a year before, the North Carolina State Legislature passed the Speaker Ban, the "Act to Regulate Visiting Speakers," which prohibited communists—or suspected communists—from speaking in state colleges. This ban created an enormous uproar. Students considered this act a direct infringement of the First Amendment, and further, an attack on student protest itself. I read about it in *The Daily Tar Heel*, but I was diffident because I had no passion for the politics, and did not take part in any protests or demonstrations.

When the second semester of my freshman year began after Christmas and New Year's break of 1964—and contrary to my Beat lifestyle attraction—I veered in a conventional direction: I pledged Beta Theta Pi. So, instead of hanging out on farmhouse porches with Beats, drinking homebrew, and smoking dope, I spent Spring of my freshman year doing dip-shit chores for the fraternity upperclassmen, washing their cars, picking up their laundry in town, and bringing them cheeseburgers and milkshakes from the Goody Shop.

Fraternity activities overwhelmed my scholastic life. My spring 1965 grade point average tanked because I failed French and Algebra, which marked the nadir of my academic career. Because of my falling GPA, at the end of my freshman year I attended the first six-week summer school session, which opened my eyes to academic possibilities. Visiting history professors from Tulane taught graduate-level courses in colonial and antebellum history. I loved these courses and earned A's. But instead of enrolling in the second summer school session, I chose to sit it out on the sidelines, looking forward to a carefree end of summer at the beach with friends.

My father, however, had other ideas. He stepped in with what he thought was a more productive program than drinking beer at Myrtle Beach.

Dad figured if I was not in school I should be working. He found me a summer job with one of his clients, and thus I became an employee at M. Lowenstein in Rock Hill, South Carolina, purportedly the largest textile printing plant in the world under one roof. At dawn five days a week I drove twenty-five miles from Charlotte to Rock Hill to work in Lowenstein's "economy department," a backup pool of general workers that management sent off to various departments of the plant to fill in temporarily when regular employees failed to show up due to illness or drink. The giant textile printing plant was enormous, hot, loud, uncomfortable, and dangerous.

A typical day at M. Lowenstein saw me carting a ponderous roll of bare cloth three feet in diameter and weighing a quarter of a ton across winding, narrow lanes through the plant, an expanse of several football fields, to the print shop. From the print shop I transported equally huge rolls of printed cloth to processing departments far on the other side of the plant. I walked miles every day back and forth, back and forth across the boardwalks traversing the plant.

In the print room, my base camp, things were different from the rest of the plant. Skilled printers in the top echelon of the plant wore sport coats into work, then changed into white coveralls in the locker room. Printers spent their days snapping their eyes rapidly and repeatedly up and down, up and down, following the patterns of cloth streaming up from print rollers, to detect flaws in color and registration and adjust the print machine. During long apprenticeships, printers developed specialized eye-motor skills and possessed the concentration and endurance of athletes. Rapid eye movement was the only way to see the cloth clearly. If you looked straight on at cloth flying up, it appeared nothing more than a blur of patterns and colors. I could not ignore that most printers were missing fingers that had been squeezed off between heavy print rollers.

Carting cloth from one place to another in the plant, passing through other departments, I observed what went on. Bleach Department men worked around deep toxic pits in the concrete floor, which might have been steaming holes to Hell. Bleach rooms stayed about a hundred degrees Fahrenheit and about a hundred percent dripping humidity. Bleach workers had white, pasty, mottled skin and white hair like albinos. God knows what their average lifespan was. I picked up my pace when I passed through Bleach. Working in M. Lowenstein was slightly surreal, as if I had stepped onto the set of Fellini's *Satyricon*.

After six-weeks laboring in the bottom rung of the textile industry I learned my lesson—have fun but stay in school all year round. My sophomore year proceeded with ups and downs, bumps and grinds. In the spring I found a delightful love interest in an affectionate, local Chapel Hill girl. in April, when I collapsed with mononucleosis, and could not stay awake in class, dear old Dr. Morgan in the student medical facility, prescribed Dexamil. It kept me alert enough to achieve Deans List. From then on out, combinations of amphetamines continued to be my study companions until I graduated.

That summer I attended both summer school sessions. On hot afternoons, I devoured history and English literature, blissfully reading in the shade of giant poplar trees on campus, just as novelist Thomas Wolfe had done fifty years before.

When students returned in fall semester of 1966, few could deny that the world of our parents was unraveling. Free Speech protests at Berkeley, Freedom Marches in Mississippi, and opposition to the Vietnam War raced like wildfire through liberal colleges across the United States. UNC Chapel Hill, an established bastion of Southern liberal values, proved no exception. Across the student body the culture of campus life quickly began adapting to a new world view. "Alternative lifestyles"—as *Look Magazine* labeled it— fueled by marijuana and LSD, were beginning to crack open the mind of the South—whether it was ready for it or not.

During that year I quit going to the barber and grew a straggly beard. Although I continued to party hard at the Beta House, I began harboring regrets that I had not joined the informal community of Beats and freaks who lived in farms and forests surrounding Chapel Hill. My interest in modern fiction, and philosophy grew. I walked around with poems tucked into my pockets that I read over again and again during the day. I began to channel Dylan Thomas and the Romantic Poets—especially Shelley and Wordsworth—into my neuro-reactive system, memorizing long poems that stirred me deeply.

Fraternity brother Don Dickson called my attention to a student job offer posted on the main bulletin board in the Ackland Art museum. I applied for and got the job: Assistant to the Preparator at the Ackland Art Museum of the University of North Carolina at Chapel Hill. Working at Ackland with Don took me to an inflection point in my life.

The museum, conveniently situated directly across North Columbia Street from the Beta House, quickly became my haven. All I had to do was set down my can of beer in the Beta House living room, cross the street and punch the clock. The preparator's staff consisted of Robbie Nuremberg—the Preparator—Don Dickson, and me. Our responsibilities entailed installing and taking down shows and exhibitions—safely packing, unpacking, and moving art objects to storage, or for shipping.

Working at Ackland drew me into contact with the wider community outside the fraternity culture of Chapel Hill, non-conformists with whom I had begun to identify. I started meeting artists, craftsmen, professors, graduate students, published writers, musicians, freaks, and dopers—acid heads, peyote eaters, speed freaks and junkies—and especially, world travelers.

✳ ✳ ✳

After my junior-year term ended in May 1967, Scott Bradley, a Beta a year older than I, invited me to drive with him to take in Expo 67, the World's Fair in Montreal. Scott proposed we invade the domain of Henry Barrow, a mutual friend, who graduated from UNC in May with a degree in African Studies. Biding his time before leaving for a Peace Corps assignment in Malawi in the fall, Henry was caretaking a private estate in North Hatley, Quebec, a few miles from the University of Sherbrooke, and seventy miles east of

Montreal. It was a promise of adventure I could not turn down. I took a temporary summer leave from my job at Ackland Art Museum and set off to Quebec with Scott.

In his VW bus, Scott drove us from Chapel Hill to New York City, detouring through the Holland Tunnel across into the Lower East Side to place an order for an ounce of marijuana with a dealer Scott knew who later in the fall fell from—or was thrown out of—his fifth-floor apartment in East 2nd Street. Scott instructed the dealer to mail the weed to Canada, to the name of our host's oldest child.

A Connecticut native, Scott had been coming alone to Manhattan since he was a teen and knew his way around. He treated me to supper at Max's Kansas City on Park Avenue South where I had my first sangria. We continued up to Darien to pass the night in the home of his parents who were vacationing in Europe.

Next day we drove straight up to Dartmouth College to visit another Beta, John Sneed, affectionately known as "John Doe," in language training for Peace Corps in Upper Volta. From Vermont we crossed the border and drove to North Hatley, Quebec, taking us back, I thought, to an earlier century. Through the windows of the VW bus I watched farmers plowing fields with teams of horses. This was my first trip outside the United States; Quebec was francophone and I spoke hardly any French at all. I would have been surprised at the time to learn that ten years later I would be fluent in French, living in Paris.

We arrived in the lake-side town of North Hatley and followed Henry's directions to the house. Henry oversaw the property and cared for the children of our absent hosts while they were away in Europe for the summer. The house was a Victorian mansion, a large white wooden building among gardens perched above clipped lawns that swept down to docks on the shore of Lake Massawippi. A fancy wooden motorboat moored beside the dock. Across the wide lake from the dock lay North Hatley, where at night loud music pulsed from night clubs on the other shore. Their red, blue and yellow party lights glimmered across the lake.

Henry's principal duty was to care for the crew of five rambunctious Blankenship kids ranging in age from eight to sixteen, three girls and two boys. The oldest, Roxanne, owned an Austin Healey 3000 but because she had no driver's license yet, her parents forbade her to drive it. Henry did have permission and he drove it with great delight. To visit Expo 67, we crammed kids into Scott's van and into the Austin Healy and drove seventy miles west to Montreal. The fair was fabulous, especially the multimedia exhibitions, such as Marshall McLuhan's "Medium is the Message." I really felt like a little country boy introduced to a global wonderland.

It came as no shock that Scott invited two girlfriends *du jour* from Chapel Hill to visit him on the estate. When the two coeds arrived, lust afflicted Henry and me. We pitched affection to the ladies, but they summarily rebuffed our pleas for intimacy. After his love interests departed, Scott did too, leaving me with Henry, five kids, and the Austin Healey 3000.

Two days after Scott left, a notice came in the mail to Roxanne from Sherbrooke Post Office about twenty-five miles away stating they held a package for her. The notice listed the contents as an "air conditioner coil" from Ace Speed Company in Manhattan. Should we pick it up? How should we weigh the risk of being arrested for international smuggling against the pleasure of having good weed?

Later in life, I heard a brain development expert cite research indicating that the two lobes of the male brain do not unite until well into the twenties. Female brains, on the other hand, he noted, mature earlier in the teen years. Does brain morphology explain why young men take ridiculous risks? Had she been aware of this research, Roxanne, just turned sixteen, should have known better. She allowed Henry and me to persuade her that customs authorities would surely ignore a young schoolgirl picking up a small package with a household air conditioner coil. To make certain she looked like a child, we insisted she dress in her boarding school uniform: a white blouse, a plaid skirt, white knee socks and black Mary Jane shoes. We laughed over the wordplay: Mary Jane = marijuana.

The plan was simple: take Roxy to the post office to pick up the package, scoot back to North Hatley and get stoned. Henry drove, Roxy sat in front protecting her hair from the wind, and I crouched in the narrow back seat. We pulled up in front of the post office, which resembled the Department of Justice in Washington, DC, flights of stone steps flanked by Corinthian columns, and massive metal doors. Roxy got out and walked up the broad, stone steps.

From a bar across the street, Henry and I ordered beers and waited. We waited. We waited. We drank beer after anxious beer. *What happened to Roxanne?* Finally, through the bar's wide plate glass window, we spied Roxy stepping down the post office steps in her schoolgirl outfit, a small cardboard box swinging from her hand.

She entered the bar. "What happened, Roxy?" Henry demanded.

"They opened the package."

What! Henry and I freaked out. Hair-standing-on-end-freaking-out! We threw a wad of cash on the counter, grabbed Roxy, flew out the back door of the bar, and leapt into the Austin Healy. Blazing out of town like Bonnie and Clyde running from the Mounties, we blasted along back streets and rural gravel roads, skidding on dirt roads cutting through fields and forests.

Finally, the wild ride ended. The Austin Healy braked to a halt, resting in wheel-ruts in a muddy tractor path beside a corn field. We listened for sirens. Nothing but breeze rattling corn stalks.

We turned again to Roxy. "What happened?"

Quite casually, while Henry and I were still catching our breath, Roxy began her story.

"After you dropped me at the post office, I went inside. I entered a large room with a high ceiling with metal tables in the middle and along two sides, cashier counters with ornate iron grills, like cashier windows in an old bank. I approached the first window and showed the postal agent the post office receipt. He noted the number on the slip. 'Bring back a paid receipt,' he said, 'and retrieve your package,' pointing to a cashier window on the far side of the room, where I paid two dollars, Canadian, and the cashier stamped my receipt.

"When I walked back to the first window with the paid receipt to get the package, the first agent now stood at one of the zinc-topped tables with a package before him. He pulled out a pocketknife and cut it open."

"*What!*" cried Henry and I in unison. Panic returned.

"Yep. He cut open the shipping carton—this one here—and dumped a brown bank envelope on the table. He unwound the string on the envelope and a couple handfuls of green marijuana spilled on the table."

"*What!!!!*" I could feel my heart pounding.

"I'll tell you *What* if you give me a chance," said Roxy. "To tell you the truth, I was petrified. The customs agent stirred through the marijuana with his fingers, '… can't find any air conditioner coil or anything else in this package except for this packing material. The company must have neglected to send the coil,' and with his hand he swept most of the weed back into the box along with the empty bank envelope. Some of it went on the floor. 'Young lady,' he said to me, 'please take this receipt back to the cashier. We will refund what you paid. The post office does not charge you for what you didn't get,' he said, and canceled the receipt with a red ink stamp.

"As he instructed me, I took the red-marked receipt back to the lady at the cashier counter, and she gave me back my money. Then as I was leaving, the first agent called out to me, 'Young lady, do you want to take your package?' Thinking this might be a trick, I replied, 'No, Sir, not if it's empty.' He held out the package in his hand. 'Please take it with you. We have too much trash around here as it is.' I took it from him, left the post office, crossed the street to the bar, and … here we are. In a cornfield."

An utterly amazing and horrifying story—a tragic catastrophe barely averted. Henry and I looked at each other and shrugged. What just happened? Sherbrooke was a university town; how could a postal agent not know the packing material was marijuana? Inconceivable. By pure luck did Roxy encounter a hip customs agent, a "viper" himself? Henry fired up the Austin Healy, and we backed out of the cornfield in the direction of North Hatley—driving away much more slowly than we had driven in.

✳ ✳ ✳

Two weeks later Henry and I left North Hatley, but before we did, we water skied daily on Lake Massawippi, and we hit the music clubs and bars across the lake. Parting North Hatley, Henry drove the Austin Healy to Edenton, North Carolina, where the Blankenship family would return when summer ended. After that Henry was to leave for Peace Corps training in Malawi.

Back in Chapel Hill, major changes awaited me. In a storeroom in the Ackland Museum basement, Robbie convened a meeting with Don and me. He pitched the idea of opening a new art gallery and invited us to go in with him on the enterprise. We respected Robbie and agreed on the spot to join him.

Robbie found us suitable gallery space in three rooms at the top of a flight of wooden stairs at 133 ½ East Franklin Street across from the Varsity Theatre and the Carolina Grill. At the far end of the hall, David Honigmann's Chapel Hill Leather Shop occupied two rooms by the fire escape. Robbie, Don, and I debated pros and cons of names we could call the gallery. We settled on "The Other Ear Gallery," partly in homage to Vincent Van Gogh, and because the name suggested we were hearing the beat of a different drum.

Although I come from a family of artists on my father's side—my grandfather, Lazar Raditz, had excelled at the Pennsylvania Academy of Fine Arts in the early 1900s under the tutelage of William Merritt Chase and Edmund Tarbell to become a sought-after portrait painter in Philadelphia and New York—yet as a kid I had little interest in fine art. You might think my DNA would predispose me to art, but no evidence supported that notion. When WWII began, Dad had dropped out of engineering school at the University of Pennsylvania, enlisted in the Navy as an airplane mechanic, and was stationed at Camp Croft in Spartanburg, South Carolina. That is how he came to flee a well-off, respectable family in the arts in Philadelphia and marry my mother, Virginia Cleveland, a young widow, nine years his senior, a southern belle, and a DAR.

Mama taught drama, English and elocution in public high schools. She read me poems of Wordsworth, Keats, Tennyson, Matthew Arnold, Noyes,

Kipling, and plays of Oscar Wilde, Agatha Christie, and Tennessee Williams. Much later in life, it dawned on me that while Mama nurtured in me love of literature, I shared a similar frame of mind to my father's—that I had no real talent myself. But I did appreciate talent in others, and as I came to realize over the years, I did have talent for recognizing genius.

✳ ✳ ✳

My English major caught fire in a senior honors course in Modern Fiction when I read all of JD Salinger's short stories and novellas in one swoop of a week, a feat a fast reader can accomplish during a long holiday weekend. Salinger introduces the Glass family in *Nine Stories* and *Franny and Zooey*, and concludes the Glass saga with *Raise High the Roofbeam, Carpenters and Seymour: An Introduction*. The last one— *Seymour: An Introduction*—blew me away and possibly changed the neuro-molecular composition of my brain.

Buddy Glass narrates how his suicidal older brother, Seymour—a brilliant scholar, a full Columbia University professor at twenty years old, an emotional disaster from his WWII soldiering, but above it all, a spiritual savant—becomes his teacher in life and in death. Buddy relates how Seymour taught him the Zen way to play marbles. Seymour would haphazardly launch his shooter marble without aiming at the target marble. His marble would hop and twist, and with seemingly uncanny luck, strike the target marble, which to Seymour was not a big deal. When I read this in the overstuffed armchair by the Student Union fireplace, I lifted up my eyes, tilted back my head, and stared out the window. The Zen marble story sank in and profoundly cornered my attention as if the story harbored a revelatory truth.

Salinger, our professor told us, had studied Zen Buddhism, and Zen had inspired and shaped the character of Seymour Glass. He referred our class to Herrigel's book, *Zen in the Art of Archery*, from which Salinger presumably had drawn. Herrigel relates how the master Zen archer dissolves the dualist perception of here-and-there, uniting inner self and outward "reality." Archery, Herrigel implies, was to the skilled Zen archer not a martial art, but a meditative practice to achieve a transcendent experience of oneness. Archer, arrow, and target, one. Seymour, shooter-marble, and target-marble, one. Both pointed to this mystical experience. This meant something to me, and although I did not know what it meant, I was hooked.

At the same time when I was taking Modern Fiction, I enrolled in a course in Professor Shea's Philosophy of Art. This course turned out a bit more than I could chew. I struggled to understand the art criticism of Roger Fry and Clive Bell on "significant form." Heidegger's discourses on phenomenology left me befuddled, and *The Meaning of Meaning*, I. A. Richards's and C. K. Osborn's disquisition on language symbology, totally bewildered me. Step by step, however difficult this new ground, I began to understand that these writers and philosophers pointed to cultivating a state of consciousness of observing things directly—not getting lost in words, concepts, ideas and thinking. In class, I held up my hand, "Isn't this a bit like Zen?" I asked Professor Shea.

"Like Zen?" He pondered a moment, "Yes, like Zen …. Why yes, precisely like Zen Buddhism." I felt validated.

During this senior year it took an effort to balance my schoolwork with everything else that was going down. In late fall the Other Ear Gallery had a successful exhibition of the semi-psychedelic portraits of the Indian guru, Mehr Baba, by Lyn Ott, a semi-blind artist who painted portraits exclusively of Mehr Baba, who resided in Myrtle Beach. Scores of Mehr Baba devotees flocked to the show—"Baba-Heads," some called them—and the show sold out. Don and I were delighted, but harbored suspicions that Robbie had founded the gallery to give this show a Chapel Hill venue. Further, we learned that Robbie had no other well-known niche painters such as Lyn Ott queued up for exhibitions. Gallery activities slowed down. *Are we a one-trick dog?*

Aside from occasional walk-ins, mainly by artists and professors, the gallery sat dead during the day, but we had to stay open, and Don and I alternated looking after the business during the day when Robbie was working at the Museum. We hung paintings and showed sculptures by student artists—Robin Moyer set up an art object he had welded, a Nazi helmet with a stovepipe sticking up from the top. I cannot recall ever selling student art—but maybe Don or Robbie did because some of the artists were highly talented and becoming known, such as Ray Kass.

To keep from drifting into a coma of boredom I began drifting down instead to David Honigmann's Chapel Hill Leather Shop at the end of the hall. There I learned how to make sandals and use the Singer sewing machine.

David Honigmann, Chapel Hill Leather Shop. 1969. By Piper Honigmann

After winter turned to Spring, I moved into a group house with a girl I had known from high school, Julia DeLuca. The house was on Longview Street, six long blocks from the epicenter of Chapel Hill, the intersection of North Columbia and Franklin Streets. We nicknamed it the "Longview Country Club," because it became a destination for longhairs to listen to music, drink, smoke dope, hangout, and screw in the basement on second-hand couches, mattresses, and carpets. The party scene further detracted from my studies.

As I had taken two incompletes in the spring semester, I was unable to graduate with the rest of my 1968 class and needed to complete them. By typing the overdue term papers, Julia helped me immensely. Not long after, however, she fled town pissed-off about my string of infidelities. The straw that broke the proverbial camel's back was Julia coming home to discover me in the basement *in flagrante* with another lady.

Eventually turning in my term papers, I officially graduated from UNC. The Other Ear Gallery had no upcoming shows where we could make some money, nor any art students to sell art supplies to, and consequently, it went down the tube. We gave up the space at 133 ½ East Franklin Street. Left in a lurch I hung around aimlessly in Chapel Hill with townies smothering under the hot and humid Carolina summer, surviving by picking up casual gigs painting houses and working from time to time in the Chapel Hill Leather Shop. When I got paid, I treated myself to breakfast at the Carolina Coffee Shop, or lunch at Harry's, and beers at the Tempo Room. The Other Ear Gallery had served me in making the transition from frat-guy to hipster—putting me in the company of Chapel Hill artists to develop friendships that would last all my life: theater producer Kathy Fehl, artist Ray Kass, novelist Russell Banks, and others.

One day a redheaded girl came into the Chapel Hill Leathershop to get her sandals repaired. She had long strawberry blond hair, an angelic freckled face and wore a short dress showing the magnificent legs of a dancer or figure skater. While David Honigmann was replacing soles on her sandals, she waited, standing in the corner barefoot. She had perfect, round little toes. In a hair salon, stylists look first at hair; in a sandal shop, sandal makers look first at feet and legs. Everything about her was round, her toes, her limbs, her ass, her mouth, her eyes, her ears. Standing on tiptoes to look at the hair barrettes hanging on the wall by the workbench caused her calf muscles to flex delightfully. She was stunning. Shyness reined in the impulse to race up to her. I desired her intensely but lacked the courage to approach her, fearing I might be rejected or laughed at by someone so perfect. She inspected a display of leather bags, ignoring me staring at her twelve feet away, practically drooling, propping myself up against the far end of a long, stained work bench.

From his chair behind the work bench David raised his eyes and watched what was going on between me and his customer. He looked at me. He looked at her. He beckoned me over. I leaned in across the work bench as he quietly asked the obvious, "So, you want her?" My eyes popped open wide, and my lips parted. David handed me a flat-head cobbler's hammer. "You can have her now, you know. Do this. Go over and ask her what she likes about the hair barrettes. And while you listen—keep her talking—and looking her directly in the eye, stroke the hammer, and imagine you are caressing her body. When she notices you holding the hammer, keep talking—smile—and casually hand it to her. If she does not take it from you, she is uninterested. However, if she does take it, invite her to go swimming with us at Clearwater Lake this evening."

She took the hammer.

Amy and I swam naked in warm Clearwater Lake that night with others from the leather shop. We kissed floating in the lake. Naked, she took my hand and led me to the side of David's convertible. With her gaze, she measured the distance to the backseat, vaulted into it like a gymnast, flipped around, and taking hold of my wrists, pulled me into the backseat on top of her, wrapping those strong, round legs around me, clamping me to her wet, warm body. She was splendid.

Of course, I realized it wasn't magic in the hammer that caused success with Amy, but the ruse David concocted for me using the hammer as a prop. *Do the thing, and have the power*, as the old saying goes. From that day confidence began to replace my shyness and it became easier to approach strange women—and people in general—without shyness or pretense.

✳ ✳ ✳

Despite applying my newly discovered social-confidence, Chapel Hill began to wear on me. I needed someplace to go, something new to do, some rebirth of wonder. When my friend, Topper Schachte invited me to his wedding with Peggy Pringle in Charleston, I was all too ready. I threw a couple of things into my hucklebag, walked out to North Columbia Street and stuck out my thumb. At this point, a scruffy, indigent vagabond, I hitch-hiked down to Charleston to attend the Charleston society wedding.

Topper and Peggy assessed my disheveled appearance. In unkept hair and beard and wearing worn Salvation Army clothes, I was far too scruffy—they had to conclude—far too outrageous to attend the wedding, way beyond the pale for polite Charlestonian society. No tuxedo for Cary this time around, none of the fancy dress I had worn to Charleston debutante balls two years before. Topper and Peggy begged my forgiveness, and of course I understood, no apology required.

By inviting me to go shrimping with him, Baxter McLendon freed me from the embarrassment of not attending the wedding. I accepted his compassionate invitation to explore Lowcountry sporting adventures. In the maze of creeks not too far from Brunson he took me fishing and shrimping with a net across little freshwater streams. We feasted on fried bream, steamed shrimp, and blue crabs, and lots of beer.

For a day or two I stayed out at Isle of Palms with a former debutante girlfriend, Bennett, and Bennett's mother. Like many beach houses owned by Charlestonians in those days their beach house was one step above camping, more of a shack they nailed back together after hurricanes blew them apart unlike the hideous, new-money mansions that came to replace them. Bennett's ancient beach house had uneven floorboards, which creaked when you walked across the room, and it had screened sleeping porches. Decorum demanded that Bennett and I occupy different sleeping porches, but we slipped out at night into the dunes to make love among the sea oats, lying naked on a blanket under the stars. The next time I saw Bennett, six months later in Charleston, I was a crazy, flipped-out lunatic from Berkeley, and she was married to a French guy.

CHAPTER 2

Paspalum dilatatum

Summer of 1968 dragged on. In April, James Earl Ray had killed Martin Luther King in Memphis. Two months later, in Los Angeles, Sirhan assassinated Robert Kennedy. In the sticky, humid heat of Chapel Hill July the news made us feel awful, but events barely touched our dissipated lives.

After thunderstorms steam arose from Chapel Hill streets and it was so hot you could fry eggs on a car hood. I moved into a big rambling farmhouse down a dirt road off Airport Road, which Scott Bradley rented from an ex-Army Colonel named Jenkins. Aside from a few odd bucks I made occasionally painting houses, I had almost no cash. If not for yellow squash growing profusely everywhere in North Carolina I might have starved. It's a marvel I didn't turn yellow. During days when I wasn't painting houses I hung around the leather shop, and learned how to make "hucklebags"—shoulder bags named after one of Chapel Hill's notorious travelers to backwater frontiers of the Third World, Paul Hucksler.

Much of the time I hung out idly sitting on the wall in front of the Methodist church on Franklin Street with other indigents waiting for something to happen. Or I swam out in Clearwater Lake with Honigmann, drinking beer, smoking bad weed, and chasing local girls. One, the daughter of UNC's chancellor, had recently returned from student riots in Paris where she had been studying at the Sorbonne. At the lake, she stripped off her two-piece bathing suit. I marveled at her incredibly contrasted, two-toned tan from the beach, which made her dark, naked torso appear as if she was wearing a pale bikini with a dark patch between her thighs.

Then I met Deward and my life took a drastic turn.

One hot day I came upon friends clustered on the wall talking to a stranger. When he removed his gray railroad engineer's cap, his red hair fell to his thighs. Golly. When he unbraided his full red beard—turned under like a Sikh's beard—it curled to his lap so that he resembled Barbarossa, the pirate Red Beard. Speaking in the measured tones of an academic he introduced himself as Deward Hastings, from Berkeley, a scientist, printer, and chemist. Even among seasoned hipsters and freaks in Chapel Hill, Deward stood out like a light bulb in a dark cave.

Deward explained why he was in Chapel Hill. He removed a magazine from a leather satchel. "This is a 1906 Rutgers University agricultural journal." We circled him looking at each other quizzically. "Check out this article," he went on, turning the pages to a scholarly paper written about a wild plant found growing in eastern North Carolina.

"The name of this grass is *Paspalum dilatatum*,'" he read, tapping the page with his index finger. "This is it," pointing to a faded photograph of a plant that looked like an innocuous weed. "According to the article, *Paspalum* can be infected with an ergot fungus," he said, looking at us as if we should know what he was talking about. "This is where it gets good," he said, closing the magazine, "I think *Paspalum* fugus can be converted into lysergic acid—a principal ingredient of LSD." We knew what LSD was.

From Berkeley, Deward had driven cross-continent to Chapel Hill in his British racing green, vintage Morris Minor. The sub-compact provided Deward with all he needed on the road, a minimalist, transportation artform. He had removed the right passenger seat and replaced it with a narrow Japanese futon where he could crash during his expedition. In the space normally occupied by the two backseats, he stored a wooden crate with mechanic's tools, a US Army duffle bag of clothes, and essential provisions: a case of Galileo Italian Salami and a crate of Coca Cola.

Deward needed a place to stay in Chapel Hill besides his car. I found him an unlikely place a block away—my former bedroom in the Beta house. I introduced him to the few fraternity brothers hanging around between summer school sessions. They welcomed Deward and all seemed copasetic at the Beta House. Could my fraternity brothers have subconsciously recognized Deward as the harbinger of a new age, a new age that would soon engulf them from all sides, which would put an end to traditional fraternity life we had known?

Deward needed to get out in the field to collect specimens of infected *Paspalum* and mail these specimens in petri dishes to his laboratory in Berkeley. This was my chance. A recent university graduate and defunct art gallery owner with time on his hands, I gladly volunteered to guide Deward into the wilds of Carolina. Before heading off on the quest, Deward said he needed to consult a biologist specializing in wild grasses to confirm his *Paspalum* hypothesis. To that end we drove over from Chapel Hill to the agriculture school of NC State in Raleigh to find a qualified "grass man."

Using a Raleigh street map to find the ag school, we eased into an almost deserted parking lot next to a non-descript, brick university building. Wishing to downplay his eccentric appearance, Deward twisted his long, red hair under his railroad engineers cap, and braided his long, red beard, turning it under itself so it looked tidy. I crammed my curly hair up into a baseball cap Deward lent me.

We walked into the airconditioned building, which felt wonderful to us, and examined departments and teachers on a roster list thumb-tacked to a bulletin board in the front hall. We had no idea who the grass man was or if a grass man even existed on this campus. Deward clutched the briefcase carrying the agricultural journal in his hand, confident that if a grass man were here, we would track him down. We walked the halls. In a laboratory room he interrogated two student technicians in white lab coats working around a cluster of beakers. He explained our mission, pulling out the agricultural journal. Their expressions, like balloons over a cartoon character's head, told us clearly what they were thinking: *This is outside our pay grade. Who is this dude?*" The taller one motioned us out the door and pointed down the hall. "The last door on the right is the biology admin office. Maybe someone there can help you."

Deward understood it could be dangerous to divulge the goal of our research—to make LSD—if in fact *Paspalum* fungus was an ergotamine. A federal law passed only a year before classified LSD as a Class 1 Substance in the same illegal category as heroin. His Rip Van Winkle appearance did not fit the conventional image of a scientist at the University of North Carolina at Raleigh in 1968. To create a convincing pretext to explain why he was collecting this wild grass, Deward concocted a story, not far from the truth, that he was conducting commercial research to establish if *Paspalum* fungus had similar properties to ergot fungus in rye grass.

The receptionist in the admin office had no problem telling us the "Grass Man" was Professor Anderson, located in room twenty-four in the basement. We took an elevator down. At the end of the hall next to the green, neon-lit exit sign, we paused in front of room twenty-four, knocked, and heard, "Yes? Please come in," and we entered. Seated at a desk directly facing us, Dr. Anderson was reading a newspaper. He wore a faded blue buttoned-down shirt, sleeves rolled up to the elbow, and a large, steel watch on his left wrist. When we entered he checked us out, took off his watch, and placed it face up on the newspaper he had been reading. Lowering his spectacles on his nose, he inquired, "What can I do for you gentlemen?"

Deward carefully explained his hypothesis that ergot fungus in *Paspalum* had the same properties as infected rye that had killed millions in Europe during the Middle Ages.

Again, Dr. Anderson, "Ok. I understand. But how can I help you?"

"The problem is," Deward began, "we don't know precisely what *Paspalum dilatatum* looks like in the field. The actual living plant, that is." Deward opened his briefcase on a chair and pulled out the old agricultural journal and thumbed it open to the article about *Paspalum* in North Carolina. He passed the magazine over to Dr. Anderson. "This is what we have to go on."

Dr. Anderson glanced over the abstract and returned the journal to Deward. Looking up at us, he said, "Please follow me." He stood up, walked around his desk, and opened the door of his office. Without further words, he beckoned us to follow him, which we did. He opened the exit door, and we walked out into the back of the parking lot. *Was he kicking us out? Had he figured out what we were up to?* Dr. Anderson propped the door open with a brick. Ten feet away sat a large, green trash dumpster in a patch of overgrown weeds and bits of trash not far from where Deward parked his car. Dr. Anderson walked over to the dumpster. He bent over, pulled up a clump of weeds from the ground, and handed it to Deward. "*Paspalum*," was all he said. He turned, kicked the brick away from the door, and reentered the building. The door closed behind him.

Deward shrugged, looked down at the bouquet of *Paspalum*, and said, "Whoa!" Pointing to the flowering end of the grass, he sucked in his breath, "Look at this! Completely infected with a fungus. This is it!" We climbed back into the Morris Minor and zipped off. So ended the identification stage of *Mission Paspalum*.

During the next week Deward and I drove in a loop from Chapel Hill to Pinehurst, through Wilmington to Rocky Mount, to Winston-Salem to Charlotte and back. Deward wanted fifty samples, which we found over four days. *Paspalum* grew abundantly on the shoulders of roads in North Carolina and for the most part, all of it was infected with the fungus. From rural post offices across piedmont North Carolina Deward mailed specimens to his Berkeley post office box.

Collection stage of Mission *Paspalum* accomplished, Deward invited me to return with him to Berkeley. "What the hell," I surmised, "nothing for me here."

"Sure, Deward." *I am ready to go.*

✳   ✳   ✳

Leaving Chapel Hill we drove up the East Coast, staying one night in Vermont with the mother of Katherine, a friend of Deward's from Berkeley. We drove across the border to Canada the next day. When we got to Montreal we had no place to stay. We ended up crashing in sleeping bags on the floor of a group house with Quebecois freaks we met on the street in old town. In the days of the late '60s, longhairs often took in freak strangers as if they were members of the same endangered tribe.

A day later, driving through conifer forests of Ontario, the radiator sprang a leak and Deward pulled over to the shoulder to fix it. I stood by and watched him take a large, metal box of tools from the back of the car. He removed the radiator and propped it up on a large rock. I also sat on a rock and saw him bring out a propane torch and solder the leak in the radiator. "Hopefully," said Deward, "this will work until we find a decent garage." It did.

In Calgary, a foreign car garage replaced the radiator to Deward's satisfaction. From Vancouver we crossed the border into Washington State, and drove south.

As we cruised into Berkeley from Richmond and Albany, I noticed something familiar beside the road. "Pull over, Deward!" I jumped out and jerked up a handful of weeds and thrust it towards him. "*Paspalum!*" we both said in unison. Big, robust California *Paspalum* infected with gray, ergot fungus. Six thousand miles to find the thing you seek turns up in your own back yard.

CHAPTER 3

San Francisco Bay Blues

Two blocks south of Ashby, and one block east of Shattuck, the Carolina poor boy finds a new home—2136 Essex Street, Berkeley, California. I moved in with Deward and his partner Jenny—AKA, his "old lady," as freaks called their wives and girlfriends in those days—and her two small children, Ernest and Helen. Behind the simple two-story cottage, a six-foot redwood fence separated the small garden from the neighbors, and in this garden sat a little wooden garden-shed no bigger than eight by ten feet, into which I moved my backpack containing all my belongings.

Deward provided me with an Army bedroll of WWI vintage as a mattress, and a couple of blankets. This was fine for me; I would be warm and dry. Wooden steps led up from the garden to a landing just off the kitchen of the house. Standing on the landing one morning shortly after I arrived, I looked over the fence into the neighbor's garden and watched a bearded man practice Tai Chi with skill and grace. I had never seen Tai Chi performed before. And it was only one of myriads of new experiences this young freak from North Carolina would encounter in San Francisco and Berkeley, the epicenter of the cultural revolution. I felt uplifted to be part of this transformational change that had started in California decades ago but only recently crashed into the consciousness of the American public—and me.

✳   ✳   ✳

Deward's conversion of *Paspalum*-to-LSD experiment failed. After an independent lab conducted analysis on the samples, Deward was forced to confront the results—this was not a fungus that could be converted into lysergic acid. Disappointing outcomes meant the project did not warrant further biochemical tests. Deward was only mildly annoyed because he had suspected his hypothesis was weak from the very beginning. Although his vision to turn *Paspalum* fungus into LSD proved unsuccessful, it had inspired an adventure to the East Coast where he had never been before.

Deward had other projects in the pipeline in various stages of implementation. Principal among these was an underground printing business, pumping out brochures and pamphlets on a cast-iron printing press. His clients consisted of community action groups, anti-Vietnam War protesters, and even the Black Panther Party, which kept an office on Shattuck Avenue, a block away from his home. From the printing press in his basement flowed inflammatory revolutionary treatises, posters of concerts, as well as notices by food cooperatives, searches for lost dogs, this and that.

Once settled in Berkeley, I observed that Deward surrounded himself with interesting people of all calibers: community organizers, musicians, scientists, engineers, yogis, and mechanics. His lucid, encyclopedic mind attracted intellectuals. His ability to plan and implement strategies enabled people to execute their projects. His long red hair and beard alone made him physically unforgettable, and his many accomplishments and skills were renowned, even by Berkeley's highly unconventional—and lunatic—standards.

Almost daily I went over to North Berkeley with Deward. I usually smoked a joint in his workshop and walked around Berkeley to explore new territory. I enjoyed getting high and sitting in the campus eucalyptus grove reading D.T. Suzuki's book, *Zen Buddhism,* which perplexed and fascinated me, especially disquisitions on esoteric states of consciousness.

Walking back to Dewards from the eucalyptus grove one day I turned on to Telegraph Avenue a block past Sproul Plaza. A poster stapled to a bulletin board outside of Shakespeare & Co. Bookstore on Telegraph Avenue announced: *The Golden Toad, A Band of Minstrels Playing Ancient and Traditional music.* The band was performing that afternoon in Live Oak Park in North Berkeley. It took me about thirty minutes to walk up Walnut Street to the park. As I approached I heard singing, drums, cymbals, horns, and bagpipes. I sat down on the grass slope above the performance area to watch. Musicians and dancers of Golden Toad attired in Renaissance robes and ritual masks performed free-form, hypnotic dances while streaming colored silk banners. Between me and the dancers sat a hundred or more people on blankets and oriental carpets. Two people stuck out. One was a young blond woman sitting cross-legged, relaxed but remarkably erect like a stalk of celery, as the metaphor came to me. The other person was a young man sitting in a lotus position, shirtless, who folded his torso over his crossed legs to place his chest and forehead on the grass with his hands clasped behind his back and arms raised above his head. *Yes! This is yoga*, I remarked to myself, *I want to be able to do these yoga poses, too.* My wish came to pass. A half-century later I was teaching yoga in Nairobi, and remembering this Golden Toad performance in Live Oak Park, I sent *Metta* retroactively to Live Oak Park to the blond girl with the straight posture, and to the young yogi in a bound lotus asana.

Friends of Deward and Jenny found me odd jobs in neighborhood construction and remodeling projects, mainly painting houses. Ron, a small-business contractor, hired me on a crew to paint interiors of Victorian houses in Berkeley.

Mornings, we carried our tools and materials into the house: canvas drop cloths, step ladders, scaffolding, cans of paints, masking tape, buckets with brushes, rollers, cleaning equipment, and solvents. Ron taught me how to paint properly. To be competitive he took on tough deadlines. Often we worked long hours, sometimes all night. To keep us awake and active he distributed amphetamines to the crew. Using a wine bottle as a rolling-pin we crushed Dexedrine spansules into powder between pages of slick newspaper, and snorted lines with a cut straw. At dawn, after having frenetically painted all night, bleary eyed and wired to the gills, I would walk over to the Berkeley Co-op grocery store on the southeast corner of Telegraph Avenue and Ashby to buy donuts and coffee for the crew.

Ron was of Japanese descent and like Deward's, his long hair reached his belt. Whereas Deward's hair was ginger-red, Ron's hair was black, and fell from the nape of his neck in a neat ponytail. Drooping from his upper lip, a thin black Fu Manchu mustache met a wispy, pointed Van Dyke beard. Also like Deward, Ron was practical—an articulate intellectual whose hipster appearance confounded those who did not know him personally. I enjoyed watching Deward and Ron debate esoteric subjects. Both were honest and entrepreneurial. Ron kept us working and paid us on time.

Scott Bradley in Chapel Hill rang me at Deward's to tell me he had just spoken to John Whisnant, a mutual friend from our UNC days now living in Berkeley. I rang John and he invited me over. When I arrived at his house on Ellsworth Street, he was sitting on a swing on his front porch reading. The house was enormous, a brightly painted Victorian bristling with all sorts of rococo sawn-wooden ornamentation similar to houses I had been painting with Ron's crew. John had painted all the details in a full palette of bright colors.

An architecture student at Berkeley, John immediately launched into a detailed description of the historic house and its most salient features, and how he had become a student landlord. "About 1885, a sea captain built this house in the distinctive Queen Anne style you see in the magnificent homes in Pacific Heights across the Bay. Notice how the steep roof steps down to the conical corner tower. Those rooms are mine"—he pointed up to a large stained glass dormer window. "My tenants paint the house in lieu of part of our rent. The owner considers it an art object." And he added, "It truly is." I could imagine myself on Ron's crew hanging off scaffolding painting millions of window mullions and grilles with a small artist's sable paint brush.

On the fancy, black, wrought iron fence out front, a sign hung, which looked like a Filmore Ballroom art nouveau poster, advertising, "Seeking Foxy Ladies For Renters."

"I got to hear more about this," I said, touching the sign with my hand.

"Let's go inside, Cary. I'll tell you all about this LLC I set up with my partner David. It's legal name is *Broken Homes and Substandard Housing* ... "

In Berkeley weeks went by on Ron's crew painting the interiors of houses like John's, reading, hanging in Essex Street with Deward and Jenny, listening to their high-fidelity radio tuned to community rock stations like KSAN in San Francisco, KPFA, and especially KMPX, which played psychedelic bands of the Filmore and Avalon Ballrooms, the California sound, Santana, Canned Heat, Blue Cheer, Iron Butterfly, Sly and the Family Stone and others. Radio stations aired the newest releases of albums and songs, the Beatles' *White Album*, Janis *Joplin's Cheap Thrills*, Buffalo Springfield's song, "Broken Arrow," and Judy Collins' cover of "Both Sides Now." Walls and telephone poles around the Bay Area displayed posters announcing concerts at the Ballrooms—fantastically creative, psychedelic, mind-blowing art forms.

Across the Bay Bridge from Berkeley, San Francisco's hills and commercial buildings dominated the jagged skyscape. Between painting jobs I hitchhiked over to San Francisco to visit Al Stoneman and his wife, Mary, in the Madison Hotel on the corner of 3rd and Harrison under the overpass that led to the Bay Bridge.

In Chapel Hill Al Stoneman's family had founded Stoneman's clothing store on Franklin Street—a preppy icon—that came into its heyday in the fifties and early sixties when undergraduates still wore Brooks Brothers and Jack Wood Ltd. tweed jackets to class. Around town, Al Stoneman had been a wild, impetuous drug athlete. Several times I saw him stagger into the hallway of the Other Ear Gallery and the Leather Shop completely stoned out of his gourd, bragging he had taken a quadrillion microgram of LSD or had been up for days on speed. Every time Al came up to 133 ½ East Franklin Street, he was high on something or another as if he were challenging his capability to function as a human being when stoned. I never really dug his behavior.

Al was never more than an acquaintance until I got to Berkeley, when Paul Davis, infamous Chapel Hill Leather Shop sandal maker, took me over to the Madison Hotel and reconnected me with Al, who in turn, introduced me to his charming wife, Mary. By then Al had married and mellowed and I had broadened my social perspectives.

The Madison Hotel was one of scores of SROs—a single-room occupancy hotels—that dotted the Tenderloin and South of Market region, San Francisco's skid row. Some of the hotel's inhabitants were real, down-on-their-luck, burned-out winos, prostitutes, destitutes and addicts living on welfare. Others not so down and out also chose to live there. At night, hotel residents and their friends congregated in the hotel's halls and bedrooms—often with doors wide open—smoking dope, drinking wine, sharing bread and cheese and pizza and munchies, and roamed between rooms in a sort of free-form party house. With Al and Mary's room as my San Francisco base station, I launched explorations into the city's many neighborhoods on foot, trolly, cable car, and bus.

The *demon*-ology of the hotel's occupants constantly changed, replenished by varieties of winos, crazies, freaks, misfits, musicians, artists and writers, petty drug dealers, prostitutes, palm and tarot card readers, and various ne'er-do-well street criminals. They thrived in San Francisco's anti-establishment culture fueled by drugs, drug money, blues and rock and roll, funding their aberrant lifestyle with welfare checks, food stamps, and casual work in the underground economy. What a place, The Madison. One of the inhabitants, Dick Kermode, a professional clarinet player, later joined Janis Joplin in her post-Big Brother band as a keyboard player. Among the residents, I also found Diana.

I jotted down in my notebook: "Diana has red hair and as far as I know, no source of income other than food stamps and welfare checks. Evidently, she values her freedom more than the empty pleasure of owning things, things she could buy if she wanted to buckle-down and work. Diana is certainly bright, congenial, and intelligent—valued assets in the business world—but chooses to live on welfare rather than work at a day job. I know almost nothing about her background and how she came to live at the Madison. Interesting lady, Diana."

Diana was good company and easy to be with. I slept with her from time to time. She had a pure redhead's body, white and slightly freckled, with pink nipples and a pink pussy nestled in a patch of strawberry-blond curls. I adored the way she looked, the sweet, musky way she smelled and tasted, a particular scent, which I noticed in other ginger girls. Peaches mostly taste distinctly like peaches; red heads distinctly taste like redheads, at least in my limited research.

One of Diana's friends, Nancy, worked as a secretary at the Japanese consulate. In a conservative grey business suit and black heels she walked in to visit Diana one evening, and stood out distinctly among us. I was immediately drawn to Nancy, and with an enthusiastic grin, impetuously said, "I want to sleep with you." Smiling, Nancy accepted my frank proposal. Arm in arm, we took the N Juda bus to her place.

Nancy lived on the second floor of an apartment building on the Great Highway next to the Bay, a few blocks north of Golden Gate Park. Her door opened off a common balcony facing the Marin Headlands, which gave me respite from the stuffy confines of Al and Mary's hotel room and my garden shed in Berkeley.

In my notebook I wrote: "Nancy is a cross-cultural thrill-seeker, an enigma—she looks the part of a conservative but has a taste for the underbelly of San Francisco. She cultivates friendships among hotel residents without embracing their criminal ways or revolutionary worldviews, but enjoys peeking into the street world of drugs, wild schemes, and dubious deals. I can picture her as an escort to San Francisco's Pacific Heights aristocracy, but here she is, South of Market, among lowlifes at the Madison Hotel, dredging her social life from the bottom of the city's fish tank."

After Nancy left for work in the morning, I would either thumb back to Berkeley, or head over to 3rd and Harrison to hang out with Al and Mary. If Diana was in her room I would climb in bed with her. Had I been more persuasive I could have coaxed Diana and Nancy into a three-some, but as it was, I was reluctant to pitch it to them—no use risking good friendships for a fleeting sexual adventure. They had no jealousy problem sharing me and I doubted I was special, probably only one guy among many lovers. It didn't bother me in the least.

Al Stoneman entertained myriad business schemes. He enlisted me to join Mary and him to sell the *Berkeley Bard* newspaper in San Francisco's financial district down on Montgomery Street. Al, Mary, and I picked up bundles of *Berkeley Barbs* at dawn, split up what we carried, and took up stations on strategic street corners. Occasionally, we would rob bundles of *San Francisco Chronicles,* which legitimate newspaper dealers had not yet picked up. "Buy the *Berkeley Barb*!" we shouted to get the attention of the breakfast and lunch crowds, or "Buy the *Chronical*" for the news stand price. Keep yelling, "Barb the Berkeley Buy!" Stand out. Be loud. Sell papers. "Berkeley the Buy Bard" and other nonsense phrases to raise a smile and coax a purchase. That was the idea.

At the time it would have been unimaginable to consider that four decades later I would be one of the suits—a Chartered Financial Analyst— entering the doors of a prestigious office building on Montgomery Street to lunch in the private club of a director of a multinational bank.

But in San Francisco in 1968, in no way did I resemble an international banker and I was selling newspapers instead of institutional investment services. I wore high-waisted WWII navy bellbottomed trousers from an Army and Navy Store over black English riding boots, a red and black checked wool lumberjack shirt over a t-shirt, and to top it off, a Stars and Stripes bandana. My hair was long and curly, worn in a droopy Afro. Mary generally wore homemade skirts and blouses fashioned from what she collected from second-hand stores. She secured her long, brown hair with a beaded headband. Al usually wore a tattered, olive drab US Army jacket and jeans patched at the knees.

After the financial district lunch crowd cleared, we had pretty well sold out our papers. The proceeds covered our nut, and earned us enough to eat, buy weed on Polk Street and go to a Filmore Ballroom concert. In the afternoons, we dumped whatever papers we had left, and walked up Montgomery Street into Chinatown for a late lunch of noodles, rice and sautéed vegetables. Supper was often brown rice at the hotel or chili dogs from a Doggy Diner, which had a big orange plastic dachshund statue on the roof.

Most nights pugnacious Bill Graham stood guard at the front door of the Fillmore Ballroom, greeting friends, and barring those he didn't like, while studying the incoming audience for celebrities and potential troublemakers. One night at the Filmore we saw Canned Heat open to the Grateful Dead. Al led Mary and me on a twisting line-dance, coiling between bodies seated on the ballroom floor until we were right next to the stage. He artfully intercepted a fat joint that was passing around hand to hand and shared it with us. Mary had slipped a quart of Red Mountain Wine under her dress to make sure we were well lubricated. Weed, wine, loud music, swaying shuffling dancing hippy girls wearing beads and feathers, smoke, stumbling, did me in ... and so fucked up, I even slept on the hardwood floor through the hypnotic Grateful Dead performance that night.

When not hanging out in Berkeley or painting houses I explored San Francisco. I drank cappuccinos at Vesuvius Café in North Beach, browsed the shelves at City Lights Bookstore, and walked through the Haight into Golden Gate Park. In those days San Francisco buses and cable cars cost 15 cents a ride, with two transfers. It was easy and cheap to get anywhere in San Francisco.

Nancy and Diana kept me company in San Francisco, but I didn't have a steady girlfriend in Berkeley, although I did get laid from time to time by sheer luck. One day with house-painting earnings, I went shopping for hiking boots. At a shoe store on Telegraph Avenue a dark-haired girl named Amy waited on me. When she bent over to extract a shoebox from a low shelf, I could not ignore the enticing contours of her magnificent caboose. When five o'clock came I met her and we walked back together to Essex Street, out to my garden shed. A few days later when I visited Amy in her apartment, which happened to be directly above the shoe store, I met her roommate, an attractive lady breastfeeding an infant. Amy made me coffee. When I asked for cream, her roommate opened her blouse and proceeded to squeeze breastmilk into my coffee cup.

✳ ✳ ✳

Friends from Chapel Hill arrived: Paul, the sandal maker, and Stanley, a small-time thief, along with George, from Charlotte. George had serious photography projects on his agenda and needed a place near the Haight where he could install his darkroom. He leased a spacious apartment on steeply sloped Willard Street near Parnassus, a few blocks west of Golden Gate Park. Paul and Stan moved in with him as non-paying roommates. I began hanging out with them and their freak friends, and when stoned, I dug through piles of *Zap Comic Books,* assorted issues of *Doctor Strange,* and other Marvel Action comics.

Everyone in the house was shooting speed except George and me. Paul and Stan were druggies, fond of heroin and methedrine, not addicted, but "chipping" as they say. But mostly we smoked weed and drank Red Mountain jug wine, reclining on carpets and cushions to read and listen to music. I didn't realize it at the time, but my association with Stanley and Paul was leading me on a dangerous path into a criminal subculture.

Once I asked Paul to hit me with meth. As the spike went in my vein, I got scared. "Paul, pull it out." He got pissed. Rather than waste a shot, he withdrew the needle from my arm, recooked the contents of the dropper in a spoon, and did it up himself. Sharing needles as we did, how did we escape death from hepatitis? Some of us didn't, and some of us lived with it for years. I tested positive for hepatitis C three decades later. *But that's another story.*

One night Paul led the household to a Japanese sushi restaurant in the Fillmore District. The only gaijin in the place, we sat on stools at the counter across from the sushi chefs. The menu had no English on it nor did any of the pictures of sushi on the banner that hung across the kitchen wall. This was the first sushi I'd ever had, except for bream I had caught and eaten raw from Carolina ponds when I was a farm kid, without rice, tamari, and wasabi.

Another day we crowded into an old Ford station wagon and drove up through Marin to the Point Reyes seashore. We built a fire on the beach with driftwood, and took what was said to be mescalin, and spent the night stoned telling stories as waves lapped up on the stony beach. I got stoned but didn't have a psychedelic experience so maybe it had been bogus mescaline. A lot of bogus drugs were sold on the street. You never really knew what you were getting unless you got it from a reliable source, and we were far removed from reliable dealers. We lived as drifters, urban hunter-gatherers, pleasure seeking freaks without clear goals other than to get stoned day to day, week by week. But for me, my days of vagrant-drifter were going to change cataclysmically.

※   ※   ※

1968 was an election year. Political activists put on events all around the Bay Area. Before the election Yippies Jerry Rubin and Abbie Hoffman held a Youth International Party rally in Golden Gate Park on a blue-sky day—music, crowds, militant speeches, and Black Panthers. Yippies were running a pig for president named *Pigasus, The Immortal*. Paul, George, and I pushed our way close to the stage. Face painted mime-white under a wild Afro, Abbie Hoffman ranted to the crowd, while beside him, Jerry Rubin stood whacked out on stage by the podium, next to Pigasus, obviously out of his mind, a war-party-painted face, eyes staring inwardly. We were all, each in his own way, immersed in the hippy fantasies of a new world order, stoned out, dreaming of utopia, and like Jerry Rubin, staring into space.

CHAPTER 4

Arising & Passing Away

From her balcony, intimately holding hands, Nancy and I surveyed a sweeping view from the western tip of the Headlands of Marin to the northern expanse of the Golden Gate Bridge. An avalanche of Pacific fog mounted the Headlands and rolled eastward across the bridge and into the Bay. Long whips of kelp strewed across the beach where we took long walks up to the Cliff House and back. On the nights when we slept together at her place, and when I came to know her better, I understood more fully the scope of the controversial two lives she straddled, working in a prestigious foreign consulate during the day, and at night, hanging with musicians, freaks and drug addicts in welfare hotels.

On weekday mornings Nancy walked up the Great Highway to the N Judah streetcar stop clothed in conservative business attire and heels and rode the streetcar all the way across San Francisco to the Japanese Consulate near the Embarcadero. She explained to me that convenience and privacy compelled her to establish physical distance from both diplomats and lowlifes. Nancy spoke fluent Japanese. I appreciated her expertise in finding a perfect job where her Japanese was a huge asset. In the parlance of her lowlife friends, "This chick has got it all together." As for me, the critical capacity to recognize talent had not yet dawned in me, although mysteriously, I was drawn like a magnet to extraordinary people like Nancy.

After she left for work, I got up, drank coffee she left for me, showered, and dressed. I continued to read Suzuki's *Zen Buddhism* or listened to music on her reel-to-reel. When it neared noon, I took the N Judah into the city. I usually thumbed back to Berkeley if I had work painting houses or hung out in San Francisco at the Madison with Al and Mary, or with George, Paul and Stan by Golden Gate Park, or went back to the Great Highway to keep company with Nancy.

On a Friday in late October, following several days of wine, dope and snorting speed with Paul and Stan, I was simultaneously edgy and fatigued. Nancy had given me a key to her apartment where I took refuge. When she came home from work, she changed clothes, and we took a stroll on the beach. We had seen an ad in the newspaper announcing that Chet Helms and the Family Dog were throwing a special Halloween bash at the Avalon Ballroom, featuring the Velvet Underground. Even though the Velvet Underground had played the Avalon two weeks earlier, Chet had snagged them again for a Halloween party. Even though Nancy was tired, and I was wired, we thought this would be an event too special to miss. The Velvet Underground in San Francisco on Halloween!

The N Judah carried Nancy and me into San Francisco and we walked up to the Avalon Ballroom at Sutter Street and Van Ness. In the streetcar coming in Nancy and I dropped blotter acid Al had laid on me days before. We stood in the queue at the door among those in full Halloween garb. Of course! We should have realized; we were in street clothes, underdressed for the event. We paid at the window, got our hands stamped, walked in, and elbowed our way through the costumed throng onto the ballroom floor. The air was festive.

Charlie Musselwhite and his band opened the evening. His harmonica and Chicago blues put the crowd in a groove, people clapped and hooted. The lights came up, the Musselwhite band exited the stage, and the lights dimmed again. Lou Reed mounted the stage with the Velvet Underground. Stage lights focused on them, dressed in black, faces painted stark white. Wow. Spooky. The acid started coming on. Nancy got nervous; I could read anxiety in her face. "I have an appointment tomorrow," she pleaded, "I have to go to bed." A feeble excuse as tomorrow was Saturday. She was scared.

OK, I was getting high, too, but it wasn't a full-blown acid trip, yet. *Maybe I'm still hungover from the speed I've been doing for days.* We left the

Avalon early after the Underground's first set—they played the New York themes—"Heroin," and "I'm Waiting for the Man." In our streetcar on the way back, freak Halloween revelers in full costume, faces painted white or in color, danced in the aisles and sang. I became unnerved as their bodies and faces contorted and pulsed in neon tones—smiles became sneers, sneers became fanged snarls—a ghoulish apparition. Nancy clung closely to me.

Descending from the streetcar at the N Judah stop, we walked down to her place. Nancy was clearly rattled. She immediately retired into the bedroom to try to sleep off the acid. Left to myself, I smoked some weed in a wine-filled water pipe and drank some of the foul liquid in the bowl. Bad idea. Naked, I was sitting cross-legged on her couch in a full lotus position—a yoga asana I had never assumed before. On her high-fidelity reel-to-reel I was listening to Steppenwolf, "… take my hand if you don't know where you're going/ I'll understand, I've lost the way myself …."

Seated immobile, head hanging over, staring down at the blue and red Persian carpet, I became fixated on its intricate design pattern. My eyes became zoom lenses and locked on to the carpet pattern that completely eclipsed my vision, and the geometric pattern began to pulse and glow with what seemed to be supernatural luminescence. Instantly, the perspective changed. I was looking into an all-absorbing inner space that converged foreground and background. The carpet disappeared and I lost all external objectivity, including for a moment any sense of "Self." There was no "Me," or "Myself," nothing but a pixelated, pulsing geometry of colors that absorbed my total mind. Awareness itself became the experience, so fantastic—identity dissolving into direct experience, a true acid trip—which I had heard about and read about but had never known before. For a moment the space was exhilarating, but quickly and decisively, the surreal trip plunged into Terror.

The mind went into overdrive, a panic like barreling down a twisting mountain road in a truck with no brakes. My thoughts went wild. Perhaps this discombobulated body on this couch represented the ghost of a person who had died. *Maybe that body was me.* Reason pulsed in and out, exacerbating creepy suspicion. One moment I was logical and investigating phenomena, the next moment, the mind-stream flushed with a torrent of dread, and the body shook convulsively. Seizure-strength tremors racked my body. The inner voice of Ego trembled: "You poisoned yourself by drinking poison sludge from the water pipe, you stupid idiot!" as Ego grasped desperately for a stable reality: nothing was stable—neither mind, nor body, nor point of view. Perhaps I was dead in Purgatory? The more I struggled against the terror, the stronger physical and mental anxiety intensified.

Oh no, I am dead!

"Not dead, but going-to-be-dead," declared Ego-Fear of Death.

"What if there *IS* a Heaven and Hell? Am I going to Hell?" spoke the inner voice of fear and dread: demons, death, and trembling fear. The Devil! and God!—God and the Devil visited me!

"Am I in hell now? *Is this Hell? Have I always been in Hell?*" I got vivid flashbacks to an automobile accident I had when I was sixteen and skidded my '57 Chevy off a dirt road by the Catawba River into a tree. I slammed against the steering wheel, the emergency brake shattered and its metal shaft pierced under my left knee and penetrated into my quadricep muscles. The metal floorboard crumbled like aluminum foil crushing my left foot while burning oil dripped on it. Neighbors called the police. An ambulance arrived and they cut my bloody body from the wreck with a jaws-of-life machine. Because of a possible concussion, the ambulance staff could not administer painkillers—when they jerked me free from the penetrating brake handle, I unleashed an unholy scream of pain that seemed as though the scream was coming from outside my body.

I ran into Nancy's bedroom as if to escape this horrific flashback, but it was everywhere. I was visualizing ambulance technicians wheeling me into the emergency operating room at Presbyterian Hospital in Charlotte, where doctors operated on me without anesthesia. When I closed my eyes a red field pulsed behind my eyelids, like the red blood that had plastered the interior of the wrecked Chevy. The Ego-mind seized these flashback episodes as evidence I had actually died on that operating table and all my life to this point was nothing more than a drawn-out, post-death delusion.

Nancy was awake and terrified. Thoughts ran wild. *Is she a demon witch controlling me? Is she my savior?* I imagined the impending presence of the Devil, and I prayed to God that I be delivered from Evil. I made a pact with God. I promised to devote myself to helping the poor and sick, as my mind raced in and out of reason. *Was I now commanded to sacrifice her?*

During a momentarily lucid pause I jumped out of bed and pleaded, "Nancy, call 911! I am afraid I could hurt you! I'm having a hard time. Go lock yourself in the bathroom!" She did. Soon policemen—who by this point I saw as orc-demon servants of the Dark Lord—handcuffed me, manhandled me down the steps, and threw me into the back of a police car.

Minutes later, police deposited me in the psych ward of San Francisco General Hospital where I joined dozens of other freaks who had been brought here from acid trips gone bad on Halloween night, along with heroin and speed overdoses, gunshot wounds—all the nutcases, the human detritus of San Francisco freaking out. In the waiting room, they injected me with Thorazine, and I passed out.

In the morning, I felt chipper. I organized calisthenics with other patients. Hospital staff observed me, questioned me, and concluded that I was ok. They discharged me before noon. Deward picked me up and took me over the Bay Bridge to Berkeley, to my Essex Street garden shed, my home.

To this day, I remain uncertain of the timeframe or what activities I might have engaged in over the next few days. But one late night, a few days after the bad trip, while everyone in Essex Street had gone to bed except me, I was sitting at the dining room table, sketching in my notebook. When I draw with pens, sometimes I get into a focused state of mind that watches a line automatically take form on the paper. That evening, the automatic drawing became macabre. The stream-of-consciousness sketching produced werewolves. Werewolves had frightened me since I was a kid. *Fear.* I became terrified; paranoia and strong vibrations surged through my body, just like I had experienced in Nancy's apartment.

"What is causing these tremors, this shaking?' Ego-mind demanded. "Am I about to have an epileptic seizure?" I had seen seizures happen to people on the street. Right before Halloween, I had witnessed a man on east Haight Street convulse in a body-shaking fit, as his friends struggled to jam a wallet between his clenched teeth. The mind flashed back to that episode in the Haight, "Do the vibrations indicate an impending fit of epilepsy?"

I flailed around the room like the madman I was, screaming and pounding on Deward's bedroom door and on the other bedroom doors commanding people to help me. "Raditz!" shouted Deward's voice through the closed door, "Shut up! Go outside! Go to sleep! We don't care!"

What was I to do? I stopped beating on the doors. *I need help.*

In the alcove next to the kitchen hung a wall phone. On the bulletin board beside it, roommates had thumbtacked notices and menus from fast food joints and posted a list of emergency phone numbers. Trembling and terrified, I dialed the number of the Berkeley Hot Line. A pleasant female voice answered, "Hello, Hot Line, how may I help you?" I began to babble incoherently, loudly, and hysterically about seizures, Hell, werewolves, Thorazine, epilepsy, death …. The voice on the Hot Line stopped me, "Whoa, Man! I can't understand you. Slow down! Get control of yourself! Get someone else to call back and explain the situation so we can help you."

I placed the receiver back in its cradle. Still shaking—but pausing—I reflected, "If I am going to get some help from the Hot Line, I should pretend to calm down."

Ringing the number again, I heard the same voice answer, "Hello, Hot Line, how may I help you?"

Putting on an air of sanity and composure, I said, "Hello, may I speak to you about someone in this house who needs help …?"

Suddenly, everything stopped. *Emptiness.* Silence. Calm.

In this instant, standing in this alcove speaking into the receiver of this kitchen phone, the center of "my consciousness" dissolved, or imploded, and my conditioned-mind went "*Poof*" and whoever or whatever I thought I was … *disappeared.*

The experience was as if I had been sleepwalking all my life, and suddenly woke up. Woke up from a dream of life into real life for the first time in my life.

I said calmly and coherently into the telephone, "Thank you, Miss. Everything is ok, now." And I hung up.

Total silence—silence I had never known before.

Gone was the audible droning like the low background humming of a refrigerator motor that goes on all the time, a buzzing you never notice, never realize it exists until it goes away. The silence—the emptiness—was truer than anything I had ever known. All anxiety in the body, vanished. Whatever aspect of consciousness was witnessing this, it was surely not the old "me," the Ego-mind, the unique, discrete personality-with-a-story. No "Cary" entity, only pure, unconditioned awareness coming and going, in and out of itself, from nowhere to nowhere—an arising and passing omnipresence—impermanent, totally and completely alive.

Further, the first-person point of view—the "witness"— noted that all the wishing and hoping that my ordinary mind had concocted in my day-to-day life had been nothing more than nonsense, a soliloquy from *Macbeth*, Puck's prologue in *A Midsummer Night's Dream*. Hey! The insight was: *all the late trains in my life I thought had been late, had been on time.*

Things are never going to be different from the way they are.

In addition, the witness presaged that the Ego-personality would reinstate itself and would dismiss all the awakening insights that everything is perfect. And, ironically, that denial by Ego would be perfect, too. *That's what happens.*

This insight episode passed away over the ensuing hours, but I would never be the same person afterward. *Never.* The experience of oneness had been more real than anything I had ever experienced. It had shaken my unexamined faith that "I" was some sort of permanent entity when my sense of personality had dissolved into a stream of all-encompassing awareness. Was this flash of profound insight the same as the "rebirth" experience Christians talk about? Was this instant illumination the "*Satori*" awakening that Suzuki wrote about? *A step toward ultimate Enlightenment? Nirvana?*

Mysterious wonder and bliss persisted that night and for perhaps a day, then subsided, and turned back on itself with fury. Ego-personality was trying to objectify and hold onto an experience of impermanence. As the witness had noted, Ego-personality reemerged and brought along its consort—*Fear*.

Years later, meditation teacher, Daniel Ingram, wrote about "Dark Night phenomena"—that fear, misery, and disgust predictively follow in the wake of certain illuminating states of insight. Accordingly, I began to shake with fear, creepy dread, with the trepidation that the terror would get worse. When I closed my eyes, I was afraid to go to sleep: *Sleep = death?* Peace, understanding, and serene silence totally disappeared, leaving me in a whirlwind of fear—*bat-shit crazy*.

In a state of manic frenzy I hitchhiked over the Berkeley hills to Canyon and scared the bejeezus out of my friends William and Catherine. Mustering sublime equanimity, they listened to my rantings and ravings, and watched me strip off all my clothes and boots and run up and down the forested Canyon hills barefoot and stark naked, howling like a werewolf though redwood forests and eucalyptus groves for a night and a day. Then it passed. I thanked William and Catherine, dressed, and hitchhiked back to Berkeley.

But it was not over. The craziness changed to occult weirdness. To a stranger in Peoples' Park, I gave away my black riding boots. I roamed the cold November streets barefoot. When I encountered other people, my unique identity lost firm boundaries. I became transparent. Sometimes it seemed as though I could read peoples' minds and know what they were going to say before they said it. Walking barefoot through Shakespeare & Company on Telegraph Avenue, I touched spines of books on the shelves and felt as though I could grok their meaning in the entirety. I descended into unworldly realms of fantasy. I lost the roadmap to reality. I was unmoored in space and time. In ordinary terms—*I had gone insane*.

For days and nights—it felt like eternity; certainly, it could not have lasted very long— barefoot I stalked the cold, wet streets of Berkeley. In a momentary harbor of reason I phoned Dad and begged him to get me out of this, to bring me back to North Carolina. It was a delusional idea, as if going home could rescue me from madness. Dad came through. He instructed me to go to the airline desk at San Francisco airport where a ticket to Winston-Salem awaited me. How did I get to the airport? A bus? I can't remember. Did Deward drive me? Anyway, by the time I got there I was a raving lunatic again.

Once inside the terminal I became further disoriented, sat down on the lobby floor in front of the ticket counters, crossed my legs, and proceeded to die. At least that's what I told the cops when the concerned airline folks pointed me out to them.

"So, you're gonna die here, Buddy, sitting down in the middle of the airport, huh?" said the fat one.

The tall one said, "Ok, Pal, let's walk downstairs and discuss this," or something like that.

"Oh no! Not Downstairs!" howled my crazy, gushing Ego-thought-stream, "the Evil Orc dressed like a cop means to take me to Hell!" and I resisted arrest, as the arrest document would state. Resisting arrest turned into a scuffle; they packed me yelling and kicking into the squad car, and hauled me off to the cooler, that is, Redwood City jail. In the clinker, I put up such an ungodly racket even seasoned junkies told the guards to put me somewhere else. *Total lunacy!* What happened after that, after a blurred series of crazy fiascos, I ended up in a loony bin part of the jail system where they pumped me full of tranquilizers that brought me around. What I noticed, in the parting of the madness clouds, even sedated I retained some of my insane superpowers. For example, I remember playing ping pong. Acuity sharpened, the ball seemed to float in slow motion, and my reflexes reacted with high coordination. I easily won every game I played.

Dad came out to Redwood City, bailed me out, and flew me home, the first time in my life I had ever flown in an airplane. Way above the clouds, above the corn fields of Iowa, the irony of being "high" did not escape me.

CHAPTER 5

Mad Man: Ad Man

When I arrived in Winston-Salem from San Francisco, I was a mess. First on the agenda I had to get my head straight. The lingering effects of the San Francisco bad trip, the "*awakening*" event in Berkeley, and its subsequent *Dark Night* agony, made me question what I had experienced. Had it been authentic? Had it been spiritual, or sacred, or mystic? Or merely ordinary, pedestrian psychosis?

Jim, a senior Beta fraternity grad from Winston, referred me to a psychiatrist friend, who had a "good reputation," with whom he played golf.

Here I was, November 1968, twenty-two years old, taking refuge with my parents, to be treated for mental illness by a golfer, for God's sake. Surely this was the epitome of failure. The psychiatrist decorated his office *feng shui* style. On *faux* rice-paper walls hung ink wash prints and on polished shelves, sat brass Buddhas. Lao Tzu's *Tao Te Ching* lay on the side-table next to a book of Walt Whitman's poetry. "Copasetic," I said to myself. At least no photographs of Sam Sneed on the wall.

The psychiatrist—I think his name was Jeffery—invited me into his *feng shui* office.

After small talk about our mutual friend, Jim, his golf partner, he went to the point. "What brings you here, Cary?"

"I think that I have been suffering from amphetamine psychosis."

"Really? What is it like for you having amphetamine psychosis?"

"Doctor, it's very much like sitting here talking with you." His eyes popped wide open, pupils dilated, and I thought I detected a slight trembling in the hand as he wrote me a prescription for an anti-psychotic.

I made a quick assessment, "This shrink is a lightweight. My situation may fall outside his realm of expertise." Unfortunately, I didn't know how to precisely identify the realm of expertise my condition required. *Maybe I need a Zen monk.*

First step: get tranquilized. Next task: find a job. I turned to the want ad section in the *Winston-Salem Journal*. Davy Tree Experts was seeking climbers and crew. Why not? At 7 a.m. next morning I showed up in the supermarket parking lot where Davy did their recruiting, and they hired me on the spot. My crew consisted of a foreman, Stanley Harding, a short country guy with the build of a wiry, featherweight boxer, and two others. A fighter he was, Stanley, a descendant of John Wesley Harding, he told us. Once when he was thrown out of a bar, he went out to his truck and got his chainsaw. Cleared the bar instantly. The two other guys on the crew were also country boys, friendly guys, laborers who could barely read or write. And me.

The scope of work consisted of clearing limbs and brush obstructing Duke Power electrical lines. Over the early winter of 1969, I cleared brush and sapling trees under power lines, ate brown rice, studied yoga, and watched the mind cycle between heaven and hell with lots of sub-stations in between. Mystical wonder pulsed in and out with the vibrating edge of fear still hovering just beyond the periphery of my perception, but with far less intensity than before. I muddled through crazy phenomena like I was teetering on the edge of a Hunter Thompson delirium. At least I was functional.

Clearing areas around power lines entertained me and provided good outdoor exercise. Lingering aftereffects of my awakening experience produced a physical upside. In this manual tree work, I discovered I could effortlessly call up heightened concentration. When chopping out brush under power lines with my bush ax, I could aim at a tiny imperfection on a shrub tree and strike it with a *chi* force, strong, relaxed, and focused, slicing it as if it were no more than a tall stalk of asparagus. While other guys flailed along with bush axes, hitting shrubs hard, again and again, exhausting themselves, I took one cut at a time, shearing the target sapling in one blow, and calmly moved on to the next. *Is this the kind of focus golfers dream they could bring to their game?*

In a couple of weeks Stanley promoted me to apprentice climber. "Is this a good idea?" I wondered. After all, from the time I was a little boy, I had had a fear of heights. When I neared a high window, for example, I would recoil from the edge as if I were fighting some inner demon compelling me to leap to my death. *Climbing trees? Bad idea!* But I said to myself, "Yes. Bring it on. I have met fear and it is internal and not out in the external world of circumstances."

Stanley taught me the ropes, literally. I learned to tie the taut-line hitch on my climbing harness, allowing me to safely control descent. Oddly, I discovered, height didn't really bother me; I got used to it quickly. What did bother me was the risk that became manifest when Stanley, hoisting himself to stand on a limb without harness and belay, fell thirty feet to the forest floor. The whole limb parted from the trunk of the tree, and he rode it standing erect all the way to the ground like Slim Pickens riding the a-bomb down in "Dr. Strangelove." Damp pine needles on the forest floor cushioned Stanley's fall. He stood up uninjured, shook himself off, and went back up the tree. This bizarre accident didn't freak me out, or stop me, but it did give me pause.

Lunchtime we ate at fast food, take-out places, usually barbeque joints. Usually we ate in the truck. At first I brought brown rice and chopsticks, which the others thought was hilarious. It was. Over time good Carolina barbeque won out and I ate what they ate and drank RC Cola. Overall, they were good guys with good country ways. The crew admired Stanley for his bravado, his work ethic, fairness, and his schemes. Once a week at least, a resident from the neighborhood where we were working would ask if we could cut down a tree on his property. Although officially improper, because we were Davy Tree Expert employees, we would take an extra unpaid hour after work and do the after-hours job quickly. Then Stanley would split the proceeds evenly among us.

Gradually, as I became more rational, I sought a more suitable job. In the closet of my parents' house, I found all my Southwick suits and sportscoats, silk ties and Alden shoes that I had acquired working after school in Jack Wood Ltd in Charlotte. I owned corporate clothes, consequently, looking good at a new corporate job would be no problem. The problem I had, however, was I lacked corporate experience. Besides selling clothes at Jack Wood, owning a defunct art gallery, working on farms, loading trucks, working in factories part time, and clearing powerlines for Davy Tree, my resume showed no solid business experience.

In the *Winston-Salem Journal* I spotted an ad for Manpower, the headhunting agency. I rang and made an appointment. Two days later I walked in the Manpower offices wearing a fine herringbone suit and filled out an application. A lady in a dark business suit introduced herself as Joanne Brown and led me into an interview room, where she had me perform a typing test—on which I did poorly—and then handed me an envelope containing a business aptitude test.

"This is how this works," she explained. "I will time this test. You have 30 minutes to complete it." She walked out of the room and closed the door. I opened the envelope and saw the test consisted of problems in math, critical reading, and basic logic. I took the test, feeling remarkably relaxed and focused. When she walked in to tell me time was up, I scribbled nonsense on the bottom of the test, such as "I would like to sleep with you," folded the test, and inserted it back into the envelope. As she had instructed me, I laid the envelope in the tray beside the receptionist and left the building.

Out on the street I stopped dead and practically slapped myself. "What the fuck are you doing, you moron?" my rational-self confronted my impulsive-self. "Your goal is to get a job, not to get laid!"

The next day she rang me at home. I was glad it wasn't the police. She said, "Cary, this is Joanne Brown, director of the Manpower office, whom you saw yesterday. I've got three things to tell you. First, your typing does not meet acceptable standards. Second, you scored the highest anyone has ever scored on that test in this office. Third, I accept your proposition."

Thus, I came to fall in love with Joanne Brown, the director of the Manpower agency, and she fell in love with me. Joanne took me under her wing and helped me to find a job—a safe, creative, professional job—an ideal job for a recovering madman with an English honors major from UNC: *Advertising*.

✽   ✽   ✽

"Cary Wingfield Raditz," stated the name plaque on my desk—junior copywriter at Winston-Salem's prestigious, boutique advertising agency, Long, Haymes and Carr. I liked seeing my middle name on my name card, an old family name from Albemarle County, Virginia, a fulcrum between "Cary," also a family name from Virginia, and "Raditz"—a name known to art historians, but not a name from the first families of Virginia. LHC had an outstanding reputation serving local small businesses, top corporations, and North Carolina industries—textiles, tobacco, and furniture. I felt my full name would be an accoutrement, like my fine suits, to bolster my image in the business world.

I was super grateful to Joanne for finding me a job, convincing a fine company like LH&C to hire me. She was a wizard, conjuring up this job out of pure intention. She wished me well, wished me to have a good job, and wished me success. To address my obvious madness, Joanne even introduced me to her best friend, Katrina, a psychiatrist who took me on as a patient. Joanne and Katrina mentored me, thank God, in the ways of the corporate world. I had no idea what I was doing.

Copywriting proved a great job for an English major who loved to write and create. Not too bad, advertising. Despite its tarnished image, I liked it. Account representatives came on as flashy, well-dressed salesmen, fast talkers, good old boys in Madison Avenue suits. The art department was looney. The art guys built model airplanes, WWII fighters and bombers, British Hawker Hurricanes and Spitfires, German Messerschmitts, and Dorniers, Heinkels and Junkers, which they suspended from the ceiling in a tableau representing the Battle of Britain. When working on projects, often they turned their slanted drafting boards against the wall, swiveled their chairs to face one another, yacking and sharing artwork. The art department was the creative playground in the agency, yet when these guys attended meetings, they showed up dressed as corporate citizens wearing sportscoats and ties. Directors seemed patrician in comparison, but they were all friendly and approachable. I was grateful to have a job in a great ad agency—and a salary.

Working at LH&C marked a giant leap from working for Davy Tree Company, a monumental step from my degenerate life last year in San Francisco and Berkeley. Not everything had fallen in place, however. I was 22 years old, I had landed a solid professional job, but I was still living with my parents.

With my first paycheck I moved out of my parents' home and rented a single room in a boardinghouse on a quiet, tree-shaded street in a respectable neighborhood not far from the agency. Dad took me car shopping. An ex-Navy airplane mechanic, he had worshiped cars since he was a teenager in Philadelphia. For $600, Dad got me an incredible deal on a black 1960 Mercedes-Benz coupe with red leather upholstery and a polished teak dashboard. I adored this little Mercedes whose rounded shape resembled a London derby hat, or the lumpy cars that first-graders draw.

Boardinghouse rules prohibited parties or entertaining visitors in bedrooms, so Joanne never came over to visit me, but it didn't matter; I visited her. She and her twelve-year-old son Grayson lived in a bungalow on a quiet side street near the Winston-Salem School of the Arts. Joanne was pretty, smart, managerially adept, and affectionate. The first time I stayed over with her we made love all night long, not even unhitching for a break between orgasms. Her son sleeping down the hall made me uneasy; I was closer to Grayson's age than his mother's. What made me even more uncomfortable was the threat of her ex-husband, Ray.

"We can only do this while Raymond is out of town on business," she told me, taking off my shoes. "Even though we've been divorced for four years, he is still jealous. He carries a pistol." Shit, I liked Joanne fine, but I didn't cotton to the idea of getting beat up or shot by Ray.

Joanne became interested in my circle of artsy friends. One Saturday, I took her to a party in Chapel Hill at Robin and Donna's house on Longview

Street, just across from the group house where Julia and I had lived a year ago. Walking through Robin's front door with Joanne on my arm struck me as awkward. Thirteen years older than I, Joanne dressed and held herself with the poise of the career executive she was, while all my friends were hip, academic hipsters in torn jeans wearing boots or sandals. Even so, Joanne seemed to feel right at home. She talked to everyone with animation and curiosity. All my friends liked her and welcomed her. We slept together on a mattress on the floor in Robin's spare bedroom. She loved it. Why then did I feel uneasy?

Does dating a thirty-six-year-old bother me? No, it wasn't age. Maybe being with Joanne in Chapel Hill among my Bohemian friends made me realize that advertising was not what I wanted. The world was exploding with possibilities, and I felt stuck in Winston-Salem. At the time, my friend Robin was starring in a university play titled, *Dionysus Wants You*! I took the theater poster back with me to Winston-Salem. *Is Dionysus speaking to my inner being?* Decades later, I hung it in the long entry hall of my 21 East 21st Street apartment in Manhattan across from the *Mingus* prints Joni had given me—the poster of Robin Moyer as *Dionysus*—shirtless, crowned in a myrtle and ivy wreath, pointing his finger at me.

Despite lingering doubts about the future of my career in advertising, I got into my work at LH&C, even the most banal. In my cubicle, I wrote ads for Bunny Devereaux's Shell Station, "Ladies, does your car go 'bang, bang, bang'? You may have a serious engine problem. Go see Bunny"—photographed, kneeling on one knee next to a gas pump in front of his Shell station—"Bunny Devereaux will attend to all your automotive needs." *From here, nowhere to go but up.*

I cooked for myself in the boardinghouse's common kitchen. Was I the only one in the house who really did? Judging from the kitchen trashcan contents, other residents appeared to subsist on fast-food, canned food, and Swanson TV dinners. Living in Berkeley had taught me about macrobiotic diets. In a health food store near School of the Arts I bought miso, short-grain brown rice, seaweed, almond butter, and olive oil. I bought a large cast-iron pot in a second-hand shop to cook brown rice and pasta, and to make lentil stew. My go-to meal became rice with hunks of steamed cabbage, onion, and vegetables, on which I dribbled tamari and ate with chopsticks. Happy, hippy macrobiotic comfort food.

When I drove over to Chapel Hill alone on weekends—Joanne stayed in Winston-Salem—I crashed with Scott Bradley out at Jenkins Farm. Scott was running the revolution in Chapel Hill. As Director of Chapel Hill's Student Nonviolent Coordinating Committee, he organized protests and strikes at the university, one of which involved raising pay for cafeteria workers. The strike worked and the cooks and staff got their raises. That was an occasion to celebrate.

Out at Scott's farmhouse, it seemed a party was going on all the time. I'd gifted Scott my collection of record albums that were mostly folk and blues, Bob Dylan, Cisco Houston, Woody Guthrie, Charles Lee Guy, and others. Dylan had just released *Nashville Skyline*, a big shift of style and attitude from earlier *Blond on Blond*, and *Highway 61 Revisited*. The turntable spun Bloomfield, Kooper and Stills on *Super Session* late into the night, "… must be the Season of the Witch." As we danced, the old wooden floors of the farmhouse bounced and creaked. We drank beer and cheap wine and smoked bad homegrown weed. Seems like bad weed was the only weed we had. I was at the party at Scott's, celebrating the successful cafeteria workers' pay raise, when I met Holly Black.

A serious science student, Holly. She had a twisted smile that gave the impression she looked on life with cynical curiosity. Holly surveyed lifestyles beyond the campus culture of dorm life, fraternities, and sororities. Although in favor of the SNCC protests and other current social and political events of the day, she thought critically about issues and held her own counsel. She was about 5'9"—a little taller than me—with long brown hair down her back, full breasts, and long legs. Although affectionate, she initially kept me at bay. When she accepted my invitation to camp at the Union Grove Fiddlers Convention northwest of Chapel Hill on the border with Virginia, I was pleasantly surprised.

We walked together through the big, gravel school parking lot, where from every tailgate, bluegrass musicians played extemporaneously. Women in aprons laid out trays of fried chicken, buttermilk biscuits, coleslaw, and barbeque. We approached a small crowd clustered around the back of a pickup truck where Doc Watson and his son, Merle, jammed with other musicians. Smoke from barbeque grills filled the air. Holly and I ducked into tents to drink wine and smoke dope. In one tent, waiters from Harry's Restaurant on Franklin Street were shooting speed. *No thank you.* Holly and I moved up to the bandstand where a band composed of youngsters included a girl in a yellow dress who played fiddle while clogging. These kids appeared as accomplished as the adults performing in the parking lot.

That night at Union Grove, Holly welcomed me into her sleeping bag. After that weekend, we started dating regularly, and I drove over to Chapel Hill on weekends to be with her. She had already made plans to take the first semester of her junior year abroad in Germany, to intern at a pharmaceutical company, and so we tried to savor every moment until she left.

In Winston-Salem, Joanne and I stopped sleeping together. She didn't resent Holly taking over the love-light in my life—she had already resigned herself to our breaking up—it seemed inevitable, yet we were both sad about it. Anyway, parting ways with Joanne relieved the anxiety that Ray might gun me down.

Holly left for Munich in early June. I didn't go back to Joanne, but continued my work at LHC, felt lonely and sorry for myself, and wrote Holly every week. One day, a letter arrived from her, postmarked München. When I opened the envelope at my desk, a $100 bill fell out on the floor. In the accompanying letter, Holly said she missed me, and invited me to come over to Germany. That declaration of affection—secured by a $100 bill, which was a lot of money in those days—sealed my decision. Next stop, Munich.

Mr. Haymes' secretary showed me into his office. He stood to greet me, "What is it, Cary? Everything okay?"

"Mr. Haymes, I've only been at Long, Haymes and Carr a little while, and everyone has made me feel welcome. I appreciate every moment I've worked here. But, Mr. Haymes, I regret to tell you that I've decided to retire."

"Cary, sounds like you are quitting. What? 'Retiring'? You're only what? Twenty-two? How can you say you are retiring when you've barely started a career? 'Retiring?' You mean resigning?"

"Well, Mr. Haymes, I am actually twenty-three. 'Retiring' is precisely what I meant."

"What do you plan to do, Cary?"

"Travel. I want to travel. Life is too short."

"Travel. Ha! God bless you, Cary! I wish I had done that when I was your age!"

Mr. Haymes wished me all the best, then he personally escorted me around the agency to see Mr. Carr and Mr. Long, the other copywriters, the artists, the secretaries, and the janitor. "Cary's leaving us to travel to Europe." They practically applauded. And that was the way my career in advertising came to an end.

A week after I gave my notice to Long, Haymes & Carr, Robin Moyer enlisted me into a road trip to the Atlanta International Pop Festival over the 4th of July weekend. Robin and I, and his friend, Sam, drove six hours from Chapel Hill to Atlanta. Robin loved my little black Mercedes and I put him behind the wheel. Fleecy clouds and towering cirrocumulus dotted the pale blue skies as we crawled bumper to bumper into the hot, dusty, red clay infield of the Atlanta racetrack. In the exhaust of slowly moving traffic, the Mercedes crept its way through a jam of cars, vans, and tents as we looked for a place to park. Along the road, popup food booths were serving the usual festival fare: hotdogs and pretzels, as well as hippy food, granola bars and fruit. Queues of long-haired red necks waited in front of clusters of porta potties exuding the acrid stench of chemicals, urine, and decomposing organic materials. Robin squeezed my little coupe into a space between two Volkswagen vans and we pitched our tent. Then the trouble began; after parking, the little Mercedes refused to restart.

Disaster! Had it not been for the creative, problem-solving genius of my pal, soon-to-be-famous, *Time-Life Magazine* photographer Robin Moyer, I might still be down there in the infield of Atlanta racetrack kicking the tires, cursing my fate. He got me into the mess, and by God, he was going to get us out! Robin sprang to action. Climbing in, under, and around the engine compartment, he performed rudimentary diagnostics with tools he borrowed from a neighboring van owner. He determined the condenser had died on my car. Then he fixed it.

Remarkable how he did it. Robin persuaded two college girls to drive him to a foreign car garage off Interstate 85 to buy a replacement condenser. Several hours later the ladies returned with Robin, a Mercedes condenser, and a case of Pabst Blue Ribbon. I've long forgotten the details of the festival itself, the bands and music—I can't remember if I even approached the performance stage or not—but I'll never forget how Robin rescued my Mercedes 190, and saved my ass at the 1969 Atlanta International Pop Festival.

By mid-August, I was working as a landscaper in Northport, Long Island, staying with my friend Roger and his folks, trying to earn enough money to join Holly in Munich. Roger and I pruned shrubbery and mowed lawns around Huntington in the hot muggy days of midsummer. On our knees weeding flower beds, or while bending over to spread mulch under scrubs, Roger and I spied our employer, landscaper Ed Lombardi, lounge in the front seat of his Dodge station wagon, air conditioning running, listening to baseball games on the radio, drinking. Every evening about quitting time, an empty fifth of Smirnoff sailed out the station wagon window and plopped on the lawn.

In mid-August Roger's friends invited Roger, Shaft, and me to crowd into a VW van with them and go to the Woodstock Festival. I did not have to think about it; I turned the offer down flat. I swore I could still taste the red clay dust from the Atlanta racetrack infield. The way I saw it, if the Woodstock Festival was going to be anything like the Atlanta Festival, it would likely be crowded, hot, dirty, and unpleasant. Instead of going to Woodstock, I decided to stay put in Northport with Roger and Shaft and churn out a few more paydays of landscaping for Ed before flying off to Germany.

A week later, Roger's friends returned from Woodstock, elated, telling outrageous tales of amazing music, rock stars, drugs, sex, and naked bodies rolling around in the mud on Yasgur's Farm. Although some folks attending Woodstock found it awful—as I expected it would be—not Roger's friends. For them, it had been an ecstatic, life-changing event despite the crowds, rain and mud.

Missing Woodstock? I never regretted the decision for an instant. Further, it made me double-swear to avoid music festivals in the future. That vow, however, did not last very long.

CHAPTER 6

Parable of the Coin

If you don't know where you are going, any road will get you there.

Woodstock was far from my mind when I stepped off the Air Icelandic flight in the gray and chilly Luxembourg airport. As I passed through customs, my new passport received its first-ever immigration stamp. I lifted my backpack from the baggage carousel and changed two twenty-dollar American Express Travelers' Checks into deutschmarks at a currency booth in the airport terminal. That left me with $110 in travelers checks in my wallet. Exiting the airport terminal, I breathed in the fragrant morning air of Northern Europe. For me, a new world.

Except for a month in Quebec two years earlier at Expo 67, this trip marked my first time outside the United States. Would being in Europe create a new beginning for me, a grand adventure, or would it result in a dismal failure, causing me to creep back with my tail between my legs to my copywriting job in Winston-Salem?

Now here I was in Luxembourg. My worries disappeared. Exhausted from the flight, I shouldered my backpack and began to walk in the direction of the campsite recommended by the guidebook, *Europe on Five Dollars a Day*. I carried no tent, only a leather hucklebag, and a REI pack frame containing a down sleeping bag, a skinny camping pad, a thin ground tarp, a toothbrush, and several changes of clothes.

As I entered the camp late in the afternoon, ominous clouds darkened the skies. I dreaded the prospect of spending the night shivering in rain, huddling in a soggy sleeping bag in the mud. A mosaic of tents of all sorts, sizes and colors filled every square foot of the campsite grounds. A few small trees rose above the collage of colored tents, brick service buildings, a fast-food canteen, rudimentary toilets, and shower stalls for men and ladies. As I trudged along between the rows of tents, a few campers looked up from what they were doing and greeted me. I stopped to say hello to the friendliest and asked if they had room for me. *No?* Fortunately, a young Danish couple standing off to the side overheard my conversation, and my American accent, and invited me to sleep with them in their tent.

They made room for me and I shoved in my pack frame and hucklebag. I unrolled my sleeping bag next to theirs. They wanted to hear about Woodstock, "Did you go? Was it wonderful?" they asked me. "No? You didn't go? Why not?"

They were on their way to the Isle of Wight Pop Festival to see Bob Dylan, the Band and The Who. They listened eagerly to my automobile misadventures at the Atlanta Pop Festival. Though the tent was a bit cramped, I was grateful for their kindness, and for their tent that kept me dry, out of the rain. Casual in their nakedness, they undressed in front of me and snuggled into their joint sleeping bag. Despite my boho nonchalance, the sweet innocence of their candid nudity surprised me and endeared me to these young Danes.

Rough, hard ground dug into my shoulders and hips despite the camping pad, but I was exhausted and slept straight through the night. Groggy, I awoke as the first sunrays of dawn illuminated the tent walls. Beside me my hosts still slept, entwined in their one sleeping bag. As the early morning fog lifted, I began stuffing my sleeping bag, rolling up my pad, and arranging my pack. The couple awoke and sat up in their sleeping bag. It took supreme effort for me to avoid staring at her breasts whose nipples I swear were winking at me. We said goodbye, good luck, happy travelling, enjoy the Isle of Wight Festival, enjoy München. My new Danish friends gave me a granola bar and a bottle of orangeade. I took advantage of the campsite's relatively clean latrine facilities, filled my water bottle at a standpipe, shouldered my pack, and set off to hitchhike to Munich.

Just outside the Luxembourg city limits the main street turned into a two-lane country road. From 7 a.m. until noon I walked. Rows of hardwood trees lined each side of the road that cut through cultivated fields of wheat and barley where farms and small hamlets populated the countryside. A new universe, its beauty astonished me. How different it looked and felt from suburban Long Island, which I had left two days ago.

I stuck out my thumb at every car and truck that passed. I wished I had made a sign that said, "München." As I walked along the right shoulder I looked over fields, woods, and villages so perfect they could have been plucked from a Lionel model-train landscape. It was almost noon, I had been walking nonstop for five hours with no one offering to pick me up. Not accustomed to hiking with a backpack—or hiking at all—my shoulders, feet, back, knees and thighs ached. The straps bit into my shoulders. I was getting tired.

At a simple auberge outside a rural hamlet, I crossed the road, entered the restaurant, and took a seat at a table. The lady who served me spoke German-accented English, more grammatically correct than most Americans. She was courteous but not outgoing. I ordered steak frites for lunch, the cheapest item on the menu. I was the only person in the restaurant until two cars pulled up and customers seated themselves at tables. The steak frites hit the spot.

Well-fed and exhilarated at being in a foreign land and ordering my first meal, I returned to the road to hitchhike. Almost immediately a transport truck stopped and picked me up and two hours later, dropped me off outside Saarbrucken. When I hiked across the bridge over the river Saar in late afternoon, my *Europe on $5 a Day* directed me to an inexpensive pension.

Few people appeared along the narrow cobblestone streets. Finally I spotted the sign of the pension and rang the doorbell. A middle-aged lady wearing a white lace apron greeted me and invited me in. Because she spoke almost no English, she summoned her lovely daughter, Kristel, to translate. We worked out the arrangement for the night; I received a bed in a small, single room and breakfast in the morning. Instead of a top sheet the bed had a wonderous, high-lofted down comforter and a long firm bolster for a pillow. I stripped off my clothes, bathed in the sink with a washcloth, brushed my teeth, and collapsed immediately into the bed.

The next morning, well slept, I breakfasted with Kristel and her mother. Kristel spoke heavily accented but remarkably fluent English. I found her attractive. We chatted over breakfast. "You look like you might be an athlete, Kristel. Do you play sports?"

"Oh, yes, I play football—what you Americans call *soccer*, yes? I like all sports with balls, from ping pong to basketball."

Charmed, I fell for her on the spot. *We could have a ball together.* She carefully wrote her address in my agenda book. We said goodbye at the door and promised to write each other. What a beautiful little town, Saarbrucken, at least the residential quarter where I was staying; the rest of the city was heavily industrial. Recrossing the Saar, I walked up to the main road and resumed hitchhiking. After a half-hour a commercial truck picked me up and took me east, half-way across Germany to slightly past Karlsruhe. The driver apologized that his load had a southbound destination. An hour later he dropped me off at a fork in the road. I immediately got picked up by a salesman in a Mercedes who represented a company that manufactured plumbing equipment. He was eager to practice English with me.

At twilight I was still hitch-hiking along the skirt of the highway with no idea where I would spend the night. I searched with a critical eye each farm and field I passed. *Would it be prudent to crash in a barn or under the eaves of a haystack?* As night began to fall I spotted a spa and coffeehouse at the top of a winding driveway leading off the main road. This was worth a try. I knocked on the front door. A middle-aged man in a sweater answered the door and invited me in. He was the proprietor, spoke good English, and apologized that he had no rooms to rent; however, for 10 deutschmarks, I could sleep on the wooden benches of the unheated sauna. I unrolled my sleeping bag onto my pad on a wooden sauna bench and went right to sleep. The next morning I paid and walked back down to the highway. Straight away a trucker picked me up and drove nonstop to the outskirts of Munich, letting me out next to a trolly stop. *I have done it!* The trip across Germany to Munich had taken me three days and two nights.

Verifying cross-streets on *Europe on $5 a Day's* München map, I pinned-down that I was on the western side of Munich. I saw the trolly stop had a schedule posted. Soon a trolly car with the correct Swaabing-bound number approached, and I scrambled aboard. Transferring cars once, I got off on Ungerstrasse across from the abandoned furniture factory that Holly had described in her letters. As I walked up to the factory, a hand-painted sign stapled to a telephone pole read: "Desolation Row." Relieved but wary, I passed through the open gates of Desolation Row into the stone paved courtyard of the factory.

Clutching Holly's instructions I located the first building on the right where a stack of concrete blocks stepped up to a window serving as a door to the apartment where Holly supposedly stayed. Her host, she had written, was Jonathan Clarke, a British electrical engineer with counterculture tastes who worked at the Siemen's research institute in Munich. *Where was Holly?* I peeked inside the open window, where seated on a chair, a blond woman with a ponytail was sewing a Hofbräuhaus patch on a Levi jacket.

She glanced up, smiled, and greeted me in American English, "Hi there! I bet you are Cary. Are you Cary? Far out! I'm Susan. Holly told me to expect you, but she didn't know exactly when you would arrive. On the spur of the moment, she went off with German friends to the Isle of Wight Pop Festival. Bob Dylan was playing! Far out! The festival was over yesterday so she should be back in a day or so. Please climb in, Cary. Here, hand me your backpack. Holly's bed is the lower bunk at the top of these stairs," she went on, pointing to a narrow wooden ladder going up through a square hole in the ceiling, "put your pack up there and come down. Take a nap if you want. The toilet is in the warehouse over there. Are you hungry, Cary?"

I climbed the ladder and plunked down backpack and hucklebag beside a bunk bed with a futon covered in quilts. A bookbag with "HB" hand-embroidered on it hung from a hook on the wall. Sitting down on her bed, I felt disappointed. *No Holly—casualty of another rock festival.* First the Atlanta Pop Festival, then Woodstock, now Isle of Wight. *Beset by a scourge of rock festivals!*

Susan called out from below, "Cary, do you want some bread and cheese? We have beer." I descended the ladder. "Jonathan is expecting you. He works until six and will be back some time or another. One never knows, with Jonathan. Make yourself at home. Holly was really excited about the prospect of seeing Bob Dylan at the Isle of Wight. She knew you would love it and wished you could have gone with her." *Me, too.*

Cutting cheese and slicing bread, Susan told me she was from Louisville, Kentucky, and was taking the summer and fall off from college to travel in Europe. "Staying with Jonathan is free. It is too good. I like Munich. I've made some German friends who have been showing me the city, the monuments, cheap restaurants, beer halls and clubs in Swaabing—the swinging neighborhood of Munich. Travelers hear about the Factory and come here to crash and get their bearings." She laughed, "But all good things come to an end. I must start moving again. I have a student Eurail Pass I've barely used."

Paperbacks in English, German and French left by visitors filled a bookshelf near the open window. I pulled out William Burroughs' *Naked Lunch*, sat down and dug right in. "Do you have any drugs?" I asked Susan.

She shook her head. "No. Hashish turns up in the Factory every day or so. A couple Munich freaks stop by almost daily to chat and to check out new additions to the costume storerooms. They almost always have hash and other drugs, too, like acid, opium and pills."

My ears perked up—*Opium?* Before I left Chapel Hill for Long Island, I had started chipping at heroin with Paul Davis. I wanted more. "Heroin?" I asked.

"Haven't heard of any but I wouldn't mention it around Jonathan. He doesn't want the Factory to become a haven for junkies. Nothing but trouble."

Jonathan's pad had a turntable and several dozen record albums, Celtic folk songs, German classical, Mozart, Beethoven, Brahms, Wagner, but mostly rock and roll. Susan put on Joe Cocker, *Mad Dogs and Englishmen*, and sat down next to me with a beer. *This could be interesting.* I put my arm around her shoulder. Immediately, she recoiled and pulled my arm away.

"Cary, Holly is your girlfriend and my friend, too. Don't come on to me!"

"Sorry, Susan, nothing intended," I lied. *So much for that.* I withdrew to my *Naked Lunch.*

Later that night curling up in Holly's bed I thought I could detect her distinctive scent on the sheets. I wished she were beside me. Thank you, Susan, for shooing me away. Screwing her would have been bad, awkward at best. And disastrous at worst.

The next morning, Susan introduced me to Jonathan as he was rushing off to work. A pleasant guy, small of statue, very British, very hip. After café créme, bread, butter and jam, Susan led me out through the Factory gates across Ungerstrasse and down a wide sidewalk to a stretch of bakery and grocery stores to buy brochen, butter, wurst, fruit, vegetables, and beer. We were unpacking groceries back at the Factory when two German guys dropped by as Susan had predicted. They climbed in and sat on the windowsill facing us. Both guys, Hans, and Werner, spoke English quite well and offered us a big conical joint of hashish mixed with dark cigarette tobacco. Susan smoked with them and I declined. Hash with tobacco was way too harsh for me and besides, cannabis was not my drug of choice. It sometimes made me anxious.

"Got any heroin?" I asked them.

"We haven't seen heroin for weeks," Werner said. "Theater people in Swaabing sometimes bring it in from Amsterdam. Usually, Hans and I try to score ampules of pharmaceutical morphine. Right now, we've got a few vials of dilaudid left. Want one?" He pulled out a labeled glass ampule from his bag. "Ten deutschmarks?" He asked, raising his eyebrows. I handed him a 10 DM bill.

"Do you have works?" I asked.

"No, but I will go by the Swaabing pharmacy to buy you an outfit—a syringe and a pack of points," he said. "But not today. Tomorrow. Got another 10 DM for the outfit?"

Shortly after the Germans left, Holly arrived. Coming through the window, she hauled in her backpack, kissed me, and fell into my arms. Susan greeted her and immediately withdrew into Jonathan's bedroom, declaring, "I'm outta here. You two need to get reacquainted," and closed the bedroom door.

Ah, Holly in my arms. Obviously exhausted, wearing dirty clothes unchanged in days, she stank of dried sweat. I kissed and embraced her, squeezing her butt. Feeling my insistent ardor, she pushed me away.

"Cary, I am filthy! Behave while I clean up."

Stepping into the kitchen alcove, she talked to me as she poured water from a gallon jug into a big electric kettle and turned it on. She asked about my hitchhiking across Germany, and I gave her a synopsis. In turn she told me about her trip to the Isle of Wight festival. When the kettle started whistling, she stripped off her dirty jeans, socks, panties, and t-shirt, tossed them on the floor. From her backpack she pulled a towel, and grabbing an empty metal bucket, a bar of soap and bottle of shampoo, stepped out naked through the window onto the stone courtyard outside.

"Cary, come. Bring the hot water." I followed her out through the window with the kettle. At a standing pipe across from Jonathan's apartment, she opened the tap and filled the bucket with cold water into which I poured the boiling water until it became lukewarm. Dipping in a washcloth, I soaped down Holly's lean body, lingering around her ample breasts, nipples, ass, and fuzzy pussy. She squirmed and laughed, "Not so fast, Tom Cat!" I shampooed her long dark hair while she squatted on her heels on the paving stones. With a big plastic cup, I poured warm water over her, rinsing her hair and body. "Ahhh," she moaned. "Now you." I took off my clothes on the spot and she soaped me down, using the rest of the water in the bucket to rinse me off. By now I had a throbbing hard on, which she gently squeezed. She handed me the towel and climbed back naked through the window leaving me standing naked and aroused on the cobblestones to dry off. When I stepped inside she was halfway up the ladder to her bed. *What a delight!*

The next day Hans came by to deliver the outfit. Holly had never seen anyone shoot up before; she asked if she could watch. To tie myself off, I stripped my leather belt out of my jeans, wrapped it around my left bicep, pulled it snug until the veins stood out on the inside of my elbow, and held the belt with my teeth. I popped the glass nipple off the ampule and drew up the clear dilaudid liquid into the syringe. Holding the syringe upright, I pressed the plunger slightly until all the bubbles were expelled. I slipped the point into the main vein in my elbow, and with forefinger and middle finger of my right hand, drew back the plunger just a bit until a ribbon of red shot up into the syringe. Then I slowly shot all the dilaudid into the vein. As that amazing feeling began surging through my body, stronger than any orgasm, I dropped the works into a drinking glass, and fell back into Holly's arms.

※ ※ ※

Susan left for Italy leaving Holly and me the only people crashing at Jonathan's place. When he was around Jonathan was good company, a pleasure to talk and drink beer with. Holly had completed her internship at Bayer before she left for the Isle of Wight. We settled into the scene around the Factory and around Munich.

Jonathan, Holly, and I were not the only inhabitants of the Factory. Other groups of people squatted in rooms and warehouse spaces in this abandoned furniture factory. Across the courtyard from Jonathan lived members of Amon Düül, a German longhair, political art-commune rock group. The Factory served as a stopping place for travelers coming from and going to destinations in eastern and southern Europe, North Africa, the Middle East, India, Nepal, and South Asia. The Factory took in travelers from Commonwealth countries, Australia, New Zealand, and South Africa, where after lycée or university, young people customarily traveled for a year or two on what they referred to as a "Walkabout," working on farms or as casual laborers, dish-washers or waitresses all over the world before returning to their home countries to settle down, establish careers, and start families. The Factory had become legend among these travelers and news of it spread by word of mouth. Susan had called it the "Underground Railroad" of the boho traveler sect. The Factory provided a cheap place for folks to crash for a few days, meet fellow travelers, swap drugs, and share stories and news of the road.

Holly and I got on fine with Jonathan who enjoyed having visitors crash at his place. Some folks stayed for months or more, like Holly. Jonathan had moved from Oxford to Munich when he finished graduate school to work as an electrical engineer at Siemens. When he found he could squat at the Factory, he moved out of his apartment and installed himself in the factory offices, which he remodeled and currently occupied. Fluent in German, French and Spanish, and pursuing a professional career; nonetheless, he harbored an eccentric streak, and threw himself into the boho life of Swaabing.

The factory was a world unto itself. We ate all the plums from the two pitiful plum trees growing next to the water faucet in the courtyard where twice a week we bathed. There was some truth in the "Desolation Row" sign nailed to telephone pole outside the Factory gate; we lived there illegally but no one evicted us. From time to time utility company workers would climb the electrical poles outside the Factory and disconnect it from the grid. It was the same with the water supply. As soon as workmen left, rock group roadies would reconnect us to the grid and to the Munich city water supply. In the Factory several Swaabing theatre companies stored props and costumes in warehouse storerooms that presumably Amon Düül oversaw.

Swaabing, Munich's equivalent of Greenwich Village, the neighborhood nearest to the Factory, sported a full array of jazz clubs, international restaurants, German beer houses and the grand English Gardens. Swaabing theatres stored sets, lighting equipment, and costumes in the Factory warehouse, costumes which people pilfered for day-to-day, fancy dress—including us.

One day Holly encountered a German American couple picking through theatrical storerooms at the Factory. They introduced themselves as Stefan and Louise, university students who worked part time for a media production house in Swaabing. Holly invited them into Jonathan's apartment for tea, where they told us how we could earn some deutschmarks.

"This week," said Louise, "we will be shooting German soap opera episodes in the English Gardens. Several days a week our company hires extras for movies, TV productions, and theatre. If you go down to Swaabing tomorrow morning, we can meet you at this address"—she wrote it down on her notepad, tore it off and handed it to Holly. "I'm sure they will hire you. I'll see to it. They don't ask for work visas or anything. They pay extras 100 DM a day. The work is dreadfully boring because you don't do anything except stand around for six hours a day while the production crew shoots and reshoots scene after stupid scene. But the pay is not bad, considering your only job is adding background color to the *mise en scéne*."

We met up with Louise and Stefan next morning in front of a low office building in Swaabing. They introduced us to the producers, who hired us and a half-dozen other people, some dressed like hippies, some not. We signed releases and they gave us ID badges. Ironically, our role was playing hippies. The producers had a particular hippy look they sought to copy, Louise explained, which to us—real freaks—seemed ridiculous. They gave me an embroidered Afghan sheepskin vest to wear and a beaded headband. They outfitted Holly in a hilarious tie-dyed raincoat, a long silk scarf, and a wide-brimmed, floppy hat. Louise told us these were the costumes they were selecting in the Factory storeroom when we met them yesterday. They also gave us props to share—one, a wine bottle filled with grape juice, and two, a long-stemmed pipe filled with tobacco, not cannabis.

For a week, Holly and I stood in costume under trees in the English Garden and made out, kissing, and hugging, and drinking grape juice from the wine bottle, and smoking the fake pot pipe. In one scene, glamorous German actors portray a three-way intrigue between a handsome man, his stunning mistress, and his suspicious wife. The man and his mistress are passionately embracing under an ornate gazebo among flowering shrubs, when his elegant wife shows up and catches them at it. The three scream at each other, the mistress leaves in tears, and the married couple make up, sit on a stone bench by the gazebo, kiss and talk. While this scene was going on, the director instructed Holly to kiss and grope me by the trees behind the gazebo, drink directly from the wine bottle and smoke the pot pipe. Holly translated the German lines into English for me, rolling her eyes to express her disgust with the soap opera direction, writing and acting. This scene alone was reshot at least a half-dozen times. Silly as it seemed to us, each making 100 DM a day—the equivalent of twenty-five dollars—that provided the wherewithal to go out to clubs, and to eat in restaurants.

Over the last six months working as a paid intern at Bayer, the multinational chemical company, Holly had acquired a beat-up Volkswagen bug and a marvelous one cylinder, 200cc, BMW motorcycle. We had more mobility than we needed. Together, Holly and I explored Swaabing, went to music clubs, ate cheaply at Indonesian restaurants, which seemed to be everywhere. Once a week we hopped on her BMW and blasted into Munich for free lunch at the Lowenbrau factory, which hosted tours. We figured out how to slip away from the organized tour group, bypass the customary show and tell, and detour directly to the factory bar for beer, brochen, and wurst before the rest of the tour arrived.

I liked exploring Munich on my own on the BMW. One afternoon leaving the Hofbrau House on Ungererstrasse bloated and half-drunk on beer, I dropped the motorcycle in the middle of a roundabout in the midst of cars and trucks flying by. Traffic parted around me as if I were a rock in a stream and kept going. Scared and humiliated, I struggled to get the motorcycle upright before traffic ran me over. Fortunately, a kind pedestrian in a business suit and umbrella helped pick up the BMW and move it over to the side of the road. I thanked him profusely. "Bitteschon," he replied, and walked away. Thoroughly embarrassed, I remounted the BMW and continued out to the Factory. *Death narrowly averted once again.*

✹ ✹ ✹

September slipped into October. As it came to pass I realized that I had the phone number of US Army Second Lieutenant Bill Barton—a Beta brother—and his wife Eunice, who were stationed in Pond Barracks, a US Army post in Amberg two hours north, close to the Czech border. I rang them up and Bill invited Holly and me to be their guests at Munich's Oktoberfest. They drove down from Amberg on a Saturday morning and picked us up in a Mercedes 190 sports car at the Factory. We easily found parking near the festival grounds.

Oktoberfest presented a mass spectacle of gluttony and mirth, performed by drunken, reeling crowds. Lederhosen clad men and women in bright traditional costumes locked arms and swayed together at long tables, guzzling beer, and singing to the brass and accordions of live polka bands. Howling with laughter and song, revelers filled the long tables in the big tents, ate huge plates of wurst, potato, and sauerbraten, which they washed down with huge quantities of beer. Stout blond, buxom beer maidens in bright costumes, sleeves rolled past elbows, clutching four hefty liter beer steins in each fist, steered their way between tables to thrust steins of frothy brew in front of loud, fat, red-faced drunks and their drunken, corpulent, big-bosomed wives. We ate and drank too, modestly in comparison, amazed by the beer festival activities unfolding around us.

When Bill and Eunice drove us back to the Factory, Holly gave the Bartons a short tour of the repurposed furniture factory and the costume storerooms. "Come back to Amberg with us," they said. Without hesitating we accepted their warm invitation, crammed into the back of the Mercedes, and drove straightaway to Amberg. For two days Holly and I stayed with Bill and Eunice, mostly walking around the town, and enjoying the Gothic architecture and history. During the day Eunice volunteered as our historical and cultural guide while Bill worked at the post. Holly and I thought staying in this old, Gothic Bavarian town might be cool. We even battered around the idea of renting a tiny room within the ancient stone wall fortifications surrounding the medieval town.

Eunice—the voice of reason—pointed out, "… but it might get cold living in that stone wall when winter comes."

Yes. Whatever were we thinking? Already days were drawing shorter. At night chilly winds nipped through our sweaters. Looking ahead, how were we going to fare in Jonathan's poorly heated rooms in the Factory in winter?

As we noodled these questions, Eunice drove us back to Munich in the Mercedes taking a circuitous detour through Austria. Holly and I took turns riding up front with Eunice while the other hunkered in the back seat. We flew along the Autobahn at 160 kilometers per hour while cars passed us as if we were standing still. Eunice graciously treated us to a night's stay in a well-appointed traditional mountain inn, sensing this would be a real treat for us, given the pathetic way we lived in squalor in Desolation Row. It was. After supper Holly and I bathed and shampooed each other in the tub and then luxuriated under the down comforter in a big, high bed. All clean and pink, entwined beneath the warm covers, we blessed our good fortune and blessed Eunice Barton's sweet generosity.

The next afternoon Eunice drove us back to Munich, depositing us at the Factory. We decided we had to leave Germany soon to seek warmer climes. Oktoberfest was over and the weather was turning increasingly chilly in Munich. Bathing naked on the cold cobblestones in the Factory courtyard was becoming unpleasant.

On 21 October 1969, German voters elected Willy Brandt Chancellor. Concurrent with the election, the Bundesbank—the central bank of West Germany—revalued the deutschmark from 4 DM to the dollar to 2.5 DM. Devaluation of the dollar relative to the deutschmark practically halved our purchasing power over night. We didn't make much money as it was playing extras in German TV productions, and although we could economize some, and dine out less often, winter would soon be on us. As the days shortened, during gloomy afternoons we talked about how much we craved warmth and sunlight. It was high time to flee Munich and flee winter, we decided—time to find a winter abode someplace warm and cheap, maybe Spain, maybe Greece, maybe Morocco. We advertised Holly's VW and the BMW for sale on bulletin boards and sold both in a single day.

Holly and I were conducting research on warm places to spend winter, consulting *Europe on $5 a Day* and asking travelers what they recommended. Some said Spain, some said Morocco, some said Lebanon or Israel, some said Greece. Some said India and Nepal. All the choices left us undecided where to go.

Holly debated whether to return to UNC for the Spring semester, or to go back in the autumn. "It depends on where we go next and how we feel about it," she said. "You would no doubt say, 'Let the Fates decide.'"

We packed up our few belongings, and said our goodbyes to Jonathan, Amon Düül and the others at the Factory. Packs on our backs, we hopped on a trolly outside the Factory. Holly made a semi-comic figure wearing a full-length fur coat over a calico dress and hiking boots. Her dark hair fell to her waist. I wore Levi's, a yellow chamois cloth shirt and a leather vest that I had made in Chapel Hill. But I had no fur coat like she had, only a tan corduroy sport coat I had found in a Salvation Army store. Our backpacks were piled high with sleeping bags and a bulky pup tent.

I had been reading *Tropic of Cancer* at the Factory. What an inspiration, Henry Miller. Living one day to the next, Miller survived as a bum in Paris for years, hand to mouth, often not knowing where he would get his next meal or where he would spend the night, "I have no money, no resources, no hopes. I am the happiest man alive." Like Henry Miller, on the best of days, we felt happy, uncluttered, and free to accept whatever came our way. On the worst of days, we cursed, we suffered, we prayed for deliverance, and we muddled through.

This was a best-of-days. At the end of the trolly line, we transferred to a city commuter bus that took us down to the south side of Munich where the highway forked. We got off the bus just before the fork. Our scheme was pure flipism. But instead of flipping a coin, we let a fork in the road determine our course. If a car picked us up and took the left fork in the road—Greece it would be. If our ride took the right fork—then Spain, Formentera and Ibiza, and maybe Marrakesh. "Destiny, be my copilot!" I shouted to the sky. We stuck out our thumbs. A truck picked us up and took the left fork. We were on our way to Greece.

✳ ✳ ✳

In twilight that first evening on the road, we set up the Army pup tent in an Austrian pine forest overlooking the lights of Innsbruck, the pungent fragrance of pine needles around us. Spreading out cross-layers of little branches, we fashioned a springy pine mattress to support our ground pads. We crawled into the tent and arranged our sleeping bags. We slept on top of one and covered ourselves with the other like a down quilt. Naked, we were quite warm cuddled together. We had escaped Munich. We were escaping winter.

The next morning we broke camp and walked out of the forest to the road. We soon caught a ride to Bologna in a truck, and from there, hitched a ride with a refrigerated meat truck on its way to Rome. Holly sat next to the Italian driver and I had the window. The truck driver's hand rested on her thigh and her hand rested on his—restraining or encouraging his hand—it was difficult to tell. When I asked her about it later, she said she herself was of mixed mind at the time, knowing that I didn't care one way or the other, which was not entirely true. But I was intently curious. Last spring when we started dating she seemed demure, even naïve. *Not now.*

As we entered the outskirts of Rome just before dawn, the truck dropped us at a roundabout within sight of the Forum. Alone on the deserted streets, Holly tucked her arm in mine and squeezed me to her. Her smile expressed joy; its warmth touched my heart.

In foggy predawn haze, yellow streetlights illuminated streets devoid of cars. An occasional motor scooter putted past, taking its rider home from night work, or from the soft bed of his lover. As we walked along the sidewalk, the sun peeked above the horizon, and traffic suddenly erupted like a hatch of mayflies on a quiet lake. At the roundabout, two cars raced into the traffic circle, went three-quarters of the way around, and sped out the other side. Almost immediately scores of other cars, scooters, motorbikes, and trucks flew into the roundabout, jockeying for position. As the torrent of traffic increased so did the frenzy. Careful not to get run over, we continued trekking into Rome center to find the pensione our travel guide defined as simple and inexpensive. But first, we wanted to get to know Rome, because our journey would continue tomorrow and who knows if we would ever come back. Holly took off her fur coat and threw it over her backpack, which made her look like she had an enormous cat draped across her shoulders.

Walking past the Forum we cut through crowded streets to the famous Spanish Steps, a central location where students and travelers congregated, rendezvoused with friends, scored drugs, and shared stories of the road. Grubby longhairs hung out on the Steps, some panhandling, others offering hashish and pills. People on their way to work or to shop—to do whatever Romans do during the day—threaded their way around the freaks littering the Steps. We talked to some travelers about getting to Greece. What they told us confirmed what we already knew.

Consulting the Rome map in *5$ a Day*, we located the pensione on a side street in an old neighborhood, booked a room, bathed each other at the sink in the room, redressed, and ventured out. From the pensione we walked over to the Coliseum where immediately a young Roman descended upon us, looking like an early Elvis with greasy black hair combed back in a pompadour and wearing pointy black boots. He boldly proclaimed himself a guide, and while I was reading the short history of the Coliseum in the guidebook, managed to lure Holly off into a little alley. Moments later, she flew out with him in pursuit, turned and pushed him away. "Asshole!" she yelled and gave him the finger. As we walked away, he stood and shrugged his shoulders.

When I questioned her, she told me, "Sure, I wanted to see his prick, and yes, I did touch it, but when he pushed me up against the wall and tried to pull down my jeans, I freaked out!" I thought about that. Holly was willing to handle dicks in public but not fuck in public; obviously, she had morals. It was dawning on me that Holly's attitudes and demeanor were evolving day by day as if she were competing in a race with me to determine who could be more outrageous, more adventurous, and more libertine. *Oh well. Rome.*

We walked over to the Vatican, but the queues were too long, and we were too tired to wait in line. At a grocery store we bought some bread, cheese and grapes, and some pizza consisting of a thick, stale, spongy bread smeared with tomato sauce and olive oil. "Ugh. They should go to New York to learn how to make real pizza," Holly joked. It had been a long day. Back at the pensione we took stock. We had done some sightseeing, handled a prick, and had a simple but disappointing supper. We tucked in for the night. *Rome!*

The next morning, the matron of the pensione served us good pastries and strong coffee. She directed us to a street corner where we boarded an eastbound bus to its terminal stop on the outskirts of Rome. From there it was a short hike to the highway. We thumbed to Bari and Brindisi and spent the night in a cheap guest house. In the morning we bought tickets to Patras, Greece, at the ferry office. I remember almost nothing about that crossing except the joy I felt arriving in Greece. After that our journey seemed a blur of nonstop travel activity, repeatedly getting on and off buses. One bus took us east to Athens, where our *Europe on $5 a Day* guided us to the downtown youth hostel. With few exceptions, all the signs on streets, in shops, and on menus in restaurants were printed in Greek, which we tried to find the English translation in the dictionary.

Truly we felt as though we had landed in a foreign land, far from Europe and way farther from the United States, culturally as well as geographically. Yes! We had almost reached our goal. In the afternoon we took a taxi across Athens to the port of Piraeus, bought tickets, and boarded the overnight ferry to Iraklion. Finally, Holly and I were heading to our winter destination: a small harbor located on the southeast coast of Crete named Matala.

View of the caves from the hills across the harbor

CHAPTER 7

Gulf of Messara

At dawn the ferry chugged into the Iraklion harbor. Holly and I had spent a long night sleeping on deck under the brilliant stars of the Milky Way, lulled to sleep by waves slapping against the hull of the ferry. As the ferry began to dock, we surveyed the morning skyline. A crenellated geometry of buildings, blue, white and cement grey, cut across the panorama of the Iraklion harbor, below which we spied a conglomeration of port equipment: cranes, fork-lifts, dock vehicles, and miscellaneous rusting machinery. Hoisting backpacks, we stumbled down the wide gangplank, elbow to elbow with other passengers, mostly Greeks returning to Crete from Athens. The guidebook map indicated the Matala bus stop at the top of the embarcadero.

When we walked up the hill, porters were tying down baggage on top of the bus with ropes and rubber strips made from inner tubes. Porters heaved our backpacks up to nest amid burlap sacks of grain, suitcases, trunks, wooden crates, a cage of chickens and some chairs tied together. It was Halloween, 1969.

Stepping up onto the bus, we threaded our way down the narrow aisle nodding to four other young travelers wearing funny costumes and took seats near the back. Celebrating Halloween, the other travelers, young Brits, had painted their faces white and wore colorful Gypsy clothes, bandanas, and ragged shawls. We struck up a conversation with one dressed up like Tinkerbell with paper wings sticking out from her shoulders. She told us that they were going to Matala where they had been living for the past few weeks. The day before, they had bused up to Iraklion to shop, to shower in warm water at the youth hostel, and to fete their friend's birthday. The birthday girl, her face painted like a clown, pink dots on her white cheeks and a red rubber nose, spoke in a strangely deep baritone voice. During the next two hours on the bus the four of them told us about Matala, the culture of the little village, and how to live in the cave community.

Tinkerbell asked where we were coming from.

Holly replied, "Munich."

The birthday girl inquired, "Munich? Did you ever go out Ungererstrasse to visit the furniture Factory, they call, 'Desolation Row?' Friends of ours crashed there."

"That's exactly where we were living!" said Holly and I in unison. "In the Factory."

"Wow! Far out, man!" They were impressed.

Halloween. An uneasy feeling suddenly hit the pit of my stomach. Somewhere swimming below the surface of my mind stirred the memory of Halloween a year ago when Nancy and I, stoned on LSD, shared a N Judah streetcar with similarly attired Halloween revelers, as we rode out to her place on the Great Highway for a bad trip—my unscheduled rendezvous with Death.

The bus stopped at several small villages along the way to discharge and take on passengers and baggage. About two hours later the bus crested a hill and we saw below orchards and a hodgepodge of buildings set back from a small harbor bracketed on either side by cliffs. We had arrived at Matala.

Exiting the bus in Matala's unpaved *plateia*, its village plaza, we bought yogurt and bread at the bakery on the corner. North across a long pebbly beach, perhaps two hundred meters from the *plateia*, a cliff pocked with caves sloped up the valley from the sea. Shouldering backpacks, Holly and I crunched across the stony beach till we arrived at the base of the cliffs, which seemed much steeper and higher the closer we got. A small group of longhaired freaks lounged around on the rocks reading, talking, and smoking.

We asked these folks if any caves were vacant. A girl wearing only a bikini bottom replied, "You are so lucky. A Dutch couple just moved out of one up there," she said, pointing up the cliff at a large recess that encompassed three small caves. "See? Just inside that big space," she pointed, "you will find their recently vacated cave on the left. Feel free to move in."

In times past the large space had been a multiroom complex enclosed by the cliff face. Perhaps during a storm or earthquake, the front cliff had collapsed leaving an open cavity containing three smaller caves. Two caves—straight back and on the right—had proper door openings. The third was a doorless indenture sunk several feet deep into the wall. That indenture—that nook—was ours, a starter cave, so to speak.

The cave was not much bigger than a shallow pocket in the rock, perhaps five feet by seven feet. The ceiling, if you could call it that, was so low you couldn't stand up straight. Barely large enough to unroll our sleeping bags and hang up our clothes on pegs; nevertheless, the cave fit our immediate needs; it was dry and sheltered from rain, sea spray and wind. A tattered red and blue Cretan carpet covered a springy bed of dried reeds that leveled and cushioned the uneven rock floor. Previous cave dwellers had left us a lamp—empty of kerosene—and a few candles to light our first night in Matala.

At the rear of the large common cave a reed door opened into a multiroom cave housing three people: Americans, Mark and Barbara, and a Brit, Ethan. To enter their cave you had to stoop to pass through a square hole in the rock wall that issued into a spacious anteroom, that in turn had two interior rooms coming off it—sub-caves in a complex cave warren. That evening Mark and Barbara invited us to share bean soup, olives and bread in their cave. Ethan did not join us. He was a bit of a loner, a blond Viking lost in time.

Mark had lived in Greece for years, initially stationed at the US Air Force base east of Iraklion. He spoke Greek and Arabic. Of medium height and lanky frame, he looked like a cowboy, long hair tied in a ponytail, wide smile accented by a full handlebar mustache, ends twisted in the fashion seen in portraits of Cretan patriates of 1921. After his discharge, he opted to stay in Crete and take up residence in the caves of Matala. Mark spoke Greek in Cretan dialect, and Greeks often mistook him for a Greek American.

Barbara was about Holly's height and build, but strong like an athlete—full breasts, long, dark hair, and tan skin softened with olive oil. A hippy Earth Mother, Barbara often sat naked on cushions reading in the big cave, laughing, and joking with visitors who dropped by. Like Mark, she came from Indianapolis. They had been living together in Matala for two years since he retired from the Air Force. Barbara seemed to get along with everybody, always cheerful and hospitable. When guests called, she treated them to wine, hashish, fresh fruit, dried figs, and nuts.

Ethan, the Viking-Sadhu, read spiritual literature and burned incense. A devout vegetarian, he subsisted on chickpeas, vegetables, and rice, which he cooked on a kerosene stove in the common area of the Big Cave. Handsome with a stocky build, his blond braids fell to his chest, which was covered in a blond, animal fur like the rest of his muscular body. Ethan wore a rustic sackcloth vest over a sort of Iroquois loin cloth and hung strings of Gujarati beads round his neck. I could see why the hippy ladies liked this Mr. Natural. Although he proved pleasing enough company once we got to know him, I rarely spent any time with Ethan at all. And neither did Holly, at least not during our early days in the caves.

Barbara told us that Phil Lawson, a black American musician, lived directly across from our nook in another real cave, a rectangular cuboid—imagine the inside of a sandstone shoebox—equipped with a roll-down, reed door Mark had made. Phil was presently away in Athens putting together some song and dance projects.

Not long after we arrived, a November wind picked up, blowing rain came from the west across the Gulf of Messara, and the temperature began to fall. With cooler weather, tourism further tapered off in the tourist destinations of Crete, including Matala. Businesspeople on holiday had gone back to their stifling office jobs, and students to their universities. As winter drew near travelers departed Europe to winter in India, Nepal, Ceylon, or Southeast Asia. Even so, Matala was far from abandoned. Longer term cave residents like Mark and Barbara convened in tavernas at night with town folk, fishermen, farmers, and the shepherds.

Forever industrious, Mark always was fabricating something; he was a natural, perhaps compulsive, craftsman. I got Mark's total attention when I told him about the history of the Other Ear Gallery, and how I came to learn sandal-making at the Chapel Hill Leather Shop.

"Mark, ever make leather goods?"

"Made belts, a knife sheaf …. Let's see … and this leather bracelet," holding out his wrist encircled by a braided leather band.

"Nice. Ever make sandals?"

"No, but I'd like to learn how. Shops in Greece sell sandals to tourists but the ones I've seen are cheap and poorly made."

"Yes, I agree. Poor quality leather and cheap workmanship. We could do better … much better."

"You think?"

"I know. I made these sandals myself," I said, removing one I was wearing, and handed it to him. "Check out the jackboots local men here wear. Those boots have good leather. The soles are what we call 'oak', or 'oak-tanned' leather. Good boot soles and good harness straps on horses and donkeys mean good leather exists in Crete. Do you think we could find suppliers?"

"I know bootmakers in Iraklion. Maybe they will turn us on to leather venders." The conversation turned into a plan.

When we arrived in Iraklion by bus the next day, we went directly to the bootmakers' workshop on a side street off the main shopping drag. Mark greeted the leather workers who were busy making shoes and boots. Each shook my hand while Mark explained to them that we wanted to buy leather to make sandals. From my hucklebag I pulled out the Chapel Hill Leather Shop sandals I had made. The boot makers sold us leather—a sheet of heavy oak-tanned bottom sole, another in a lighter weight for belts, a sheet of harness leather for straps, and some supplies. They wouldn't sell us heavy strap buckles, so we bought what we could find from market stalls.

Thus began the Matala Leather Shop. We started making crude sandals in the big cave. We sat in the rectangular cavity in the stone floor next to Mark's cave. We positioned an abandoned wooden boat hatch in front of the hole as a workbench. We struggled to cut the heavy oak with sharpened metal blades we wrapped with cloth as handles. That's the knife the bootmakers used to cut bottom soles. We had no stamps to cut holes and slots, but we improvised to produce a sandal, not a very good product, not anywhere near the standard of the Chapel Hill Leather Shop, but a functional sandal—barely functional.

Before I left for Munich, Henry Barrow had told me about living in the Matala caves after he left Peace Corps Malawi. Now—fortuitous for us—he was living in Provincetown, the Mecca of sandal making. Chapel Hill sandal maker, David Honigmann—who had taught me—had worked at Zebo's in Provincetown. Against my IOU, Henry shipped us good leatherworking tools and supplies in care of the Iraklion bootmakers—brass buckles, brass rivets, carbon steel leather knives, skives, slot stamps, a cobbler's hammer, and a pair of heavy-duty leather shears. To further equip our shop-in-hole, we bought general tools in hardware stores in Iraklion. Within weeks, when Henry's package arrived in Iraklion, Mark and I were making and selling sandals that we bragged were the best handmade sandals in southern Europe.

※   ※   ※

The little Matala harbor sheltered a half-dozen fishing boats moored to rusty iron rings set in stone piers. A few steps above, a simple corniche extended across the harbor from Delphini Taverna at the north end—a sidewalk along a strip of stone and cement block shops—to the Mermaid Café on the south side. Most shops were boarded up for the winter except one selling candles, cheap flashlight batteries, matches, cigarettes, playing cards, kerosene, bottles of wine, raki, and ouzo.

Like bookends, the Mermaid Café framed one end of Matala's short corniche while the taverna, Delphini, sat by itself at the other end. Both served food and drink, both were owned and operated by Greeks, and both had generators. Delphini faced the beach with a concrete patio out front, where Cinzano umbrellas shaded two tables and chairs. At Delphini, fishermen and shepherds came to dance *pentozali* and Cretan dances in the evening, displaying athletic prowess, picking up tables in their teeth and such.

If Delphini was a wild party scene, the Mermaid Café was a milder version, concentrating more on great food and hip ambiance. Stelios Xagorarakis and his British girlfriend, Dora, ran the Mermaid, which catered to a wider range of European and American travelers, backpackers, and tourists. Sliding glass doors opened on the concrete corniche. Inside, six wooden tables could seat about two dozen comfortably.

Mark and Barbara welcomed Holly and me as neighbors. When Mark and I had no leatherwork to work on, we took on projects around the caves or helped Mark's farmer friends in the fields. If we decided to eat in the cave, Holly and Barbara cooked everything on little kerosene camper stoves, which limited them to making brown rice and beans, and stir-frying vegetables. A couple times a week the four of us took lunch or dinner at a taverna.

One evening we went down to the Mermaid for supper just as it was starting to pour. Waves dashed against the rocks and fishing boats bobbed up and down at their moorings. As we entered the Mermaid, gusts of wind flung spray across the harbor pelting the Mermaid's sliding doors like BBs. We hung our wet coats on the back of chairs and inhaled the rich aroma of the open kitchen, fresh apple pie mingling with the kitchen smell of sautéing onions, zucchini, fish, lamb chops, and garlic.

Stelios did everything. He cooked and bartended, assisted by Dora, his Isle of Mann girlfriend, who—to everyone's delight—baked apple pies daily. Stelios, a native Cretan, embraced the new age culture of his traveler guests. A scratchy Creedence Clearwater Revival 'Proud Mary' played on the battery powered record player. Under the light of pressure lamps, four bearded cavers played poker at a square wooden table on the far wall. In the other back corner, two tables of Cretan shepherds and fishermen smoked cigarettes, drank raki and talked among themselves.

Stelios was talking to a German girl when we came in. He looked up and greeted us warmly. We ordered moussaka, dolmades, salada, apple pie and wine. Rain hitting the glass doors sounded like a snare drum; rivulets streamed down the glass. Beyond—storm and darkness. "No better place to ride out the storm than the Mermaid," remarked Mark, saying exactly what we were thinking.

After an hour rainfall diminished to an easy drizzle. Having finished dinner we walked back down the corniche toward the caves. Passing by Delphini we heard loud voices, laughter and clapping. We spied light showing through the cracks in the shutters and under the wooden doors. Did we detect the smell of hashish?

The next day Mark told us a story he had heard from Dora about a rivalry between Italian cavers, Jason and Andre. Jason—we were never sure if it was his real name—slept in a rough cave on a top level of the cliffs. At a level below lived Andre, a sweet skinny guy from Milan, an apprentice fashion designer, who could be found during the day reading at the Mermaid. In the evenings he could be seen at his cave playing with his pet cat—a feral cat he had tamed and fed on leftovers from his plate. Whereas Andre was skinny with a wispy ponytail, Jason was hefty, dark bearded, and hirsute, resembling Captain Haddock from *The Adventures of Tin Tin*. He carried a bow and quiver of arrows, hunting hares and anything else he could kill in rocky sagebrush hills south of Matala, sometimes kipping at night in crude, stone shepherd huts in the mountains.

Every few days Jason came into Delphini after hunting. He held court at the bar, drinking expensive beer, eating the rabbits the cook cleaned and grilled for him, and telling crude jokes and stories. Jason was a mercenary, speculated cavers. But if he were, Dora questioned, "Why would he choose to live in Matala instead of in Marseille, or in Corsica, where mercenaries typically congregate? No one," she confessed, "not even I, dares interrogate him about his identity."

Yesterday—in the tale Dora told to Mark—Jason swaggered into the Mermaid. He plunked himself down at Andre's table, facing him, grinning, "Buongiorno, Andre."

Andre, taken aback, put down his book, and returned greetings, "Buongiorno, Jason." "What gives me the pleasure of seeing you today?" he asked in English, inching his chair back from the table.

Jason leaned in toward him, and with a sardonic smile, said, "Andre, they say I have been unkind to you. It is true. I come here today to apologize. Please come to my cave for dinner." He turned to Dora, "Two red wines, please."

Andre cautiously replied, "Of course, Jason. I accept your apology. I would be pleased to dine with you."

"Andre, I prepared rabbit cacciatore. I shot a fat one this very morning and simmered it in marinara sauce for hours."

Andre, "That sounds wonderful. I love rabbit cacciatore. When should I come by?"

"Right now, while it is still warm." They drank another glass of wine and set off together toward the cliffs.

When they sat down on the flat stones Jason had arranged in front of his cave, Jason ladled cacciatore and spaghetti on their plates, plates which Andre noticed were the same as the plates at the Mermaid. They chatted amiably about Rome and World Cup prospects while picking apart the rabbit with their fingers and devouring the pasta. Wiping up sauce in his bowl with a hunk of bread, Andre declared, "Jason, this is the finest rabbit cacciatore I have ever eaten. Please give me the recipe."

"The recipe? Yes, why of course, Andre. The recipe!" Jason grinned, and slowly leaning toward Andre, looked directly into his eyes: "it was not rabbit: it was *cat*. *Your cat* Andre! Get it? *Cat-i-atore!*" he howled. Andre threw down his bowl and scurried down the goat path sobbing while Jason shrieked with laughter.

Mark: "That's how Dora said Jason told the story at the Mermaid last night, laughing so hard he fell down on the floor."

✳ ✳ ✳

Behind the corniche the *plateia* served as the public square where the Iraklion bus came and went. On the square's eastside, a charming, middle-aged woman named Anathula ran a bakery popular with tourists and cave dwellers alike. She baked bread in the morning and again in the late afternoon, and folks lined up to buy fresh loaves of flaky crusted, white *psomi* straight from the oven for five drachmas. She sold cups of tart yogurt for five drachmas, and for half a drachma, dribbled a spoon of herbaceous, wildflower honey over your yogurt. "Mamma," as everyone called her, had earned a reputation for teaching squeamish hippy girls how to kill, pluck and butcher chickens. She braided their unruly locks to make them look presentable, as Cretan culture considered long, loose hair on women unseemly.

From the bakery on the public square, the street continued south into a wide gravel track shaded by plane trees until it petered out at the doors of a rustic Orthodox church built into a cave. In front of the church, and directly behind the Mermaid, sat a small unnamed taverna. I liked to drink here when I tired of tourists at the Mermaid. The owner of the taverna—Tomas was his name—a rough fisherman about sixty, dressed in traditional Cretan black shirt, red cummerbund, and black jackboots to the knee. He poured shots of cheap ouzo for two drachmas and raki for one drachma, which he served on a wooden table with two crude chairs set up in the street outside his shop. When he talked he had a nervous habit of twisting his big dark mustache like a comic-strip pirate. Many misunderstood and disliked him because of his gruff demeanor. In that way, Tomas was the opposite of Anathula. He had a streak of mischief bordering on mayhem, which offended many of the love-and-peace cave-hippies. But I understood him, or pretended that I did, because I considered myself a rough guy, too.

One afternoon Mark and I stopped at Tomas' shop for a raki and a cigarette. Tomas sold individual cigarettes for five lepta apiece. He brought out a bottle of ouzo to the table and instructed Mark to translate for me.

Mark listened to him and then said, "This is nuts. Tomas proposes that if you drink the entire bottle of ouzo while you sit here, he will waive the ten-drachma price. Not a good idea, Cary," said Mark. "Don't do it." He considered Tomas's offer repulsive. When I told Tomas *endoxi*—"okay," Mark got pissed, stood up, and walked off toward the Mermaid leaving me sitting alone at the table.

After spending an hour at the Mermaid playing cards, Mark returned to find me crawling around in the dirt next to the table. He roused me and pulled me out of the street where I threw up under a bush.

"Tomas does this kind of shit all the time," Mark explained, helping me to my feet. "He gets a perverse kick out of seeing people make fools of themselves."

※ ※ ※

One evening in early December, three bearded Germans in embroidered sheepskin coats who had just return from Afghanistan held court at Delphini. Vangelis barred the door and shuttered the one window. On a table in the middle of the room, the Germans spread out a trove of gems and jewelry they had acquired on the trip. They placed piles of bracelets of blood red agates and square-cut lapis lazuli stones next to a mound of silver moonstone rings. They lined up ten gold rings set with dark blue lapis lazuli, "the best Afghan lapis lazuli," the tall one said.

Holding up a flat lapis gem half the size of his thumb, the ugliest German commented eloquently, "Look how lapis draws you into its depth, into an ultramarine night sky of gold stars. Magic!" Each German wore a massive gold ring set with a block of beautiful lapis.

Checking that a timber securely barred the door, the Germans brought out a hunk of black Afghan hashish the size of a deck of cards to share with the dozen or so of us cavers. Hashish was not rare in the caves. Some black hash came in from Turkey. Israeli travelers brought in blond hash from Lebanon. Travelers from Pakistan smuggled in hashish embossed with an official seal from government stores in Peshawar, hashish laced with opium.

A few cavers smoked hashish in human thigh bone pipes they hung on lanyards around their necks. I had one around my neck that I rarely used.

The biggest German Visigoth tamped down the hashish-tobacco lump into an Indian clay chillum pipe, which he passed around the room. Although I liked the romance and ritual, I didn't like smoking harsh hashish tobacco, but I took a toke anyway.

Pungent smoke hung in clouds in the taverna. My eyes watered and throat hurt. The Stones' "Satisfaction" played on the record player. Through all this, the Germans commanded the spotlight. I loved the boisterous stories they told and how they carried a bearing of authority and purpose. Along with the jewelry and hashish, they said they had shipped back trunks of embroidered sheepskin coats and vests to wholesale to Frankfurt shops. Tales of their entrepreneurial adventures seemed tales lifted from literature. The whole spectacle enthralled me.

That night, well fed, full of wine, and groggy from hashish, I left Delphini walking the two hundred odd meters across the beach to the caves. As I stumbled drunk along the pebbles, just above water line, crunching step by step, I looked ahead to the caves. Could I make out a light from Mark's cave that faced the town? Across the face of the cliffs, pale yellow dots of candles and lamps flickered. I imagined people in the caves, sleeping, making love, reading, thrashing around awake thinking of tomorrow. After supper Holly had returned earlier to the caves. I wondered if she was still awake, maybe reading a trashy German novel by the kerosene lamp and waiting warm for me in the sleeping bag. The Milky Way slashed a broad stroke of speckled whitewash across the sky, and high above the cliffs, stars shone brilliant and alive in the deep, blue heavens, sparkling like the lapis lazuli the Germans had shown us in Delphini.

In Matala caves turned over often and cavers came and went. Some left overland for India or Southeast Asia for the winter, to be replaced by newcomers like John Flemming, who cruised into town on a red Triumph Bonneville accompanied by several of his friends in a van. John and I quickly became drinking buddies. He paired up with a lovely, dark-haired beauty, Francine, from Paris. For years I kept Francine's address in my notebook, "Rue Rosa Bonheur." The name evoked warmth, light, and made me happy just looking at it, "Rue Rosa Bonheur." I didn't know until years later when I lived in Paris that it was named after a legendary 19th century female painter and sculptor. John became a famous mask maker in New Orleans and a lifetime friend. *But that is another story.*

As for Holly and me ... we slept together ... most of the time. She had her affairs with strangers, and I had mine. We were both in favor of free love. But like seasons and cave demographics, all was changing. Back in Munich, Holly had debated when she would go back to Chapel Hill to resume her studies. One morning, in our sleeping bag in our stone nook, she asked me, "Do you want to go back and have Christmas with me in North Carolina, or do you want to stay here with Mark and Barbara? I see how much fun you and Mark are having with sandal making. If you want to come back with me, we will need to decide this week. Because you have an Air Icelandic return ticket we will need to fly home from Luxembourg."

I thought about it during the day. If Holly left Matala, sure, I could winter here with Mark and Barbara, Stelios, and Dora. But what would Matala be without Holly—without her affection, her wry smile, her innocent, inquiring brown eyes, her good humor, and sharp mind? I realized how special she was as my friend, lover, and companion. *She is a better person than I.* I felt grateful that she had befriended me. And if we part ways ...? Another thing weighed on my mind. *Would going back to Carolina feel like a defeat? Do I want to return to my job as a copywriter in Winston-Salem?*

✳ ✳ ✳

A Californian named Luke and two other Americans, Gary and Jeff, drove into Matala in a Volkswagen van. I ran into them at the Mermaid and learned they were bound for Kabul. Like the Germans I had just met in Delphini, these guys were smugglers. They planned to smuggle Afghan hashish into the Bay Area and sell it to buy land on the Russian River for their commune.

Later that evening, after many glasses of ouzo, Luke, Gary, and Jeff invited me to travel to Kabul with them. "Let me sleep on it," I said. As I walked back to the cave, I weighed my options. *This is ridiculous. I'm practically dead broke. But ....*

The next morning Luke showed me the VW van. "As I told you, this van is special," he said, thumping the side panel with his fist. "Really solid. We bought it used in Frankfurt a three weeks ago and took it to Amsterdam to be customized by an auto shop specializing in refitting vans for camping, and for smuggling. The shop welded hidden compartments into the body of the camper van to hide twenty, one-kilo blocks of hashish, triple-sealed in wax and plastic."

I quickly estimated the street value of twenty kilos of Afghan hash. *Wonder how many acres of Russian River forestland you can buy with $200,000?*

I discussed with Holly, Mark, and Barbara the pros and cons of going to Kabul with these guys. "What have you got to lose?" Mark asked. "Nothing much going on here, and it will stay slack until March and April when it warms up and people start coming back to Greece. But, Cary, suppose our shop had other things to sell besides sandals and leather goods, such as Afghan jewelry and textiles, wouldn't that be cool?" Holly looked at me and shrugged. *If it were her choice, at Christmas we would be in North Carolina kissing under the mistletoe.*

The main constraint I faced was working capital. In Matala I could squeak by making sandals for fifteen dollars a pop, but in no way did I have working capital to acquire an inventory of Afghan gems, jewelry, embroidery, and other treasures to resell in our shop. At this point I was almost flat out broke, and Mark had no cash to stake my buying trip. The idea of going to Afghanistan broke was pure lunacy.

How can I pull this off? It dawned on me that if Dad could sell my precious Mercedes 190 sedan in Winston-Salem, proceeds from selling the car would fund the Afghan venture. I immediately mailed Dad an aerogram asking him to sell my car and wire me the money in Kabul. Albert Raditz was a supportive father, and a closet adventurer—I was living out his dreams of adventure—and I had no doubt he would agree. I wrote him that although I would not hear from him before I left Crete, he could send me a telegram in care of poste restante in Kabul to inform me which bank he had wired funds to so that when I arrived, I would be flush.

Holly gave me all the cash she had—fifteen dollars. We said our goodbyes in our cave, kissed, and hugged tightly. I felt my heart clinch with a sob. In the time it took to walk across the beach, I was in the back of Luke's van. *So long, Holly. So long, Matala.*

With fifteen dollars in my pocket, a backpack, my hucklebag, my passport, and my leather knife on my belt, I boarded the ferry from Iraklion to Piraeus. It was mid-December 1969. I was leaving for Afghanistan in the company of three guys I didn't know well, in their Volkswagen van customized for smuggling hashish. With crossed fingers and prayers, I set off on a lunatic, wintertime venture to Kabul.

CHAPTER 8

New Year's Eve, Kabul: 1969

Spume sprayed across the deck from waves slapping against the ferry's starboard. Curled up against a bulkhead, I journaled, "Prudence dictates one should not travel with strangers from Athens to Kabul in the winter, with only $15 in the pocket. Wisdom, however, falls unwelcome on the ears of fools. If a journey of a thousand miles begins with one step, what if that first step is a misstep?" The rocking of the boat lulled this fool to sleep.

When the Volkswagen van rolled off the ferry's gang planks in Athens, my traveling companions, Luke, Gary, and Jeff, took it to a garage for an oil change and a mechanical checkup. They planned to spend the night at the Athens Youth Hostel. Should I go with them? A light bulb flashed in my mind. From my hucklebag, I withdrew my notebook to find the Athens phone number Willie Gilbertson-Hart had given me in Matala a month before.

What the hell? From the garage I dialed the number. The phone rang twice; Willie answered in his posh Russell Square accent, told me to come crash with him tonight, and gave me the street address. When I arrived, half-expecting to find him in some sort of derelict slum, his address turned out to be a multi-rise apartment building with balconies in an upscale Athens neighborhood.

Willie buzzed me in and I walked up four flights of stairs toting my backpack and hucklebag. He was waiting for me with the apartment door wide open. We hugged. He turned and introduced me to his two flat mates, Christine, and Julie. Again, I was shocked. Willie, the ridiculous, ragged, corncob-pipe-smoking vagabond who spun yarns in Matala about "living with two beautiful English girls in Athens," was in fact living with two strikingly beautiful English girls in Athens. The ladies, I discovered, spoke fluent Greek, and were doing quite well for themselves teaching English to Greek businessmen. That evening kicked-off a lifelong adventure with Willie Gilbertson-Hart that would endure more than fifty years.

The next morning, I cooked breakfast for Willie, Julie, and Christine, "bear eggs," as we called them as a kid, eggs broken into holes punched out in thick slices of bread and fried in fat—in this case, olive oil. Afterwards, Willie and I said goodbye. I took a taxi over to the garage to meet my fellow travelers.

Van all checked out, oil changed, tires inflated, we departed. Luke navigated the VW van through noisy and polluting Athens' traffic, eventually emerging on the coastal road to Thessaloniki where we stopped for the night. The "commune guys"—as I was now calling them—stayed at a cheap guesthouse. In exchange for food, lodging and travel expenses along the way, I agreed to sleep in the van, to guard it from thieves. God knows what I would have done had any thieves come to call.

The next morning we left Thessaloniki early, driving north along the east coast of Greece. Late in the afternoon we crossed the Turkish border, and got our passports stamped. Following an Istanbul street map Luke plunged the van into a maze of streets, locating his target hotel on a steep side street. The three guys rented a dormitory room for the night.

Luke did not happen upon this hotel by accident. Back when he was getting the van customized in Amsterdam, a mechanic turned him on to a hashish dealer he knew personally who habitually hung out around this particular hotel in Istanbul. His *shtick* involved helping smugglers prepare Turkish hashish for shipping overseas. Following up on the lead, Luke bribed the hotel desk clerk, who sent a boy to locate this known dealer. Within thirty minutes the boy knocked on our door and introduced the guy. Jeff let him in. He resembled a character from a vintage black and white French gangster film.

Creepy in black leather jacket and jeans, pointed black Italian shoes, dark hair combed into an oily pompadour, he had sideburns and trimmed mustache, looking in all aspects like a drug dealer from central casting. In fact, he closely resembled the Elvis look-alike guide Holly had fondled in Rome in October. Once inside the room he immediately closed the curtains, and peeking out the window, peered up and down the alley, presumably checking for someone tailing him. His act looked rehearsed, but sometimes truth resembles fiction. All drug dealer theatrics, I figured, but entertaining, nonetheless. He took off his leather jacket, pulled out a stubby revolver from the waistband of his jeans and laid it on the windowsill. From inside his shirt he pulled out an elongated, black leather folio, and opened it flat on the table revealing a stack of wax-paper-wrapped bars of hashish. Jeff bought ten 10-gram bars for $100.

The dealer proceeded to tutor us how to send this back to the States without getting busted. My traveling companions, willing students, jumped into action. Using a wine-bottle as a rolling-pin they flattened the pieces of hash between pages of a magazine into thin, rectangular wafers they double-sealed in plastic sleeves provided by the dealer. They glued the hashish wafers into greeting cards and put them into envelopes they bought downstairs from the hotel clerk along with Turkish postage stamps. It was getting late. I went downstairs and slept in the van.

We went out for breakfast the next morning to the garden of the notorious Pudding Shop, a gathering place for travelers, backpackers, freaks, junkies, and drug dealers. After wolfing down strong coffee and pastries we drove over to the main Istanbul post office, where Luke posted the stamped envelopes to ten different California addresses—altogether a hundred grams of hashish, one tenth of a kilo. This was ridiculous. What were they risking their lives for? To sell grams of hashish on the streets of Mill Valley for $10 a pop? In smuggling circles, a thousand dollars was pocket change.

After the post office, we bought fruit, bread, and cheese at a stall inside a covered bazaar near the Sultan Ahmed Mosque. A young boy, looking no older than seven or eight, managed this stall. He behaved in all respects like an adult. Though small of stature, he spoke with an adult's authority, bargained with customers, and made change from sales. This kid left a strong impression on me. Funny how expectations for children differ from culture to culture. In the States a boy this age would be treated as a child. *Maybe kids in developing countries grow up faster.*

From Istanbul we drove east toward the Black Sea, up and down roads cutting through dark forests. From swingout turns in the switchback road we got glimpses of the Black Sea stretching to the horizon. When the mountain road leveled out we stopped near Samsun to eat at a roadside restaurant overlooking the water. I had lamb chops and stuffed grapevine leaves. A cold wind cut through my corduroy jacket. Shivering, I vowed to buy a sheepskin coat when we got to Afghanistan, when I would receive money from Dad.

I asked Gary. "How much does a sheepskin jacket cost in Afghanistan?"

"Oh, about $15 or so," he replied.

"Oh, Man!" I muttered to myself. "Am I ever broke!"

The next day, ascending the mountains past Trabzon, we pulled into a little Turkish village to get petrol. It was cold and windy, and wisps of snow blew along the ground and frosted branches of dark evergreens beside the road. A few timber buildings surrounded the roundabout in the middle of the village square. We turned into a petrol station next to three small shops. One, a dry goods shop, sold wine and liquor. Grey smoke blew sideways off its stone chimney. I announced, "Hey, anyone want to duck in that shop for a raki and warm up by the stove?" No takers.

Entering the shop I nodded to the mustached shopkeeper standing behind the wooden counter and studied the line of bottles on the shelf behind him. I pointed to a bottle of raki and asked him in Greek, "*Poso kani*? How much?" miming an imaginary glass to my lips.

"*Deka lira*," he replied.

"*Deka*? Ten lira?" I roared. "Outrageous!" as if shouting was a way to haggle over prices.

Considering the Mermaid charged three drachma for a glass of raki—about fifteen US cents—the ten-lira price he quoted was outrageous—about $1.25. In this little shit village, in the middle of nowhere, this shopkeeper had the audacity to charge me ten Turkish lira for a raki. "Raki is nothing more than cheap moonshine," I said to myself.

Whatever specie of insanity possessed me at that moment, I don't know, but I drew a five-lira bill out of my jean pocket, placed it on the wooden counter, and stabbed it with my sheath knife.

Silence.

The shop keeper looked down at the five-lira bill with my knife quivering in it, looked up into my eyes, shrugged his shoulders, reached under the shelf, and slapped a humongous, nine-millimeter automatic pistol on the counter next to my knife. We both looked down at the pistol and the knife. Our eyes met. He smiled.

He turned his back to me, reached up to the shelf, and brought down a bottle of raki. He placed two shot glasses on the counter and filled them. He slid one glass over to me and raised his in a salute. We drank. An involuntary spasm shuttered down my back. *This raki was powerful—maybe ten times stronger than Matala raki!*

He pulled my knife out of the five lira note, smoothed out the bill with the heel of his hand, and put the bill into a box under the counter. He handed me back the knife, hilt first like a gentleman. I took it, nodded thank you, *efkaristo,* in Greek, opened the door, and walked out to the van, legs wobbly. What have I done? He easily could have shot my ass. Once more, Hubris had led me into the Valley of the Shadow of Death, and somehow—miraculously—Fate led me out again, unscathed.

We drove southeast to Erzurum and from there crossed into Tabriz, Iran. Stopping in Tabriz for some minor repairs required us to spend the night. In front of the guesthouse I discovered marvelous street food. A street vender was cooking lamb kebabs over charcoal in an upturned truck hubcap. I pointed at liver and kidney on his chopping block, which he cubed and threaded onto steel skewers alternating meat with thick slices of onion. Squatting on my heels, I watched as he fanned the charcoal glowing red with a woven fan, turned the skewers above the coals, and laid a round, flat bread directly on to the glowing coals.

Later a Persian friend told me this thick bread was called *tabrizee,* a smaller version of Persian and Afghan *sangak,* a rectangular naan, cooked on stones in a walled oven in the ground. Finally, the meat vender raked meat and onions from the skewer onto the toasted tabrizee, rolled it up, and offered it to me on a page of newspaper. I sprinkled on rock salt he kept in an open coffee can beside the fire and devoured it. Satiated, I wiped my greasy hands on the paper.

After a night in Tabriz, and more street kebab, we drove to Tehran and continued directly to Mashhad, arriving on Christmas Eve. While I was shopping for bread, cheese, fruit, and nuts in the covered market next to Goharshad grand mosque, I bumped into a tall American in jeans and a tan trench coat. We looked at each other and smiled. A missing tooth gave him a goofy look. I liked him immediately.

Sticking out his hand, "Ken Overstreet. Where are you coming from?"

"Cary's the name. We started out in Crete last week. Tomorrow we're driving to Kabul."

"Hey, it's Christmas! Come and have Christmas dinner with my wife and me."

This is how I met Kenneth Overstreet and his French wife, Agate. Christmas dinner consisted of hamburger stew and rice at their apartment. My travel companions stayed in a hotel while I slept on Ken and Agate's couch. They told me they were engaged, but because of Middle Eastern and subcontinental mores, in public they had to call each other "husband and wife." Now she was pregnant and it made sense to get married. Agate wanted to get married in France and have the baby at her parents' home in Provins, outside Paris.

I got back with the boys on Christmas morning, and we continued driving across eastern Iran toward the Afghan border, in a festive mood, laughing and singing Christmas carols. A spark of outrageous holiday spirit came upon us, and we pulled off the side of the road. Gary cut up a cylindrical tab of Owsley "orange bucket" LSD into four pieces. Each of the three put a quarter tab under his tongue. I got a wild idea and dissolved my portion in a spoon. When I injected it, immediately the acid came on—not in a full-blown hallucinogenic way—but it certainly opened my doors of perception.

Perhaps heating it had diminished its strength. Why I acted on this impulse is beyond me, recalling the awful acid freakout in San Francisco last year. Fortunately, this time the acid trip was exhilarating and not horrific.

Passing through the last village before the Iranian border, high on acid, laughing and singing—bang! We drove directly over the curb and careened across the middle of a roundabout, barely missing the flagpole, and bounced over the far curb on the other side. We howled with laughter. At the border, Iranian immigration guards stamped our passports. For the next fifteen miles or so, in a silly LSD state of consciousness, we barreled down the unpaved road through a disputed DMZ no-mans-land between the official borders of Iran and Afghanistan. To us, we could have been piloting a spacecraft across a Desolation of Doom on a faraway desert planet.

Suddenly, directly in front of us colored lights flashed, red, yellow, and blue. Crash! Bang! Only too late we realized that we had just smashed into the Afghan border gate festooned with fancy bicycle reflectors and had knocked it off its hinges; splintered, it fell to the ground. This struck us as deliriously funny, and we tumbled out of the VW van, rolling around in the dust, laughing hysterically. At that moment, Afghan border guards with rifles rushed out of the guard house, which resembled a large black, red, and green outhouse, looked at us rolling on the ground laughing, looked at the roadblock gate lying broken on the ground, lowered their rifles, and they, too, began laughing. Helping us stand up, they led us into the guardhouse, gave us chairs, asked for our passports, and stamped them with entry visas to Afghanistan. They served us strong black tea and offered to sell us hashish, which we politely declined. *Welcome to Afghanistan.*

At dawn we hit Herat, passing by the Great Mosque as the morning sun reflected off its blue tile walls. Luke pulled the van over to the side of the road beside the bazaar where shop owners were rolling up the steel shutters of their shops, preparing for the day. Gary, completely stoned and disoriented, opened the door of the van and fell into the concrete ditch bordering the street, the *jube,* a narrow canal filled with liquid sewage. Shopkeepers watched this disgustingness unfold, without expression, as we stood astride the *jube* and helped Gary scramble out. His pants up to his thighs were soaked with foul, stinking sludge. Jeff borrowed a pail of water and helped Gary wash off the filth. It was imperative we find a hotel as soon as possible with a shower so he could bathe and wash his trousers. We looked around and saw a guesthouse across the street. The shower, heated by a woodstove, cost 20 afghanis, as much as a room cost for the night. The guesthouse had two toilet facilities. One, a Turkish toilet where you squatted to shit, was blocked up, leaving only the informal one, the flat roof of the guesthouse where you had to climb out through a hall window and shit in view of the other rooms. *Welcome to Herat.*

We all took showers. Exhausted from the aftereffects of the LSD, but still wired and awake, I crossed the street and walked into the open bazaar, a conglomeration of shops and covered stalls. I entered a shop selling furs, ducking under animal pelts hanging from a beam—fox, sable, and wolf. The merchant greeted me in English, "Hello, Sir. Welcome to fur shop."

"Where do these furs come from," I inquired.

"From the mountains, in north," he said, pointing. "My shop here make you fur coat, make you fur hat," he offered. I declined, putting my right hand over my heart.

"I make you wolfskin coat. Very warm," he said, lifting a lush wolfskin pelt from a pile.

"Sorry, but I go tomorrow to Kabul," I said, pointing in the other direction.

"When you come back, Sir, I take you wolf hunting," he said, grinning.

Wolf hunting in the mountains of Afghanistan? I imagined myself on a horse with a rifle scabbard beside the saddle, and trussed behind, a wolf trophy: fulfilment of a young Carolina country boy's hunting dream. As a kid, I read everything in the Charlotte Public Library about hunting and trapping, from the Ozarks to the Yukon. But a wolf hunting expedition in the mountains of Afghanistan—the retro-fantasy of a twelve-year-old boy—it was never destined to happen.

※ ※ ※

We arrived in Kandahar, having passed through the *Dasht-e Margo*—the Desert of Death—and located the principal guesthouse on Kandahar's main street, a wide, unpaved boulevard running through the town. It could have been a setting for the Sergio Leone western, *The Good, the Bad, and the Ugly*. To complete that *mise-en-scéne*, as we were driving into town, we passed a horse-drawn wagon hauling a load of burlap sacks southward.

The next morning, drinking tea and eating eggs and naan in the guesthouse chaykhana, I spotted Melissa, an American I had met in Matala. She was sitting with three guys at a table across the room. I left my companions and walked over to her.

"What are you doing here?" we both asked each other at the same time. We laughed. I had admired Melissa when she was living in Matala, but never dated her. *I can't recall why not.* I told Melissa how this trip had come about, setting up the leather shop with Mark, my desire to collect lapis lazuli, the VW van—I did not tell her about smuggling—even among thieves one must be discrete.

Melissa said, "I've been in Kandahar most of December with these ugly Danes ...," smiling and sweeping her hand with upturned palm to introduce three big, handsome blond guys dressed in Afghan *shalwar kameez* surrounding her. "We are buying carpets, antiques, and other Afghan treasures to sell in Copenhagen. It's exciting. I am learning so much!" she gushed.

"Everything in Kandahar is far cheaper than in Kabul. And life is cheaper here, too," she continued, lowering her voice, and putting a hand on my shoulder. "Last week we witnessed a gunfight in the street. Can you believe it? We were sitting right here drinking tea when we heard gunshots outside. We ran to that window—a pretty stupid thing to do!—and saw two men running down the street"—she pointed down the boulevard—"one chasing the other. The guy being chased turned around and shot at the other guy over his shoulder. The guy chasing stopped, aimed, and shot the guy in the back. God! We couldn't believe it! A crowd came out into the street ...

Anyway, so happy to run into you here, Cary, after ... how long ... a couple of months? Oh yeah, you were living with that beautiful American chick, Holly? She was really cool. I really liked her. Are you two still together? As I recall, Cary, you were both ... how should I say it, 'sleeping around?'"

"No, we're not together. I left Holly behind in Matala. By now, she is probably opening Christmas presents at home in Raleigh. Maybe we will get together again in the future. Hard to say ... things were ... well, you got the picture ... pulling in two directions—to leave or to stay."

"Yeah, I can get that. Hey, believe it or not I've found an interesting community of expats and Afghans working together on joint projects in Kandahar. You should stay," she said, squeezing my hand. "There's good stuff going on here I'd like to show you."

"Oh shit! I wish I could, Melissa," squeezing back. "but we're setting off to Kabul after breakfast. What if I came down from Kabul to visit you?"

"That would be great," she said, giving me a quick peck on the cheek. I made a vow to come down and visit Kandahar, soon.

In a few hours we passed through Ghazni, a gigantic bazaar with a reputation for fine embroidered sheepskin coats and vests. Rack after rack of sheepskin coats and vests filled stalls alongside the roadway through town. Shivering in my corduroy jacket over a sweater and wool undershirt, I surely wished I had one on now. We stopped at a chaykhana for tea, naan, and roast mutton. We didn't take time to tour the market before we were off again.

In Kabul, it was already dark. Jeff located the Habib Hotel on the corner of the Khyber Circle. We checked in with the clerk named Saïd Issa, who helped move our stuff into a common room on the first floor above the chaykhana with four rope-strung charpoy beds, a table and four chairs. On the wall by the windows overlooking the street hung a calendar with a painting of a Muslim holy man in a turban. From the street, smoke arose from kebab and naan stands.

On my bed I curled up in my sleeping bag. It was New Year's Eve, 1969. The December 19th *Time Magazine* pictured economist Milton Friedman on the cover. I reviewed the table of contents: an overview of the '60s, Viet Nam war and protests, fashion trends, hippies, entertainment, politics, Nobel Prize winners, obituaries, moon landings, and predictions for the world economy. I lay the magazine down on my chest, feeling far, far away from these events and the subjects of the articles, far away from my past, as if the Volkswagen van had transported me to another planet—planet Afghanistan. *What a relief to be free from the "airconditioned nightmare," as Henry Miller had called it.* Impulsively, I heaved the magazine out into space. It sailed across the room, pages fluttering, and hit the wall—"Smack!"—and fluttered down to the floor like a shot quail.

CHAPTER 9

Les dents du bonheur

New Year's Day 1970, first day of a new decade, and I was horny as hell. I borrowed two-hundred afghanis from Jeff to take a bus down to Kandahar to woo Melissa and check out her scene. After enduring many cold nights in a sleeping bag on the floor of the bus between Athens and Kabul, I felt entitled to a loan. Melissa! Not only was I obsessed by her funny smile, her sense of humor, the hilarious way she told stories, her kisses, and her perky, round derriere, I was enticed to know more of the export enterprises she and these Danes had going.

The bus back to Kandahar took about six hours. When it stopped on the main street in front of the guesthouse, a small scrum of folks vied to get on the bus at the same time we were getting off. *Sheesh!* Inside the chaykhana Melissa sat in the same chair she had been sitting in when I left. She watched me as I came through the doorway, walking toward her across the room. Still sitting, she grabbed my belt buckle and pulled me to her and kissed me on the mouth. She stuck her nose several inches from my chest, and scrunched her nose, "I knew you'd be back; I just knew it! But, Jesus, Cary, you came back smelling like the bottom of a laundry bag." She turned to the Dane at her left, "Karl, Sweetheart, please fetch me clean pants and a shirt ... while I give this boy a bath."

Holding my hand Melissa led me up a wide flight of wooden stairs to the first floor, through a door that passed through a suite of bedrooms to a bathroom, a small bare chamber with a Turkish toilet on one wall, and a bathing area on the other, which was a drain-hole in the floor, two buckets and a big plastic cup. "Cary, give me your clothes." Curiously comfortable getting naked in front of Melissa, as if I had known her forever, I stripped off my boots, shirt, jeans, and socks, and handed them to her in a wad. "Wait here and brush your teeth with the boiled water in this cup," handing me a drinking cup, toothbrush, and toothpaste, "while I get hot water from the restaurant. That's a towel for you hanging on the back of the door, I'll be back in a few minutes." I wrapped the towel around my waist. I looked out the window facing a vacant lot next to the hotel where boys were playing football in the dirt barefoot. *Barefoot on the first of January?*

Melissa returned carrying a bucket of steaming water. "Wait a moment, and I'll join you." In less than a minute, she came back into the bathroom naked with a towel draped over her shoulder and hung it from a hook on the wall. She unwound the towel from my waist and hung it up, next to hers. It was a chilly in the bathroom, her nipples stood out from her small breasts like ripe dates. A thick tangle of pubic hair shadowed the space between her legs. My glance strayed down from her crotch to her strong thighs, her knees, round calves, and her feet. Her toes were splayed, splayed like the diastema gap between her front teeth, a facet of her allure, which Melissa shared with the Wife of Bath.

She saw me looking at her, laughed, and turned around to show me her ass. "Looks like you like what you see, huh?" nodding at my hard dick sticking straight out from my pubis. I poked my dick against her butt. She sighed, spinning around, and pushed me away, grinned and murmured, "Enough of that for now!" She poured hot water into an empty bucket and cooled it with clean cold water from the other. "Squat down."

With a cup she poured warm water over my hair, shampooed me, and massaged my scalp with her fingers. "Stand up, raise your arms." She soaped up a washcloth and washed my face and entire body. Squatting down, she scrubbed my feet. She scrubbed my back, and gently washed my genitals, making my prick almost painfully erect. "Lean your head over, Cary," she said, rinsing warm water through my curly hair. Then she rinsed my whole body and squeegeed it off with her hands.

A knock. Melissa opened the door fully naked, and Karl stepped in, handing her folded Afghan trousers and a shirt. "Thanks, Karl, please put them on my bed, Sweetheart," she instructed. I wondered what kind of relationship she and Karl had for her to be so unselfconsciously open with him. *Melissa and the three Danes: sounds like a Disney fairy tale.*

"Me, now," she said, handing me the washcloth. "No soap in the hair, Cary, and please, none on my lady parts. That area is sensitive, and we wouldn't want it to dry out, would we now?" I washed her tenderly with the washcloth, pleased as she squirmed a little in place. I splashed clean warm water on her with my hands, putting special attention to her *sensitive areas*. Then, cup by cup, I poured the rest of the bucket of clean, warm water over her.

Melissa dried me off with a towel, and I did the same for her. She led me into her bedroom. My intense desire subsided into a feeling of affection, of kinship. Maybe this fondness was due to her caring for me so tenderly. This was a comforting feeling I had not had since being with Holly in Germany. I desired Melissa with body and mind, but I wanted to prolong this pervasive feeling of affinity and pleasure. Fuck her? If anyone were going to be fucking anyone, she was going to be fucking me; I felt like a young boy seduced by an experienced courtesan.

Melissa laid me down on my back on her bed. She massaged my whole body with lavender butter. Lightly, she stroked my prick from testicles up to the tip, again and again. She strummed my nipples with her fingertips until they were as hard as hers and held them softly between her teeth. Lowering her mouth over mine, lips parting, she eased the soft tip of her tongue into my mouth. Wedging herself between my legs until my pubic bone mashed up against hers, she mounted me. Vaginal muscles clamped around my prick like a firm fist. *Oh my god ...!*

The sun was going down when we finished making love and finally uncoupled. Blissed out in her bed, I spooned her from behind, drifting into a dreamless state of wellbeing.

When I awoke she was standing beside me like an angel, hair braided in two brown pigtails, wearing a finely spun, embroidered white cotton dress that came down below her knees. She handed me clean clothes, "Cary, let's get dressed and have dinner in the chaykhana." She kissed me and helped me get dressed. I was putty in her hands.

We spent two days in Kandahar, Melissa and I, screwing, eating, and meeting merchants, but mostly we hung out in the hotel chaykhana drinking tea and chatting with the Danes. Could I potentially join their little family, play a role in their export enterprises? Even though the Danes treated me with warmth and respect, I imagined they perceived me as an intruder. Did they politely tolerate me because of their affection for Melissa? I might have stayed longer—Melissa was delectable, smart, and witty—but I needed to get back to Kabul and claim the money Dad was sending me from selling my car.

I shook hands and hugged each of the three Danes, wishing them all the luck in the world. I said goodbye to Melissa, who with grace let me slip away with an affectionate goodbye, a deep kiss and a squeeze. She bid me to return, "if the fates allow," stuffing 500 afghanis in my back pocket. I left Kandahar, thoroughly fulfilled, wondering why I would ever want to leave. I caught a ride back to Kabul with a pair of Scots in a beat-up Russian Lada they had bought in Yerevan and were driving to Bombay to sell.

Back in Kabul, I rejoined Gary, Jeff, and Luke in the Habib Hotel. I repaid standing loans, which left me with 150 afghanis. With that in my pocket, I walked over to the Khyber Restaurant to eat something decent. Just a block from the Habib Hotel, the Khyber Restaurant was to Kabul what the Pudding Shop was to Istanbul, a place to congregate, share travel stories and news, and eat green salad sterilized in dilute bleach rinse. The owners may have been Afghans, but they understood that cleanliness and good hygiene set them apart from the unhygienic restaurants of the Sub-continent, from Athens to Calcutta, where travelers inevitably were forced to eat—and suffer the ill consequences. As I walked out, it started to snow.

At poste restante I picked up a telegram from Dad. He reported he was trying to sell my Mercedes, and when he did, he would wire me the money. *How long is this going to take?* Despite the input of Melissa's going away present, I had to economize. Daily, I ate breakfast in the covered bazaar behind the Habib Hotel. Into a ceramic bowl, which I borrowed from the Habib chaykhana, the dairy man ladled yogurt, and the dried fruit stall next to him contributed a handful of raisins for 25 puls, one-quarter of an Afghani. I took my bowl of yogurt and raisins into a preserved-fruit stall, where an elderly, white-bearded man in a turban and a young boy sold fruit and syrup from five-gallon glass containers on plank shelves. The old man winked at me with his one working eye and spooned a dollop of sugar syrup from an enormous preserved-peach jar into my bowl of yogurt and raisins. Again, 25 puls. This was my breakfast. It cost pennies; a scrumptious breakfast that angels in paradise could serve recently arrived souls.

Every day in the Habib Hotel chaykhana I enjoyed green tea, *kahwah*, and spiced milk-chai, *chai sheer*, prepared on the samovar stoves common to all chaykhanas. An installed samovar was a piece of functional art, a donut shaped reservoir welded to the top of a cylindrical charcoal stove. A stove pipe ran up from the stove through its donut-shaped reservoir and extended all the way up through the chaykhana's ceiling. When a waiter prepared chai, he opened a faucet on the samovar to pour boiling water over tea leaves in an enamelware teapot. At any one time, a half dozen teapots sat half-filled on the flat, hot surface of the samovar. When you ordered *kahwah*, a waiter topped up a teapot of concentrated tea with boiling water. For *chai sheer*, the waiters added hot milk to the concentrated tea. Imitating Afghans sitting near me, I drank unsweetened tea with a lump of sugar, *qand*, held between my teeth instead of dissolving it in the cup with a spoon.

In the kitchen cooks fried eggs in mutton fat, which had made me gag when I first arrived. A side dish was overcooked-spinach in mutton fat. The longer I stayed, however, the more I grew to like greasy eggs and slimy spinach mush mopped up with a hunk of whole wheat naan.

All manner of expats and travelers frequented the Khyber Restaurant a block away, which at times resembled the Star Wars bar scene. There I met two bearded American twins, Samuel and Frank. Former Peace Corps Volunteers, they had remained in Afghanistan after the end of service. Decked out in Afghan attire—vests over salwar kameez, untied turbans draped around their necks—in appearance, they were indistinguishable from native Afghans. They spoke Dari and Pashtun and were married to Afghan women, also twins. Both twin couples shared a large house and compound near the Kabul River. Samuel mentioned they had an import-export business—I could not ignore Frank's gold Rolex. I told them about my leather shop in Crete, that I was in Afghanistan to buy tools and gems to sell in the shop. "Cool," said Frank. He invited me over to their home for lunch the following day.

When I walked up the broad, sandy avenue, Frank and Samuel's compound appeared like every other residency on the street—high stone walls enclosing a compound of several buildings. Beside the heavy, wooden door hung a cord with beads, which rang a bell inside. A moment later, an eye appeared through a little peephole in the door, an Afghan boy opened it and invited me into a courtyard surrounding a two-story mud-plastered stone house. The boy rang another bell, the door latch buzzed and unlocked the door electronically. Inside, on the ground level we faced a broad flight of wooden stairs, which led me up to yet another locked door.

The boy knocked and the door opened. I took in the unexpected décor. Afghan and European furniture filled the spacious room. Baluchi and Isfahani carpets covered tile floors. Everything—couches, low tables, floor lamps, and kilim pillows—was museum quality. On walls hung more carpets, paintings, and bookshelves, and in the corner sat modern stereo equipment, from which John Coltrane's "Love Supreme" played softly. Frank arose from a couch and shook my hand, "Welcome, Cary. Please forgive all the locked doors, but security is forever a concern in Kabul."

A lady in a striped silk pantsuit backed through the carpet drapes covering a doorway, carrying in tea on an engraved silver tray. "Myriam, please greet our new friend, Cary."

She set the tray down and shook my hand. "Welcome to our home, Cary," she said in perfect Oxford English. Her hand was covered in intricate henna designs. The door from the stairwell opened and two females entered wearing full, black burkas. "Cary," said Myriam, "may I introduce my sisters, Yasmine and Fatima." The women removed their burkas and hung them on a coatrack. Both wore designer sweaters over miniskirts. They shook my hand. I noticed Frank drank tea from a small glass like an Afghan, a cube of sugar between his teeth.

Servants brought delicacies for us, sweet *shirnee* candies, sugared almonds, *noql*, pistachios and *kulcha* pastries. I wrote down the Afghan names of the foods in my notebook where I accumulated a list of Dari words, phrases and numbers. We dined on lamb kebab, kofta, naan, and apples, followed by more tea. Myriam and her sisters excused themselves, leaving the room through the carpet-draped doorway. Frank sat back, "Would you like to smoke hashish?" he inquired. "Or a cigarette …?" pulling a pack of Marlboros from his vest pocket.

"Only a cigarette, thank you," I said. "May I compliment you on your beautiful home." He lit my cigarette with a gold Dunhill lighter.

Frank told me Peace Corps had upended his life in a good way. He didn't say much about his business, only, "It's complicated. I'll tell you more about it another time." Pausing, "I want to hear more about your shop in Crete." I told him about the woodworking Factory in Munich, hitchhiking with Holly to Greece, moving into a cave in Matala, where I started up a sandal shop with Mark.

"What a cool story, I wish you all the best, Cary. If Sam and I can help you in any way, please let us know." After more tea, he personally showed me out to the street door.

Several days later I ran into Frank again at the Khyber. He introduced me to three British travelers he had been talking with when I came in. He put his hand on my shoulder, "Cary, could you please take our friends to this carpet shop over in Shari Naw?" I agreed. He gave me the card of the shop.

In light snow we drove over to the Shari Naw neighborhood in their beat-up Range Rover. The shopkeeper greeted us graciously, serving us tea, hashish, and sweetmeats while his assistant displayed the stock, unrolling carpet after carpet, one upon another. The Brits bought carpets, kilims, woven camel bags, and pillow covers with fancy tassels. As the assistant was loading the merchandise in the Range Rover, the shopkeeper motioned me off to the side. He turned his back to the Brits and handed me a roll of afghanis.

"What is this?" I asked him.

"This, Sir, is your commission," he replied. *Wow! A new window has just opened in the hovel of my vagabond life. Frank, what a beautiful guy.*

During the next few days, with a wad of afghanis in my pocket, I started shopping for the Matala Leather Shop, including leatherworking tools I found in hardware stalls along the Kabul River. While I was walking back from the river to the Habib, a wrought iron anvil sticking out of the top of my hucklebag, a young man accosted me. In Kabul people constantly stop you on the street to try to sell you something or persuade you to visit their shops. This teenager asked in broken English, "What is that in your bag, Sir?"

He seemed like a good kid. I showed him the anvil and told him I was buying tools for my leather shop. He said, "I want to introduce you to my father. He is goldsmith and we have shop there," he said, pointing down the wide, unpaved street that bordered the Kabul River. "My name is Farooq." His invitation sounded refreshingly authentic. I said, "My name is Cary. Yes, I will come to meet your father."

We walked a hundred meters along the river to the shop, which had an elevated entryway chest-high from street level. Farooq's father sat cross-legged on cushions in the wide doorway-window, bending over to hand something to a burka-clad woman standing below him in the street. After she walked away he motioned to us to come inside, and we climbed up stone steps into the shop. Farooq introduced me, "This is my father, Ghulam Dastagir. And this is my brother, Siddiq," a younger boy soldering silver jewelry over a brazier of glowing charcoal. "This is Cary." They shook my hand.

Farooq brought out a thick cushion for me and placed it next to Siddiq. I looked around. Silver belts and necklaces festooned with pale moonstones hung on the wall. Farooq said, "We now make many belts for buyer in Amsterdam. One hundred agate belts. One hundred agate bracelets."

Ghulam Dastagir drew Farooq over to his side and spoke to him for a while. He came back, "My father asks you to come every day eat with us, teach me and Siddiq to speak good English. They do not teach good English to speak in school. Father say we must talk good English to get customers to come to shop. You come here for lunch every day with us? Teach us speak to customers?" I was touched. *Once more good fortune shines on me.*

Almost every day after that, I gave English conversation lessons to Farouq and Siddiq and ate lunch with Ghulam Dastagir and his boys around a common bowl, dipping torn pieces of naan into a bowl of beans with my right hand just as they did. A week later when I got sick, they bought me medicine. When I needed a warm coat, they got me a sheepskin jacket from a cousin's clothing store. They made me feel part of their family.

Farooq gave me a red, mirror-top tin can of *naswar*, a powdered tobacco-quicklime stimulant. He taught me how to dip it, just like I had dipped snuff as a kid in Carolina. You picked up a dab from the can with the edge of the lid and dropped it under the lower lip. Then you looked in the mirror to check you didn't have any ugly green stuff on the teeth.

In the goldsmith's shop I watched Farooq and Siddiq make jewelry over charcoal braziers. They heated heavy soldering irons in a charcoal brassier, squeezing hand bellows to blow coals white-hot. Farooq set agates in the bezels, picking choice, uniform, half-round carnelians, and white moonstones from bags of assorted chalcedony, throwing irregular stones into a basket. Siddiq used a hand-held alcohol lamp to direct pin-point soldering onto jewelry settings, blowing a thin pencil-lead stream of blue fire on to the soldered seam.

I dug through the irregular stones and asked them if I could set aside odd-colored fire-agates and moonstones to buy when I got my money from my dad. They said yes. "We call these colored agates, *fancy agates*, Mr. Cary." In addition, they opened boxes of dark blue lapis lazuli of the same superb quality I had seen six weeks before in Matala, lapis of the quality the German smugglers had spread out on tables in Delphini—lapis that had inspired this trip. Now, pricing the blue gems, I had to face that I didn't have a market in Matala for expensive jewelry among freaks and travelers. Cave dwellers would easily pay three-hundred drachma—about ten US dollars—for a nice agate set in a white metal ring, but not 3,000 drachma or more for a lapis ring set in twenty-karat gold.

✳ ✳ ✳

Eventually "the commune guys" at the Habib Hotel purchased their twenty-kilos of first-rate black hashish and prepared to leave Kabul for Europe. As per instructions from their Amsterdam car mechanic, they covered the blocks in paper and wax and pressure-sealed them in plastic to carefully fit into the secret crevasses in the van. After they said their goodbyes and departed, I moved out from the four-person room in the Habib Hotel to a single room above the chaykhana in the Bamiyan Hotel across the street. My room at the Bamiyan cost the same as the Habib, ten afghanis a night, about 15 cents US. A shower also cost another ten afghanis. Fortunately, since it was winter, I didn't have to shower all that often. I could bathe with a washcloth at a sink.

After lunch at the goldsmith shop I bought naan from the breadman in front of the Habib Hotel. As I turned around to cross the street, I watched two turbaned Afghan men push aside the carpeted door-curtains hung over the doorway to the Bamiyan Hotel. A cloud of steam from the hot, humid chaykhana engulfed them, making them appear like genies emerging from a magic lamp. A truly theatrical entrance. They reminded me of illustrations of thieves from Galland's *Thousand and One Arabian Nights*. These two warriors, dressed in traditional *shalwar kameez*, embroidered vests, wool blankets as scarves, and dirty-white turbans, had vintage Enfield rifles slung across their shoulders. "Wolf hunters?" I wondered, as I passed by them and entered through the hanging carpets into the warm Bamiyan Hotel chaykhana.

At a crowded table across the room near the stairs, sat a European woman in furs, gem bracelets and rings, surrounded by three guys. Our eyes locked. *She is ... splendid!* And then—as if I were commanded by a daemonic power—I crossed the room, inserted myself between the guys seated around her, reached across the table to grasp the bejeweled hands, and said, "You are gorgeous. What is your name?"

"*Je m'appel Soizette. Et toi?*"

"*Je m'appel Cary, je suis enchanté,*" about all the French I could muster at the time.

I tore a page from a newspaper on the table and scribbled my room number, "CARY-1A," put it in her hand, turned and mounted the stairs. In my room, as I was taking off my coat, I heard a soft rapping at my door. I opened it and Soizette swept into my arms. Within seconds my trousers were around my ankles, my hands under her dress. I stripped off her panties—her pussy was soaking wet. She hopped up, wrapping her legs around my waist, and my dick slipped into her as if it belonged there. We coupled standing up, the door ajar to the hall. She slammed it shut with her foot.

For almost a week, we were inseparable. Her tale fascinated me—thank God she spoke better English than my French, which at that time was *detestable*. Soizette decamped Paris three months before, after having demanded a divorce from her abusive husband who then beat her and locked her in her bedroom. With the help of the maid, Soizette fled Paris on a flight to New Delhi carrying only a Givenchy shoulder bag and her cash savings. In Goa she moved into a group house with a family of European freaks. Picking up her mail from poste restante at the Goa post office, she got a telegram from her sister-in-law telling her to be on guard because her husband had hired private detectives to locate her and force her back to Paris. Soizette decided her best move was to travel overland incognito from India to Marseilles where she had friends—lawyers—who could help her deal with her bastard husband.

"Divorce in France is *très, très difficile*," she explained. "The fucking courts always favor men in legal disputes. *Mais, je vais me débrouiller,*" I will do my utmost. "I know things about my husband's business affairs that he would not want authorities to know. I *will* get my divorce," she said emphatically, slapping her hand down on the table.

Soizette had a gap between her front teeth just like Melissa's. "I find this very sexy," I said, touching her teeth with the tip of my finger.

"We French have names for all things sensual. This space between the teeth," touching the gap with her tongue, "we call *les dents du bonheur*. We believe it is a symbol of good luck and good sex."

"I will attest to that in the court of love," I said, touching her beneath her dress.

Days of laughter, bliss, and passion, and then … Soizette was gone. She gave me an address in Paris where I could write her. We didn't get in touch again for almost two years. *Yet that is another story.*

CHAPTER 10

A Gift from the Heart

When two thieves meet on a mountain road ....

Finally Dad telegrammed that he had sold my Mercedes 190 for $1,000, more than I had paid for it, and was wiring me funds through Wachovia Bank in Charlotte to its correspondent bank, Da Afghanistan Bank in Kabul. I went down to the bank with Farooq and hit an impasse. At the counter, the clerk checked a massive ledger book and said they had no record of a wire transfer to a "Cary Raditz." I didn't know what to do except come back every day. This went on for a week.

At the Khyber Restaurant I met Lauren, an American of thirty who had a certain magnetic quality—as the French would say, "*Elle a du chien*"— roughly translated as, "although not pretty in the conventional sense, she attracts men like a bitch in heat." Long hair to her waist, she possessed the physique of a soccer player. I bought her lunch and we immediately hit it off. I could feel it in the second chakra. "Why don't you move out of that dump, the Bamiyan Hotel," she asked between bites of chocolate cake, "and come stay with me at the Green Hotel in Shari Naw? My girlfriends and I have an extra bed in our room."

That was all it took. With Lauren on my arm, I escorted her around the corner to the Bamiyan Hotel, up the stairs to room 1A, scooped up my belongings, and closed the door. *Am I imagining it, or do I detect the lingering scent of Soizette?*

I brought my stuff down to the chaykhana, paid my bill, and checked out. Lauren and I took a taxi out to the Green Hotel and I moved into a room with her and her two roommates, Karen from Omaha, and Sissy, from San

Diego. As undergraduates, they told me, the three of them had played lacrosse at the University of Maryland and had remained best friends.

Lauren made a bed for me and spread my sleeping bag on top. Karen, tugging Sissy by the arm, urged, "Let's get outta here, Sissy, I've seen this romantic comedy before. Why don't we give these lovebirds some privacy?"

Sissy laughed, "Hell no, I want to watch!" Karen dragged her out of the room and closed the door. Lauren walked across the room and locked it. Right then and there, Lauren stripped naked in front of me. She was like a Greek statue.

In the middle of the night nausea hit me. I scrambled out of the sleeping bag and stumbled to the toilet puking. A convulsive onslaught of nausea and diarrhea ripped through me. After a bit, Lauren, having cleaned up my mess, retrieved me from the bathroom, bathed me, and helped me back into my sleeping bag, "Cary, don't worry about this. Incidentally, I am a Registered Nurse. Healing the sick is my profession."

I awoke several hours later. Nausea and diarrhea struck me again and I continued to get worse as the night went on. I started to shiver and then moments later, I was sweating. Lauren took my temperature and read the thermometer, "One hundred and three, Cary. You are one sick puppy!" She put a cool compress on my forehead.

For the next day and a half, rounds of chills and fever wouldn't break. Lauren tossed my sleeping bag on the floor and covered the mattress with a ground tarp and a sheet. When I got feverish and sweaty, she sponged my forehead and body with a washcloth; when chills hit me, she pulled up a cover sheet and blanket and laid my sleeping bag on top. I couldn't hold food down. Boiled water, salt and sugared green tea kept me hydrated.

Surely good fortune had smiled upon me when Lauren walked into my life when she did. *A Registered Nurse?* If Lauren and I had not met, and if I had been sick alone in room 1A at the Bamiyan, I don't know how I could have handled it.

My illness, however, did not go down well with the roommates. Karen, whom I had initially liked, resented that Lauren wasn't paying enough attention to her. Sissy was irate. She thought Lauren should never have brought me to the Green Hotel in the first place, screwing up their happy threesome. By this point I was sure Karen and Sissy had it in for me. In nightmare deliria, I imagined they despised me because I had abducted Lauren whom they adored. I feared they could turn on me at the drop of a hat. *Will furious Harpies strangle me in my sleep?*

Then Ken Overstreet burst through the door, stepping back into my life. "Cary, I've come to rescue you," He laughed, and looking around at the grim threesome—Karen, Sissy, and Lauren—"whether you want to be rescued or not."

Ken lifted my body halfway off the cot and hugged me. The three glared at us. They gave Ken the Evil Eye when he opened his bag, withdrew syringe, points, spoon, and a glassine envelope with white power. "Doctor Feelgood has got the cure for you and it's gonna set you right."

"Don't do this Cary," Lauren pleaded to no avail. Ken ignored her. I didn't argue.

Ken screwed a point on the neck of a glass syringe, cooked up the shot in the spoon, and drew it up through a piece of cigarette filter. As Ken was tying off my right bicep with his belt, I shrugged at Lauren, arms crossed across her chest, hugging herself, witnessing what was transpiring with a sad look on her face. I felt confused and too weak to protest.

Ken fixed me in the vein in my inner elbow. Within minutes, his arm supporting me, he had me walking around inside the courtyard of the hotel. I was high as kite, smiling like my old self, except I was still running a fever, still feeling sick at my stomach. "The healing power of the old speedball should not be dismissed," Ken was saying. "It never fails to work its curative magic."

While Ken and I were in the courtyard, I heard arguing behind the door. Karen and Sissy dumped my stuff outside the room, as if it was garbage, and slammed the door. I knew Lauren was torn between loyalty to her long-time friends, Karen and Sissy and affection for me, her new lover—her new *sick lover* at that, who engendered her compassionate instincts and her professional nursing training.

Ironically, I too was caught between two sets of loyalties. I had only known Ken for a matter of hours, having stayed with him and Agate on Christmas Eve in Mashhad. Lauren ... I had only met three days ago in the Khyber Restaurant, and I really liked her. I wanted to explain to her something that I didn't really understand myself—why was I allowing this crazy drug addict with missing teeth to intrude on our love affair? By what right did he appear at the Green Hotel to claim me? I wanted to beg her forgiveness, but Karen and Sissy wouldn't open the door to let me back in the room to plead my case. Like that, it was over, Lauren and me. I felt sick in body and soul.

Ken scooped up my sleeping bag, backpack, and hucklebag from the hall floor, stuffed me into a taxi, and carried me to the Habib Hotel to share a room with him and Agate. It turned out to be the same room I had lived in with Gary, Jeff, and Luke. Funny, I had known Ken for an even shorter time than I had known Lauren, and yet he had prevailed over her. He had inserted himself into my life like he had inserted a hypodermic needle into my vein.

Now I was in bed, another bed, in the Habib hotel agian. I greeted Agate, kissing her on both cheeks in the French way. "You look like shit warmed over," she said, in her wonderfully French-accented English. Her belly was showing.

I was puzzled. "Why are you and Agate in Kabul? How did you find me in the Green Hotel?"

Ken grinned, "Old Zen saying: 'When two thieves meet on a mountain road, they know each other at once.' *What the fuck does that mean?*

"Don't look so bewildered. It's all quite simple. You do remember mailing me a postcard when you first got to Kabul inviting us to join you, don't you? Agate and I were already itching to leave Mashhad and that postcard from you put us over the top. You mentioned that you were staying at the Habib Hotel. It wasn't hard to track you down in Kabul. Agate and I have been here before. The clerk here at the Habib Hotel, told me, 'Mr. Raditz moved to the Bamiyan Hotel.'

"The clerk at the Bamiyan, said, 'Raditz move to Green Hotel.'

"The clerk at the Green Hotel pointed down the hall and said, 'Room 3.'"

Agate told Ken I needed a real doctor. "Ken, please take Cary to that German doctor who treated us for fever and dysentery when we came through here on our way from Delhi to Iran." Ken wrapped a blanket around me and put me into a taxi. At the clinic, nurses took blood, urine and stool samples and told me to come back the next day. They gave me aspirin.

Examining me the next day, the doctor delivered the diagnosis, "*Giardia lambia* is causing your intestinal distress, Mr. Raditz. A flu is causing your fever." For the diarrhea he prescribed Flagyl, and for my fever, gave me a shot of an antiviral and wrote a prescription for pills.

Back at the Habib I felt better. Soon my fever began to abate. The three of us read, drank tea, and slept. Ken and Agate smoked hash. I found I could eat plain white rice and keep it down. Ken listened to my story about my wire transfer getting stuck in Da Afghanistan Bank. Savvier than I about banks, Ken said, "Sadly, it's a commonplace problem, banks sitting on foreign exchange of foreigners. It happened to us in India and in Iran." He added, "Luckily, this is why we have an American Embassy."

Ken looked me up and down and stroked his chin, "Cary, when you feel up to it, let's visit my tailor," meaning in this case, the used clothing bazaar. We walked over the next morning.

An ex-clothing salesman, I assisted Ken choose something tasteful, a blue flannel suit, vintage I'd say about 1950, perfect for a job interview. For myself I selected a heavy worsted, grey double-breasted, pin-striped suit. We bought dress shirts off the rack. A convenient tailor in the bazaar made minor alterations to our suits. Ken generously footed the haberdashery bill, which altogether must have set him back about $10.

In our brand-new, used attire, we took a taxi out to the embassy, spoke to a receptionist, and shortly were received by the deputy economic officer in the consulate, Thomas Harding, who invited us into his office, asked us to sit, and inquired, "How may I assist you gentlemen?" Ken and I looked at each other and neither of us saw gentlemen. Nonetheless, we explained the situation regarding the delayed funds and showed Mr. Harding my father's telegram. He listened to the story, picked up the phone on his desk, dialed a number, and spoke for a few minutes in Dari. He scribbled a note on his writing pad. Hanging up, he turned and said, "Mr. Raditz, your funds are available."

Harding folded the note, hand-written on his official personal stationery, he inserted it into an embassy envelope, and handed it to me along with his business card. "Mr. Raditz, Da Afghanistan Bank is the Central Bank of Afghanistan. Please present this note to Mr. Ahmed Azizi, the branch manager; we know each other well. I am confident he will do his best to sort out your problem."

We thanked Mr. Harding, took a taxi back into downtown Kabul, called at the bank, and met Mr. Azizi. He apologized profusely for the detained funds, citing a technical problem within his foreign department. He took me over to a counter where he instructed the clerk to convert my 950 USD into Thomas Cooke travelers checks (net of fees)—for me a small fortune. Mr. Azizi arranged everything. He explained that when I needed afghanis, I could cash the travelers checks into local currency with the *sarrafs*, the money exchangers, at their tables along the far side of the Kabul River. Azizi said that when I left Afghanistan, I would then have dollars, not afghanis, which would be difficult to convert to dollars. Later, I checked out the *sarrafs* by the river. On a line of tables in plain sight, *sarrafs* did their foreign exchange business amid stacked bundles of foreign exchange—francs, rupees, rials, marks, francs, and 20 USD bills in neat, banded piles.

I hadn't seen the Dastagir goldsmith family since Soizette left. They asked where I had been and I told them I had been sick, but now I was better. "Please forgive me," I apologized to Farooq and Siddiq. "I could not teach you when I was sick. My father in America sold my car and sent me money," I said, patting the breast pocket of my suit jacket.

Farooq said, "That's okay, Mr. Cary, we were worried something happened to you. When Siddiq went to Bamiyan Hotel to find you, you moved."

We had more lessons in colloquial English. The boys took notes studiously, but I wasn't sure they got it. Farooq and Siddiq made a list of American phrases they wanted me to explain.

Farooq: "What does 'fuck off man' mean?"

"It means 'leave me alone.'"

Farooq: "What does, 'I am broken man' mean?"

"The phrase, is 'I am broke,' and it means 'I do not have any money.'"

I reminded them about our earlier conversation, that I wanted to buy commission rings set with irregular, *fancy* agates that I had culled and put aside. Siddiq brought out the basket with the agates and poured them out over Farooq's workbench. "How many agates you want to buy, Mr. Cary?" asked Farooq, assorting them into piles. "Choose what you like, and me and Siddiq will set them in silver."

"Can you set them in white metal?"

"Why you not want silver? Silver is good."

"Because, Farooq, my customers in Greece are poor and they cannot afford silver rings."

"Ok, we understand. Many Afghan people are poor, too. If you want, we cast rings in white metal and set your agates in them. No problem. But, Mr. Cary, silver is better."

"Ok, Farooq, make me fifty agate rings of white metal, and make me three special agate rings of silver, for my partner and his wife with these three fire-agates," which I handed to him. We arrived on a price of $2 apiece for the white metal agate rings, and $5 apiece for the silver. Farooq wrote this down in an order book.

"We will start on the agate rings today, Mr. Cary. They will take three days. You want lapis lazuli rings too? In silver? In gold?"

"No, Farooq, not on this trip, no lapis lazuli, but on the next trip, yes—in gold," I said, remembering the gold lapis rings the German smugglers in

Matala wore. I occurred to me that I could engage in import-export myself, like the Germans, Frank and Samuel, and like Melissa and her band of Danes.

During that week, I bought embroidered shirt fronts and so did Ken. We both bought finely woven cotton scarves and shawls. I picked up tools in the hardware bazaar and a vintage, Russian draw plate used to reduce the diameter of wires, for Barbara's jewelry making in the shop. Our purchases piled up in the corner of our room in the Habib Hotel. I needed a sturdy trunk to carry it all back to Greece. I knew just where to go.

In "Duck Street" near the Green Hotel in Shari Naw, metal workers made me a trunk fabricated from scrap rolls of sheet metal from canning factories that had colorful labels printed on them—tomato sauce, sardines, tuna, and other canned foods. My trunk was made from tomato sauce-can stock. Back at the Habib Hotel, I began filling the trunk with leatherworking tools, a kilim carpet, and embroidered fabrics.

At the goldsmith shop I continued to teach Farooq and Siddiq for an hour a day at lunch. After the rings were completed, I paid the shop by endorsing travelers checks to Ghulam Dastagir, who preferred foreign currency over afghanis. Having consummated the deal, the goldsmiths began to gift me other items from the shop—silver agate bracelets and plain silver bands—they ladled a double handful of irregular half-round fancy agates and moonstones into a velvet bag. As I was saying goodbye Farooq said, "My father wants to talk with you."

Farooq translated Ghulam Dastagir's Dari, "Thank you, Mr. Cary, for coming to our shop and teaching my sons to speak good English. You were like a brother to them. So, your father is like my brother. Here is a gift that I want you to give to your father," He slipped off a huge, gold lapis lazuli ring from the ring finger of his right hand and placed it in my hand. I couldn't believe it. They had already done so much for me. *I am unworthy.* I realized that I needed to decline the gift politely.

"Farooq, this ring is a wonderful gift, but it is too much for me to accept. Please tell your father that I will tell my father that his Afghan brother, Ghulam Dastagir, honors him with the gift of this ring. I will tell my father to come to Kabul and receive this gift directly from the hands of Ghulam Dastagir, his Afghan brother."

Of course I could not know exactly how Farooq translated my apology to his father, but I saw his father's face drop. He laid the ring down on the workbench. I rounded up everything I had purchased from them, and put it all in my hucklebag, climbed down through the doorway, and walked back to the Habib Hotel.

When I told this story much later to my Iranian friend, Morteza, his face took on a sad expression just as Ghulam Dastagir's had done. "Oh no," he said. "to quote the Persian poet, Saadi, 'Refuse my gift from the heart, deny me passage into paradise.'" I almost wept. Refusing Ghulam Dastagir's gift of the lapis lazuli ring has haunted me the rest of my life.

On a table next to the window, Ken installed his personal samovar that he had bought in Mashhad and lugged in its custom case to Kabul. About a two-liter capacity, it heated water for tea and provided clean drinking water. Using it, however, was a real pain in the ass because it required burning charcoal. Ken had to go down to the street in front of the hotel and buy burning charcoal for 25 puls from the kebab stand to heat the samovar. And then wait a half-hour for water to boil. Of course, it would have been easier for Ken to order boiling water from the chaykhana, but that was not the point—the entire process amounted to performance art. Ken had other impractical obsessions, too.

Ken nurtured romantic sentiments about the San Francisco drug culture he had left behind, the same subculture I had blundered into at the Madison Hotel with Andy and Mary a year ago. He wove a story how drug dealers, users, and cops comprised a reciprocal conspiracy—an absurd Mac-the Knife theater played out in the streets, in the Haight, Filmore, Mission District and North Beach—a kind of intrigue he could have lifted straight from William Burroughs. For example, Ken had a sentimental obsession about how to construct proper *drug paraphernalia*, as cops called narcotics outfits in courts.

With the keen attention he might have devoted to a craft activity such as origami, Ken tutored me how to assemble a proper set of *works* from ordinary grocery store items such as eyedroppers and unperforated baby-bottle nipples. Of course the outfit needed a hypodermic needle and he bought one at a pharmacy. To Ken, a proper outfit was more than a syringe substitute, it was an art object, a relic from an outdated, niche culture, just like his samovar was.

※ ※ ※

My buying mission in Afghanistan concluded, it was time to get back to Matala. We prepared to leave Kabul and return to Europe together. I would make my way back to Crete with my trunk, and Ken and Agate would go to France to get married and have the baby. I finished packing my tomato-can trunk. Ken put their belongings in another trunk and stored his precious samovar in its velvet case.

We took the bus to Kandahar, stopping for one night in the guesthouse. In the chaykhana I saw Karl who told me that Melissa was in Ghazni and would be back tomorrow. "She will be sorry to miss you." That was sweet to hear. *I miss her, too. Sweet Melissa!*

By morning we were on the bus well on the way to Herat through the *Dasht-e Margo*. What does one do for a bathroom break in the Desert of Death, when one is on a public bus with no toilet, one might ask? One character-building activity of travelling long distances on public buses in Afghanistan is learning how to defecate out in the open desert under the eyes of the other passengers. If you are prepared, perhaps you have toilet paper with you, but in the event you don't, you have learned from watching Afghans to use a tin cup of water to wash your butt with your left hand under your burka or under the long shirt-tail of your *salwar kameez*. Even the nastiest activities can be done with aplomb if you set your mind straight and develop the proper skills. I've often thought that this lesson of surrendering to humiliation—when one has no other choice—strengthens character to prepare one to undertake all kinds of outlandish stuff. Imagine asking yourself whenever you encounter anything socially risky, "What could be more embarrassing than dropping trousers, shitting in public and wiping your butt in plain view of an audience of bus passengers?"

Our travel clock seemed to speed up. We spent a night at the guesthouse in Herat, took a bus to Mashhad, stayed one night in a cheap hotel near the mosque, and continued the next day on an overnight bus to Tehran. We found a suitable room to share in an affordable hotel not far from the train station. It was cold but we had a portable kerosene heater that the hotel provided.

As soon as we unpacked, Agate went out shopping. While she was gone, Ken went down to the pharmacy next to our hotel where he encountered George, an American, a heroin addict. *Ken had a trained eye for identifying narcotics addicts.*

Ken ran back to our room where I was reading, grabbed me and together we went to visit George. A pathetic wreck, George. He lived in a windowed shed on the flat roof of an office building adjacent to our hotel that at one time may have been a pigeon cote. His hovel was as filthy as he himself was filthy. But he had one redeeming quality—he possessed a precious trove of brown Iranian heroin—"brown sugar"—which made Ken drool. When George stripped off his socks to shoot up in a vein in his foot—abscessed veins in his arms and hand had collapsed—his feet were grimy. It was an awful sight. For a few bucks we bought a half-spoon of heroin from him to "test," that is, to shoot up.

The diarrhea and fever I had at the Green Hotel in Kabul had laid me low, and although I had gained back some weight, I had no fat on my body. I was so thin I must have weighed about one hundred and twenty pounds, the weight class I had wrestled at Myers Park High School when I was fifteen. To fix me, Ken didn't bother tying off my arm, instead he encircled my skinny bicep with his fingers to make the veins stand prominent. Our quality assessment deemed George's brown heroin excellent; it stoned Ken and me to the blithering bone.

Stoned to the bone is how Agate found us when she returned from shopping. Ken was falling over himself struggling to set up his beloved samovar and I was nodding out in a chair. "Ken, Cary ... wake up! Get dressed now! We've been invited to dinner tonight at the Khademis."

The Khademis? Agate had worked in public relations at Air France and knew the chairman of Iran Air, Mr. Khademi. Once, she had helped him get a special flight home to Tehran for a family member who had been injured in Geneva. After that, Mr. Khademi felt indebted to Agate.

Agate took in how seriously Ken and I were physically and mentally impaired. We were invited to dine with Mr. Khademi, his family and friends that evening, and we were incapacitated. To call her angry would have been an understatement. If she had had a stick handy, she would have beaten us. I could barely stand up or stay conscious, had vestiges of vomit on my shirt, and Ken was in the toilet puking. She helped us dress in the secondhand suits we had bought in the Kabul bazaar, shoving, pleading, demanding, threatening us—she even kicked me to wake me up. Stuffing us in the taxi, she gave the driver the address, an exclusive residential neighborhood in north Tehran off Pahlavi Boulevard. Agate seethed in the backseat of the taxi, husband nodding out on her shoulder, while her husband's idiot buddy, Cary, slumped forward in the front passenger seat, wrecked.

Is it considered bad manners everywhere to nod out at a host's dinner table? Agate made excuses and apologized to our hosts in French. She told them I was on medications because I had been deathly ill and so forth. Since I looked like a scarecrow, perhaps they bought that explanation. Ken was a bit more alert. Most conversations among the guests were in Farsi, of course, but everyone seemed conversant in French and English; it was a cosmopolitan collection of upper class Iranians, this dinner party. As parlor entertainment, our host proposed that everyone sing a song. Invited to sing, I had a go at imitating Ramblin' Jack Elliot's version of "In the Shade of the Old Apple Tree," but in the middle of the song, when Jane "... pitches her wooden leg upon the chair ...," I got woozy and had to sit down.

Several good things came out of this fiasco of an evening. First, the chairman gifted Agate a pair of business class tickets to Paris. A godsend. And he arranged for his office to reimburse me the cash value of my return ticket on Air Luxemburg to the States. We suspected that he just paid me out of his pocket and threw the ticket away. Generous folks, these gracious uptown Tehran patricians.

The next day, Ken, Agate, and I were riding in a taxi going to the bazaar when the driver started making moves on Agate. We were getting accustomed to the aphrodisiacal effect Agate had on males in Tehran. Iranian men, pedestrians walking on the other side of the street, would spot Agate and cross over to accost her as if they were magnetically attracted. Was it the way she walked in colorful saris, or the way her long uncovered dark hair shimmied across her hips that drew them to her like moths to a flame? *I think she does this as a sport.* When the three of us walked anywhere, Ken would walk in front of Agate, and I would trail behind to fend off unwanted advances from men on the street compelled to touch her in places she did not want to be touched. But when the taxi driver turned around in his seat to grope at Agate's breasts, Ken leapt out the taxi, dragged the driver out onto the street and began to beat him up.

Almost immediately a crowd gathered to watch this one-way fight. A policeman showed up, stopped the beating, and asked the crowd what was going on. A bystander told the cop the driver had been molesting the *farangi's* wife. The policeman apologized for the taxi driver and led him away in handcuffs to the general approval of the crowd.

A day later we checked out of the hotel. Saying goodbye to one another, I patted the bump on Agate's abdomen. Instead of traveling overland by bus and train, Ken and Agate would be flying to her parents' home in the Parisian suburb, Provins, to get married. I took a train to Istanbul, lugging my tomato trunk full of Afghan purchases, imprudently crossing the border with my outfit stuffed in a toilette bag with my toothbrush, and a few pinches of brown heroin—only a medicinal amount—to ward off withdrawal until I could refill my prescription at the Pudding Shop in Istanbul.

Once checked into a hotel near the Istanbul train station, I shot up just enough to get me straight and went over to the Pudding Shop to score. I wished I had Ken with me—he could spot a dealer a block away. The Pudding Shop came up zilch on smack, but I met a scrungy guy from New York who said he had a bottle of tincture of opium in his room that he agreed to sell me. I tried to fix in his hotel room, but the tincture turned into slush in the spoon and I had to strain and re-cook it. The narcotic effect was barely perceptible, but after all, doctors typically prescribe tincture of opium to take orally to stop diarrhea, not to shoot up. I resolved to keep the stuff in case I got diarrhea again. Before leaving Istanbul, as an afterthought, I bought an aerogram from the hotel desk and penned a brief note to Agate and Ken in Provins formally inviting them to come to Matala.

I flew back to Athens from Istanbul with the tomato-can trunk loaded in the baggage compartment. The trunk and I were headed to our final destination—Matala, Crete—from where I had departed for this trip to Kabul only two months ago. It felt more like two years.

PART II

Jack of Cups

"A story should have a beginning, a middle and an end, but not necessarily in that order."
—Jean Luc Godard

PART 1

Jack of Cups

CHAPTER 11

The Worm Beneath the Nail

Rays of the mid-afternoon sun danced across the aluminum wings of the Turkish Airline prop plane as it skidded onto the Athens's airport runway and bumped its way to the terminal. Here I was, back in Greece, back from winter in Afghanistan and Iran. Clearing immigration and customs, I now had a renewed Greek visa, good for six months. I hired a porter to help me load my stuff into a bus to Athens marked "Syntagma Square."

An hour later the bus deposited the metal trunk, bags, and me in front of the American Express office in Syntagma Square in central Athens. I went inside. At the foreign exchange window, the cashier changed my Turkish lira and Iranian rials into Greek drachma and I cashed a $100 Thomas Cooke travelers' check. Down the hall I inquired at the poste restante window for possible mail waiting for me. Only an aerogram from Mom. On the way out I picked up an Athens map.

From the sidewalk I hailed a taxi. The driver stopped, got out, and hefted the tomato can trunk into his trunk and loaded my other bags and stuff onto the back seat. I hopped in beside him on the front seat, showed him the map, pointing out the location of the youth hostel. He said, "*endoxi,*" meaning okay. Lurching forward, me riding shotgun, the taxi charged through traffic as the driver threatened other drivers with shouts and curses, waving his fist and blowing his horn. He deposited me on the sidewalk in front of the youth hostel building. I rang the bell, the door buzzed open, and I dragged my stuff into the building foyer, crammed it all into the elevator, and punched the button for the second floor. The doors opened and standing before me was Speros, the manager. "Welcome," he greeted me, smiling.

Speros and I shook hands and I gave him greetings from my partner, Mark, and his girlfriend, Barbara. He exclaimed, "Ah, Mark and Barbara from Matala! *Kala! Kala!*" He helped bring my baggage into a dormitory-type room. In the kitchen Speros opened a pantry door and extracted a bottle of ouzo and two small glasses. Raising his glass, "*Yasu!* To Mark and Barbara. And you." We clicked glasses and drank. Yes. The ouzo burned my mouth, reminding me that I was back in Greece.

I took a yogurt from the hostel refrigerator and stuck five drachmas in the jar on the shelf. After a shower I retired to the dormitory room alone and climbed into the bottom bunk. No one—neither traveler, tourist, backpacker nor student—took the upper bunk.

Refreshed by a good night's sleep on clean sheets, I felt fine and happy. Speros helped me load my metal trunk and backpack in a taxi. The taxi, like the one last night, charged from lane to lane through Athens traffic to the port of Piraeus, honking all the while. At the ferry office ticket counter, I bought an open, round-trip ticket for the all-night ferry to Iraklion, figuring I'd have to come back to Athens sometime or another within the next six-months. It was nearing noon. I found a taverna down the street where the waiter invited me to follow him into the kitchen to check out what was cooking. Under the eye of the cook, I went from pot to pot, lifting lids and admiring what I saw. I ordered some oily dolmades, a mesa salad with hunks of fresh tomato and onion, slices of cucumber, and a block of feta cheese. Raw green olive oil and vinegar topped the mesa, which I sopped up with a hunk of *psomi*. I washed it down with a glass of chilled retsina. *Ah, but this Greek taverna were paradise enow!*

The waiter cleared the table. I leaned back in the chair, dozed off, then read a trashy novel until evening when I joined a queue of travelers walking down to the pier to board the all-night ferry to Crete. I ascended the ramp behind a porter carrying my tomato can trunk on his head. Ducking below deck on the stairs down to the bunks, I recoiled from the stench. The men's quarters reeked of garlic, urine, putrid wine, unwashed bodies, and sweaty socks. *Awful.* Climbing the steps, I passed the night on the open passenger deck next to my trunk. Cocooned in my down sleeping bag, I curled up to sleep under the canopy of the heavens, along with other travelers and among Greeks wrapped in blankets. *Is everyone praying like me that it won't rain?* The sea was calm. The stars shown brilliant once we sailed beyond the range of Athens' ambient light. From below deck we heard music—bouzouki, fiddle, and singing. Men were drinking and singing and dancing sirtaki. With the ferry gently rocking over the waves, I drifted off to sleep.

At dawn the ferry eased into its berth at the port of Iraklion. Enlisting the help of a porter with a cart, I gathered my things and debarked with a crowd of men, women and obedient children carrying baskets and sacks on their heads. Beside me a hunchbacked laborer pushed a wheelbarrow laden high with a mattress and household stuff. At the top of the embarcadero slope at the bus stop, the driver's assistants lashed my metal trunk, pack, and camel bags to the top rack of the bus to Matala. Matala lay about 45 kilometers directly southeast of Iraklion on the other side of the island. After delays and squabbling, the driver climbed into his seat, jammed the bus into first gear and the bus jolted through the cobbled back streets of Iraklion chugging up and down hills and coming into open countryside. The bus lurched along twisting mountain roads through a scrub terrain of thyme, herbs, rocks, and orchards of dark olives and cheerful oranges. The driver navigated the bus on roads traversing rubble stone walls, grassy valleys, and white-washed stone buildings in towns with narrow, unpaved, rocky streets. We stopped here and there to pick up and discharge passengers at village squares, to load and unload baskets of fruit and chickens from the roof and goods tied up in sacks or in thick grey shawls. A cacophony of squawking chickens, braying goats, crying babies, and shouting conversations serenaded us.

When we stopped in Mires, I stepped off the bus to buy a hot souvlaki gyro wrapped in pita bread smeared with red pepper sauce, dripping with yogurt-cucumber *tzatziki*. The gyro seller rolled my gyro up in a page of folded newspaper displaying car ads in Greek. I boarded the bus full and satisfied, my stomach telling me I had come home.

Several kilometers past Mires we crested the hill way above the horseshoe shaped harbor of Matala. I pulled out my bandana and wiped a porthole in the grimy bus window that was distorting my view. Beyond the harbor the bare Islands of Paximadia jutted out from the Gulf of Messara, resembling *Paximadia,* Crete's favorite dried bread—rough-grain, twice-baked, donut-shaped bread that hung from wooden pegs on every kitchen wall.

The bus lumbered down through orange tree orchards, twisted olive trees, and fields enclosed by waist-high, loosely stacked stone walls snaking down the long valley into Matala, and drew to a halt in the village square next to the bakery. As usual, a few Greeks and a few cave dwellers met the bus. Passengers and merchants unloaded baskets of produce and dry goods brought in from the markets of Iraklion and Mires. Amidst the loading and unloading, I recognized people in the *plateia* I knew, and spotted a larger number I did not know. In December I had left Matala for Afghanistan. Now it was late February, the season was still chilly and wet, and few tourists were coming to Crete. With all the stops, the bus had taken over two hours, Iraklion embarcadero to Matala village square.

In the bakery, I accepted the kind hospitality of "Mama" to stow the tomato-can trunk in her storeroom until I could get situated in the caves. On the way out, I bought a yogurt from her, over which she spooned a glob of wildflower honey and gave me a wide smile, "*Kali mera,* Cary!"

As I exited the bakery, wiping my mouth with my sleeve, my partner Mark saluted me across the square. "*Yasu, Cary!* Welcome back!" We hugged.

Happy to be back home, Mark and I crunched across the pebble beach to the cliffs. He brought me up to date on what had taken place in Matala since I left. People had come and gone, as they do. My girlfriend, Holly, had returned to Chapel Hill in December, a week after I had departed.

"Police got tough on Stelios when he tried to build a small extension to expand the Mermaid," said Mark. "They tried to intimidate him by claiming he is violating building codes. How ridiculous. Otherwise, it's been bleak days for the Matala Leather Shop. Few travelers, no orders, no sales revenue. Barbara hand-stitches leather vests and bags—hard work. We need a sewing machine."

As we advanced along the pebble strand, light sparkling off the sea made us squint. The fishy stench of low tide combined with fecal odor wafting downwind from the casual latrines that lay amid thorny shrubs growing from the edge of the pebble beach up the valley—"Shit Hill," as we called it.

Latrine territory to the right, sea on the left, we continued walking along lacy surf frothing among the pebbles. Straight ahead loomed Matala's sandstone cliffs pocked with a score or more of caves of varied sizes and dimensions. We stepped up the footholds carved into the rock and into the cool gloom of the whole Big Cave. On the left side was the crude, doorless cave where Holly and I had slept from November to December. On the adjoining right wall to Mark's and across from ours was the single cave where Phil Lawson had lived.

I recalled moving into the cave indenture on the left with Holly four months ago on Halloween. I looked inside. Two green sleeping bags lay side by side on a woven pallet of reeds. Two backpacks leaned against the cave wall. A white linen shirt and a red skirt hung side by side on wooden pegs jutting from the wall. In the fall, Holly and I had laid our sleeping bags on that same pallet, side by side like these, and hung our clothes side by side on those same pegs. I missed Holly. I missed waking up to the scent of her body, her sleepy breath and her long brown hair all over my face. I wished she were here now to welcome me back.

Mark and I stood outside his cave door. Hearing voices inside I approached the door, saying, "Konk Konk," scratching on the reed door like a cat. Voices inside stopped. The reed door rolled up, and an unfamiliar guy with braided blond hair smiled, put his index finger to his lips and gestured back into the cave, "Hey, Barbara, someone to see you." Barbara emerged, stood up, and her eyes got big. Crossing both her hands over her mouth, "Cary! You're back!" and flung her arms around me.

Lowering our heads to pass under the cave door, we crept into their lamp-lit cave, the ceiling barely high enough to stand up. As my eyes adjusted, I looked around to the back wall where two small doors led into smaller caves. Barbara and Mark slept in the one on the right, while they kept the other cave—formerly occupied in December by Ethan, the Viking—for visitors. The blond guy who had greeted me sat down on kilim cushions across from Barbara and another guy I did not recognize. My arrival interrupted a card game.

Pungent cannabis and tobacco smoke hung in the air. Mark rolled down the reed door behind us and made introductions. "Utah John, Stefan, meet Cary, my leather shop partner," he said, "back from travels to Turkey, Iran, Afghanistan and possibly the astral plane." I shook their hands, sat down on a cushion, and crossed my legs, home again.

"Greetings from the Astral Plane."

"Cary—Surprise! Surprise! Phil's old cave—it's your cave now," said Barbara. "Phil moved to Athens in December to produce *Hair* and launch his Greek theatre career. He asked us to save his cave for you. We have been letting people stay there if they promised to leave when you got back. On top of that, Phil bequeathed you his stove—*Uncle Stove*—lanterns, carpets, bedding, and now a fantastic new door, courtesy of Mark," she smiled, elbowing Mark in his ribs.

Phil's cave was a giant step up from the niche where Holly and I had been staying. My new cave entrance measured about meter and a half high, covered by roll-down, woven reed blinds. Inside the cave measured about twelve-feet deep and seven-feet across. At the far end, a waist-high, recessed burial crypt shelf served as a bed.

Barbara went on about Phil's cave. "A nice lady from Kent has been cave sitting for you, Beatrice, who we call Beatrice Potter, and her boyfriend, Peter, we call Peter Rabbit."

Extracting his smoking kit from a leather hucklebag Mark made for him, John pulled out his kit containing a soapstone chillum he had brought back from India, a round tin of Golden Virginia rolling-tobacco, and pebble-size hunks of black hashish. From the same tin, he dumped out three polished stone marbles and a box of wooden matches.

"*Utah,*" as Mark addressed John, "Please prepare us your best house blend."

While Utah John was dealing with the chillum, I sliced up oranges into a clay bowl. Holding up my kitchen knife dripping with orange juice, I said, "See this little blade? It almost got me killed last December in the mountains of Turkey." I told the tale of the raki fiasco, ending with the old saw: "Never bring a knife to a gun fight."

Mark lit the chillum for him. John drew deeply, inhaling the acrid smoke. He let a stream of smoke drift out of his mouth, re-inhaled through his nostrils, puffed out a perfect smoke ring, and then blew another smoke ring through it, dead-center. Coughing, he passed the chillum to Mark who passed it to me. I declined and passed it on to Stefan. I noticed he wore a gold stud in the shape of a heart in his left ear.

"Hey," I said, "I have the same heart stud. I bought it in the bazaar in Tehran two weeks ago. I pierced the lobe myself with a syringe point. But it's getting sore," I said as I touched it gingerly.

Barbara pulled my head over and looked behind my ear. "Cary, it's infected. I'm gonna take out that stud." She removed it, "It's not gold, its brass. 'Ugh,'" she said, pinching the earlobe between finger and thumb, squeezing out yellow puss. She went into her inner cave and brought back a sewing kit and a bottle of alcohol. She threaded a blunt needle with heavy white button thread and passed it clean through the infected earlobe hole and tied it in a loop. She dipped the loop into a spoon of alcohol and spun it through my infected ear to sanitize the wound. It stung.

"Thanks, Mom," I said. "I promise that I'll replace it with a high-karat gold heart when my ship comes in." Sadly, I knew that buying a gold heart stud from a jeweler would totally bankrupt me. *There were no ships coming in.*

Utah John, Stefan, and Mark walked with me over to town to help me lug the metal trunk back to Big Cave. When we got back, Barbara poured me a glass of krasi and refilled glasses all around. "Travel stories, tales of the road." she pleaded. "We want to hear all about your trip."

"Barbara, I'm too wasted and about to fall over. Can we let the stories simmer in their own juice overnight? Please?"

✳ ✳ ✳

In the morning, housekeeping affairs. My crypt needed better padding. To cushion the irregular stone shelf, I rearranged crisscrossed levels of woven reeds and covered those with overlapping layers of folded carpet pieces. I laid out a printed tablecloth from Tehran as a bottom sheet. On the floor I rolled out my new kilim over a frayed, red Cretan carpet. For cushions, I stuffed dried beach grass into camel bags.

Pacing my new cave in bare feet, I enjoyed the feel of my new Afghan kilim underfoot. I hung clothing from wood pegs driven into the walls. Around the cave I hung Cretan textiles, leather bags, and cooking utensils inherited from Phil. Bunches of thyme and mountain herbs freshened the air. Against the near wall on the left sat "Uncle Stove," a kerosene camper stove that had won cave-wide competition by boiling a liter of water fastest.

At breakfast Barbara served us yogurt from the bakery with diced dates and orange slices. Suddenly, a loud banging outside jerked us to attention. Mark rolled up the reed door and stepped out into the Big Cave. I followed him. In our work pit crouched a guy with dark greasy hair and scraggly black beard, wearing a dirty, sleeveless shirt and beaded bracelets around his wrists. He was furiously flattening a piece of sheet metal against the workbench with the precious flat-headed leather hammer we used for setting rivets and for sealing seams.

Mark and I looked at the guy and then at each other. The intruder glanced up at us and without even a nod, continued hammering. Pulling Mark aside, I asked, "Do you know this shithead?"

Mark shrugged, and gestured with his chin, "French guy. I don't know his name, but he's damned obnoxious. He falls by here all the time to use shop tools. Each time I tell him that we don't ever share tools. Then he comes back, and he does it again. What an asshole."

"Mark," I said, gritting my teeth, "We made a no-lend policy. Let's stick to it."

Mark turned, "Hey! *Toi! Arrete, alors!* Frenchie's face screwed up into a snout, his cheeks puffed, his mouth snarled, blurting out a torrent of expletives.

"Translate, Mark."

Mark: "Frenchie says we don't own these caves. We are Capitalists ripping off travelers. We should share our food and our tools with the poor. Like him."

All this rubbed me wrong. Anger surged through my body. Whereas Mark was genuinely friendly and easy-going, I was prone to fly off the handle at any moment. Right now, I was furious.

I bit my bottom lip. I yelled at Frenchie in English, "Get outta here!" Mark commanded the guy to leave:—"*Va-t'en!*"

"*Exo!*" I said as I leaned over the bench. He gave me the finger right in front of my face and I went berserk.

I slugged him hard in the face, grabbed his black, greasy hair, banged his head against the rock, and jerked his skinny body out of the hole onto the stone floor. This didn't stop him; he was stronger than he looked. With a scowl, bleeding from his nose and forehead, he came to his feet and swung, hitting me on the side of the head. We exchanged glancing blows until I tackled him and threw him to the cave's rock floor. A rage of childhood tantrums surged through me, and freeing an arm, I grabbed him in a hammer-hold around this neck and smashed him hard in the face with my fist until he went limp. A few moments later, gasping for breath, nose bleeding, blood running down his face, and still muttering under his breath, he rose and slunk out of the Big Cave.

Pain shot through my ribs. Mark helped me take my shirt off, and saw an ugly, dark bruise on my left side blossoming purple. *Shit! The fall broke a rib. Who won this fight anyhow?*

Next day, my left side hurt even more. It was hard to sleep; it hurt to breathe. Even that foul tincture of opium I scored at the Pudding Shop in Istanbul could not help; I had a broken rib, not diarrhea. I unlatched the trunk in front of Mark and Barbara's cave and spread my loot out on a carpet on the stone floor. I held up an Israeli tablecloth with Hebrew letters bought in the Tehran bazar, which I intended to hang as a privacy curtain in front of my burial crypt bed at the back of my cave. From the trunk I lifted out a dozen embroidered Afghan shirt fronts. Barbara snapped these up, "I'll make custom blouses and shirts with these."

"Hey, guys. I've got gifts for you," I said, handing them the fancy, fire-agate silver rings I had commissioned at the goldsmith shop in Kabul.

"Oh, wow!" exclaimed Barbara and kissed me.

"Nice," said Mark, giving me a hug and pat on the back.

From the heavy velvet jewelry bag I spilled out white-metal agate rings on the carpet. "We are diversifying, Mark. Henceforth, we can call ourselves, 'Matala Sandals, Leather, Custom Clothing and Jewelry Shop!'"

Sorting through the new leatherworking tools, Mark said, "Barbara and I talked to the owner of the small rock house on the cliffs on the other side of the harbor. He agreed to rent it to us for 300 drachmas a month."

Mark proposed buying a used sewing machine from the Iraklion bootmakers so Barbara could make bags and garments, which they had been laboriously hand stitching. She was delighted with that prospect. Mark and I took the afternoon bus to Iraklion and checked into the youth hostel. We ate delicious gyros from a nearby street stand, showered and slept on bunks in the dormitory. My side hurt. I gritted my teeth and thought of Frenchie and again wished that I had a taste of *Papaver somniferum*, the Latin name for opium.

Next morning we visited our friends the bootmakers. With only a minimum of bargaining—Mark had already done that—they sold us an old treadle-model Singer sewing machine, the same model I had used when David Honigmann taught me to stitch leather in the Chapel Hill Leather shop. It cost us 750 drachmas, about twenty-five US dollars. What a steal! I had ample funds remaining from selling my car.

To augment our new shop's working stock, we bought wide rolls of oak tanned leather and hides of harness leather. We gave the bootmakers a bottle of Metaxa for a present. They were pleased. We were pleased. While we collected our packs from the youth hostel, the Matala bus driver lashed the sewing machine on the top rack of the bus along with our purchases. The bus left from Iraklion over the twisting roads to Matala.

The Matala Leather Shop was a simple one room, stone house with a door and a shutter window and a flat cement roof built on the south cliffs of the harbor. Outside the shop, the afternoon light could be blinding, while inside, it remained cool, and dark. The owner had painted the exterior and interior walls white, and the door, window and exposed ceiling beams, the blue of the Greek flag.

The panorama view from the front door surveyed the Gulf of Messara, the islands of Paximadia, the harbor of Matala, and across the harbor, the beach, the cliffs, and the caves. To go down from the shop to the Mermaid Café you descended a flight of steps carved into the side of the cliff.

Mark set up the sewing machine. From driftwood planks he built a heavy worktable along the near wall. The work bench had open shelves below for tools in woven baskets. Rolled hides of leather hung from the rafters. The forged steel anvil I brought back from Kabul protruded from the tabletop. *Such a natural craftsman, Mark.* I was grateful for the fortuitous circumstances that brought us together. Without Mark's language skills and craftsmanship, there would be no Matala Leather Shop.

✳ ✳ ✳

The Karate Clan—as we called them—a commune of European martial arts enthusiasts, tried to shame people defecating in caves; they discouraged toilet paper in the scrub-brush latrines. Cave dwellers were henceforth instructed to wash themselves with water from a tin can like most people did in squat toilets in Greece, the Middle East, the Subcontinent, and Asia. Although nobody liked being told what to do, we gradually came around to endorsing their public health activities. Water hygiene, the karate folks preached, would stop shitty toilet paper from blowing around and hanging on thorn trees like hideous flags. However, cavers beware—they warned—

water runs downhill. In the rains, runoff from scrub-brush toilets must go somewhere, in this case, the surf. Therefore, washing dishes in the surf risked the peril of dysentery. Few objected to these draconian proclamations. Most were happy the strict karate commune had taken the initiative.

Living was cheap in Matala. Ouzo and raki cost pennies a glass, same price as an egg. Freshly baked bread and yogurt cost a couple drachmas. Fruit was almost free—ripe oranges and lemons grew in nearby orchards above the town. When Mark and I were walking up the Iraklion road one day, three old women dressed in black gestured us over and commanded us to fill our shirts with ripe fruit from their baskets.

Besides being inexpensive, food in Matala was exceptionally good. Mama's bread, sandwiches, and yogurt were tops; moussakas in both the Mermaid and Delphini, delicious. Both served crisp fried anchovies—*gropez* and smelt—with chunks of lemon. Tavernas served octopus, pieces of chilled tentacles with toothpicks and made *octapodi* stews. *Kokkino krasi,* cheap, harsh red wine, flowed freely. Cool retsina tasted wonderful when one acquired a taste for its turpentine flavor. Strong green olive oil permeated all the cuisine. We ate it in our food and salads and slathered it on our skin to keep it from drying from the salt and sun.

My rib still hurt but I could live with it. Frenchie had left town. Life began to look up. My cave was warm—sandstone makes an excellent insulation—and I slept soundly unless I entertained a female visitor, or unless my cave was invaded by the cluster of stray cats that roamed around Matala.

Vangelis took me on as a dishwasher at Delphini. The deal allowed me to eat free if I helped in the kitchen and bartended. The work entailed sweeping out the restaurant in the morning, hauling water and heating it on the propane stove, and washing dishes. I prepped for Mimes, the manager and cook, peeling potatoes, dicing tomatoes, onions, garlic, and cucumbers, and making salads. When Mimes discovered I loved cooking, he let me make simple dishes like bean soup and potato omelets. I began making my mother's fish gumbo, which contained all the ingredients we used in Greek dishes. Of course, I prepared Greek coffee and presided over the bar.

Delphini's kitchen plan was simple. Dividing the dining room from the seating area, a glass deli counter contained bowls of cooked food, bottles of beer, tomatoes, cucumbers, feta cheese, meat, fish, and other ingredients. The top of the counter served as the bar.

The dining room had six tables, each with four chairs. On two of the interior stone walls gas lanterns hung from wrought iron hooks. The wall closest to the sea had a large, open window space with wooden shutters and a heavy wood door that we kept open to the patio most of the time except at night, or when it was raining, or when we threw private parties. A small diesel generator behind the kitchen cycled on and off powering the frigo and the record player, which went into action at night. For Greek soldiers, fishermen, and shepherds we played Greek music, and for the cave dwellers, scratchy rock and roll.

The menu offerings varied. Almost every day we served lamb, chicken, and fresh fish. With few exceptions, townspeople, fishermen, shepherds, and farmers welcomed me with neighborly smiles and greetings. They smiled when I greeted them in my primitive Cretan Greek.

As apprentice cook, bartender, and occasional bouncer at Delphini, my drink was also free, too, as long as I stuck with the bottom-shelf stuff, wine, ouzo, and raki. For Metaxa, retsina and beer, however, I had to pay. Customers frequently bought me drinks. I loved to cook and I drank wine when I cooked. Bean soup and potato omelets were my standards. For bean soup, I soaked a pot of white navy beans for a day, picking out little rocks inevitably found in bags of beans and rice that could crack your teeth. I cooked them without salt, to keep them tender and to reduce gas, simmering them for hours until they softened, then drained them again and added fresh water, tomato paste, salt, onions, and garlic sautéed in generous quantities of olive oil. And of course, I added fresh thyme and oregano from the hills. For omelets, I kept a bowl of sautéed onions, garlic, and thin potato slices on the side.

When a customer ordered a Greek omelet, I spooned the cooked potatoes and onions into a hot, steel frying pan with a few splashes of olive oil. I turned the flame down and stirred in two beaten eggs and salt. Pulling the handle back sharply, I skidded the egg-potato mix around the frying pan, and jerked the pan back, flipping half the egg potato mixture onto itself. I turned off the burner and let it sit for a few moments before slipping it onto a plate along with a hunk of feta cheese and a thick slice of *psomi* and placed it on the countertop for the customer.

In the mid-afternoon at Delphini, lunch was over, and people were leaving to take naps. I would have liked to nap, too, especially with the freckled Danish girl who just left, but no napping for the wicked. After lunch, kitchen chores. In buckets, I hauled water, heated it in a pot on the stove, washed dishes, cleaned grease from the stove top, wiped counters and tables and swept the floors.

Word got around I was working at Delphini. Stelios came down from the Mermaid Café to say hello and toast my new job. I recruited new clientele for the taverna. I attracted cave dwellers—especially the longer-term cave dwellers— who welcomed an alternative bar scene. Besides cavers, we hosted boisterous, late night Greek shepherds and fishermen who drank a lot and performed incredible feats of athletic dancing. An added benefit of working at Delphini was it provided a convenient platform for me to market our sandals and leather goods.

Behind the kitchen-counter bar I kept a roll of butcher paper. When a customer ordered sandals, I laid out a scrap of the heavy paper on the floor, placed the customer's foot upon it and outlined its contours with a pencil, following the shape of the foot, toes, and the ankle. I marked strap style and placement. On the margin I noted the price of the sandals, the amount of the initial deposit, and the estimated delivery day. Then I took the foot pattern up to the shop for Mark to make the sandals. For basic sandals, we charged 500 drachmas, a bit over $15, a fraction of what good handmade sandals cost those days in Cape Cod. Between ours and the flimsy Greek leather sandals, which tourist shops sold for the same price, there was no comparison. We were the best. Or, at least, better than any we knew in Greece.

One day Mark and I were eating lunch outside Delphini at a patio table under a Cinzano umbrella when down the beach, a skin diver in a black rubber wet suit, yellow mask, snorkel, and black flippers waded out of the water holding up a thrashing octopus impaled on his spear. The diver looked around nervously in all directions as if he did not know what to do next. Mark threw down his napkin, leapt out of his chair, and raced across the pebbles to the diver. He snatched the octopus from the guy's spear, and with tentacles encircling his left forearm, Mark thrust his free right hand down into the octopus's head and turned it inside out. With his pocketknife he cut off guts and eyes and pushed the beak out from its head. Mark offered the diver the field-cleaned octopus. He refused it and told Mark to keep it.

Mark took the octopus to the harbor where he picked it up and slapped it down repeatedly against the stone steps. I left the table at Delphini and walked over to watch. "Tenderizing it," he told me. That evening in Delphini, I cooked *Octapodi* with my own *Kokkinisto* recipe—tomato paste, onion, garlic, red wine, thyme and oregano. Mark, Barbara, and I devoured it with a loaf of *psomi* and a bottle of *krasi*.

Delphini set up outside tables with umbrellas on it's stone patio right beside the beach. Greek parents could eat and drink while their kids played in the surf. More traditional than the Mermaid, at least during the day, at night Delphini attracted tenured cavers. Cave dwellers met new arrivals in the Mermaid, whom they took down to Delphini to join them in hard drinking, dancing, and cavorting deep into the night. As Stelios's friend I was careful not to actively poach customers from the Mermaid.

Sometimes, local shepherds and fishermen took over Delphini to dance the *Pentozale, Sigano* and the wild Zorba *sirtaki*. Among these Cretan shepherds, fishermen and soldiers, dancing was a sport. Dressed in their traditional costume, they performed wild dances as true athletes in black shirts, blousy riding britches, jackboots and woven, black *kaskol* headbands.

Ahhh, these guys from the mountains astonished us. One shepherd, for example, performed a backbend limbo with a glass of raki in his teeth, stood up from the backbend, drained the glass and spit it out to smash on the floor.

In another very cool dance move, a fisherman picked up a table with his teeth, and balanced it above his face. Onlookers awarded such feats of strength and style with shouts of "Opah!" throwing money, smashing plates and glasses to the floor. I yearned to be like them, these shepherds, to dance crazy like Zorba with a white handkerchief in my hand waving free.

On nights when the only Greeks in Delphini were the owners and their cave friends, Mime and Vangelis barred the doors and shutters from inside for private parties, When hashish arrived in town from Lebanon, Turkey, Pakistan or Afghanistan, the record player on the bar blasted rock and roll, and the most theatrical of the smugglers performed the *Benares Fire Chillum*.

To prepare a fire-chillum, the smoker charged the conical pipe with alternate layers of tobacco and hashish, and layers of shredded coconut fiber to provide incendiary substratum. Wrapping a handkerchief around the bottom of the chillum, the smoker closed his right hand around the left hand to damper the pipe. Lighting the chillum, the fire-chillum smoker inhaled the acrid smoke, and the burning coconut fiber and tobacco grew bright red. When he opened the fingers of his right hand, a fresh intake of air caused the dry coconut fiber to erupt in a flash of flame like a miniature Roman candle. *Spectacular!* Like a sadhu on the banks of the Ganges, the smuggler raised the flaming fire-chillum high over his head in clasped hands to salute Shiva—*Jai Shiva*!

Cavers fashioned chillums from human thigh bones found in caves, which we wore around our necks on cords. We smoked tobacco and hash in these bone chillums. On wild party nights, the restaurant reeked of pungent ganja. The Rolling Stones and Beatles blared out of the cheap speakers. We unbarred the shutters and doors at first dawn and light flooded the taverna gloom and its stoned-out occupants spilled out on to the patio and beach. Waves lapped up on the pebbles and roosters crowed in town. *Good morning, Matala!*

At first light, I arose. From a ledge near my cave, I dove into the freezing Mediterranean. What a way to wake up! The cold sea took my breath away. Shivering, I climbed up to my cave, drew on baggy cotton *shalwar kameez* trousers and shirt, and slipped on hiking boots. I wrapped the turban around my hair, Kabul style, and walked down to Delphini to prosecute the day.

In the kitchen Mimes was preparing Greek coffee for himself and three fishermen. In the dining room I set chairs upside down on tables and began sweeping up the floor, a mess from the night before. Good morning, morning litter! I swept up orange peels, smashed glasses, broken plates, food scraps, cigarette butts and trash. Once, I found the bottom part of a bikini bathing suit. I scraped kitchen scraps into a bucket that I dumped on the garbage heap around back, which would usually disappear during the day, picked over by goats, or carried away for compost or animal feed.

Delphini was somewhat a poor country cousin compared to the Mermaid Cafe. With American comfort food such as apple pie, B.B. King on the record player, and the convivial ambiance, the Mermaid had its regulars. Stelios and Dora created an atmosphere where you could eat Greek American dishes and hang out with friends. The Mermaid made a good refuge when I wanted a break from Delphini or when I wanted to meet newly arrived backpackers, or shoot the shit with Stelios and enjoy Dora's pies.

Fishermen and soldiers came to the Mermaid to drink and fraternize with the hippie cave girls, and some were actually successful. A small band of German girls, who were looking for more adventure than the humdrum community of travelers and cave dwellers could provide, were fair game for locals. These women were known to *elope* temporarily with shepherds and stay with them in caves and huts out on the hills. Although they would have nothing to do with us cavers, we held these Fräuleins high as heroes.

One evening Barbara invited me, Stefan, Stelios, and Dora to her cave for a birthday party for Utah John. We drank *krasi* and ate slices of a fresh apple pie that Dora had baked in the Mermaid kitchen. Stelios brought another lantern and a bottle of ouzo as a gift. Barbara turned to John, "Utah, I've known you for how long … ? but I really don't know anything about your family and background. Tell me what brought you to Matala."

Utah looked up from preparing a chillum, "Ok, I know you guys like family, I guess I should." He began his story, "I grew up on a family farm in

Sanpete County, Utah, with my parents, my grandmother, my older sister, Susan, and my little brother, Timmy. We raised wheat, sold firewood, and raised cows, sheep, goats, and chickens. Our farmhouse had a barn, sheds, machinery, and my mom kept a kitchen garden bordered by an apple orchard. Beyond the pastures, cottonwoods shaded a stream that meandered back and forth through the fields and forestland.

As Utah John told stories of his youth in Sanpete County, I saw beyond his scraggly dark beard, past the wrinkles of worry encircling his eyes, to visualize him as a boy walking with a cane pole beside a creek. Utah passed the chillum to Mark, then lay down on the carpet, and closing his eyes, confessed, "Now I am a draft dodger. I can't return ...." We looked at each other and sadness fell over the room.

✳ ✳ ✳

February was still chilly. Only a trickle of visitors and few new travelers came to stay in Matala, and if they did, most stayed only a day; Greeks only came on Saturday or Sunday. A few transients stayed for weeks. One visitor, distinguished author, Kimon Friar, arrived from Athens, bringing the legend of Zorba the Greek with him. Kimon, English translator of Nikos Kazantzakis's epic poem, *The Odyssey,* hung out in Matala for a week, visiting Cretan friends. During his days with us, Kimon drank his way back and forth between the Mermaid and Delphini and the unnamed, one-table sundry shop on the corniche where few cave dwellers drank except Mark and Kimon Friar.

Kimon was a great soul. He loved telling stories and commanded an endless variety of match puzzles and tricks. We drank with him, listened to his stories, tried to figure out his matchbox puzzles, and absorbed his charisma. I worked for hours learning one trick—how to lift a book of matches up to a top of a cigarette pack with only my index finger and little finger while keeping my middle finger and ring finger grounded on the table. Kimon especially enjoyed the company of young international travelers and openly admired the beauty of half-naked young hippie ladies sunbathing on the beach. I never remember him coming up to the caves, however, or pairing up with the ladies.

On a Sunday afternoon Kimon gave a talk on the works of Kazantzakis to an assembly of cave dwellers, travelers, and Greeks from Iraklion gathered outside the Mermaid. He had barely started his exposé when police barged in and shut down the event, citing a Junta law prohibiting public gatherings of more than ten people. Stelios argued that these people were customers, and this was not a political event; nevertheless, they waved their batons and ordered the crowd to disperse. We retired to the interior of Delphini and the police ignored us. This event foreshadowed more serious political problems that surfaced between Stelios and the police later.

Kimon donated a dozen copies of the *New York Herald Tribune* to the Mermaid Café lending library. I picked up the February 22nd issue. Forty-seven people had died in the alleged PLO bombing of a Swissair flight from Zurich to Tel Aviv. *Fucking hell! the world is falling apart.*

CHAPTER 12

Dreams of Dionysus

This world is half the devil's and my own,
Daft with the drug that's smoking in a girl
And curling round the bud that forks her eye.
An old man's shank one-marrowed with my bone,
And all the herrings smelling in the sea,
I sit and watch the worm beneath my nail
Wearing the quick away.

—Dylan Thomas
"If I Were Tickled by the Rub of Love."

Amid the turmoil of the world, life was immediate and sensual in this little fishing village. These were the days before socially transmitted diseases and AIDS quenched free, casual sex. If you liked someone, sex was almost taken for granted. It was a wonder all of us were not stricken by gonorrhea or worse. A clinic in Mires would treat you with antibiotics if you did contact a venereal disease. I never did, although I fell in and out of love several times a week. Why not? Backpackers come; backpackers go. They were looking for places to sleep in the caves and become part of the cave scene and we were all too willing to accommodate them.

One night, stoned out of my gourd, I managed to get to sleep alone in my cave and an erotic dream hurtled me into a scene lifted from classical Greek myths I had been reading. In this fantasy scene I dreamed of a Satyr kneeling on a hillside surveying the long valley over the hills south of Matala above Red Beach.

On a high rock he squats on hairy goat legs to peer below at Wood Nymphs—the nine Muses—dancing, kissing, and caressing each other, moaning and singing, playing lyre, trumpet, and flute.

The Satyr—*Dionysus*—grabs his huge phallus, an enormous goat-man cock the size of a baby's arm curling up his abdomen from a wiry patch of pubic hair springing out over fat hanging testicles, which slap against his hairy rear goat legs. Crouching on cloven hooves, he springs from rock to the glen floor below. His arrival causes a wild *Bacchanalian* frenzy and nine muses—in rapture—converge on him. Throwing down his pipes and seizing the closest muse, the golden-haired one with the zither, the satyr bites her bulging red nipple with yellow buck teeth.

The *Bacchante* turns her voluptuous rump and squirms her white buttocks up against his gigantic member. She smiles—it is the alluring, gap-toothed smile of Melissa in Kandahar!

A corpulent muse dances forth from the writhing circle of nymphs, comes up from behind Dionysus and wraps her chubby arms around his hairy chest, jamming her tits against his back. Her fingers pinch his nipples, and he grunts like a billy goat as her right-hand lifts his erect pulsing cock and rubs it up and down her sister's fat, swollen cunt. Raging wild with goat-god lust, Dionysus bites the muse's shoulder. She grins and sticks out her long, pink tongue at him.

Cum begins to gurgle from the satyr's turgid cock, which the muse smears on her sister's quivering bottom and her plump, gaping labia, and … and … Boom!

Outside, Boom! … a loud, deep, bass, resonant Boom! … Boom! startles me in my cave. I jerk up awake, bolt straight in my crypt. A fierce urge to urinate comes over me, driving me to throw off my blankets, leap right out of my bed, and scutter on hands and knees through the entrance of my cave. I sprint to the rock shelf jutting out below Big Cave to piss wildly into a foamy geyser of seawater jetting straight up in the air out of a crevasse in the rocks below. Boom!

Boom! Below, charging waves of a mini-tsunami smash against the bottom of the cliff and surge into a submerged cave that compresses the seawater to ejaculate through the crevasse to exit high following a loud deep bass, Boom!

The surf ebbs, sizzling through the pebbles, which the waves draw back and fling again and again against the high cliff. Boom! Boom! On shaky legs I shake off the last droplets and exhaling a sigh of relief, I raise my eyes to gaze into the infinite, dark-blue lapis lazuli sky where the astral brush of the Milky Way paints its whitish stroke across the heavens, a canvas stippled with pinpoints of bright planets, stars, and constellations.

Wobbling down the cliff to the beach, I scoop up handfuls of seawater to splash on face and body. I am completely stoned. Scrambling on hands and knees up the cliff face, I stop when I detect a pale glow emanating from a cave to my right.

Stupefied by the dream of satyr and wood nymph and vibrating still to the cadence of bass drumbeats of the wild surf, half-crazed on what I was told last night was mescaline, I creep naked along the sandstone ridge to investigate the dim, yellow light coming from the depth of a large cave on the level below mine. I crawl ahead, poking my head into the mouth of the cave to see a naked lady with long golden hair to her waist sitting on the edge of a narrow crypt under the faint light of a kerosene lamp sewing an embroidered patch on faded jeans. She has the full sculptured body of a gymnast, a Sheena of the Jungle, muscular legs, strong arms and an angelic face.

At first, I pause … *Is this a ghostly manifestation of Holly?* As I barge in the cave naked, she looks up, not the least bit surprised, as if she were expecting me. *What is she doing alone in this large cave that usually sleeps nine?* I look around. *Where are they? Is this, too, a dream?*

With a nod she beckons me to her side. I sit down and rest my left arm over her shoulder. I cup my right hand over her upturned breast, feeling its hard nub graze my palm. We kiss and embrace. She runs her fingers through my curly hair, and looking deep into my eyes, grabs my hair and all at once yanks me down to the cave floor on top of her. I bury my nose in her hair, armpit, and crotch—pungent animal musk, patchouli, olive oil and sage. She stabs my mouth with her hot tongue, wraps her legs around me, and we make fierce animal love on the thin carpet, never exchanging a single word.

With me curled up against her back, exhausted, she suddenly shivers, turns over, stretching wide her legs on the carpet and arching her back like a cat, pushes me away, and rolls over on her stomach to sleep. I stand up and stumble outside, reeking of her. I feel my way back to my cave to pass out in the darkness on the floor of my cave.

Late next morning when I wake up, I go back to her cave. *She is gone.* I search everywhere for her, even up the valley in the scrub brush toilets. *Gone.*

"Oh, that girl with the long yellow hair?" a cave dweller informs me. "They call her 'Sybil.' She told us she was going to sail with Theo for the Peloponnesus." A sudden shiver courses through my body. *What is going on? What kind of dreams or visitations are these?*

I never saw this Sybil again. Not in this form, anyway.

In that moment of perplexity, Matala seemed to slip away to another mythic dimension of magical realism. One day merged into the next where Ghosts of Minoans pervaded endless époques of gods and goddesses. Such unrolled the nature of Matala life: the world, past and future could contract into an unfolding *now* in an eternal present. Life was easy and rich. All the time in the world to read, to think, to talk, to eat, to drink retsina, to get stoned, to walk in the hills, to swim in the Mediterranean, to lie on the rocks in the sun, to fall in love.

※ ※ ※

Every week or so, in the early morning, I accompanied Mark into the tilled fields behind Matala village to help his farmer friend, Manoli, collect rocks from his fields and pile them alongside rock walls. There was no end of rocks. This farm work was part of Mark's ongoing community service. Mark would say, "Cary, let's go get stoned. Ha. Ha." *Very funny, Mark.* Lugging stones was demanding work. The farmer paid us in food and drink and fed us breakfast of stewed lamb head with bread, olives, paximadia and krasi from a wine skin. Lunch consisted of black cured olives, goat cheese, more wine and more paximadia.

In Iraklion we brought the bootmakers a sample of our new breed of sandals. Sitting on stools in their shop off the main street in Iraklion, they inspected one of our cave-made sandals with the same scrutiny an ichthyologist might bestow on a strange fish. Passing our sandal down the line of cobblers, each held it up to the sunlight, turned it this way and that, examining the oak-pegged soles, straps, and buckles. Grinning, they chatted between themselves. The head guy at the first bench, Ionnes, said something in Greek to Mark who laughed, turned to me and translated into English, "He said, 'This is very easy,'" We laughed.

In Matala I flogged our sandals from Delphini where I could work and socialize with taverna customers. Mark and Barbara thrived on their craft industry, making useful clothes and leather accessories. Mark loved to fashion practical things out of common materials such as reeds, driftwood, bones, shells, twine, fishline, twisted fibers and leather. He bartered reed doors for things he valued, such as fresh oranges, retsina, hashish, or sandwiches from "Mama." He was keen on seven-star Metaxa brandy. The way I figured it, Mark could have bartered his craft skills for sexual favors—surely, I would have—but he was a one-Barbara guy.

Barbara, like Mark, was an industrious craftsperson. She loved to sew, knit, and make clothing, mastering the treadle model Singer Sewing Machine. Before leaning over to spin a bobbin, thread the needle or examine a stitch, she pulled up her hair in a leather barrette to keep it out of her eyes and the sewing machine. With heavy leatherworking needles and strong thread, she turned her fashion skills to making leather goods, bags, and jackets. When she ran out of leatherwork jobs, she changed to finer needles, bobbins, and thread, and sewed Afghan embroidered shirt fronts on cotton blouses, making dresses, pajama pants, and vests from cloth she bought in the local market in Mires.

Except for the few samples of belts and bags on the wall, and my Afghan goods—agate rings, and embroidery—we had little inventory. Mark and Barbara loved the work and were good at it. Best of all, Mark and Barbara tolerated my foul, mercurial moods.

One morning Stelios sent us word by a boy to join him that afternoon in the Mermaid. When Barbara, Mark and I arrived in mid-afternoon, Stelios and Dora were at the table in the corner with Utah John and Stefan. Stelios, the gentleman, arose and pulled out a chair for Barbara. He circled the table and poured each of us a small shot glass of raki. We all raised our glasses not knowing yet what we were here to celebrate. Stelios turned to Dora, who alone among us had not raised her glass, put his hand on her shoulder, and said, "To Dora! It's her birthday! *Yasu!* Dora!"

With our glasses held high, we joined in the toast, "*Yasu,* Dora!" and downed our rakis. Stelios bent over and kissed her on her lips. Then he refilled our glasses.

Stefan arose and lifting his glass, said, "Dora, if we were in Warsaw today, I would give you flowers as your birthday present, but I don't have any flowers today, so I give you all tomorrow's flowers." And we all drank.

Dora rose and walked over to Stefan and kissed him three times on the cheeks, "Stefan, you are better than flowers." More raki.

"Dora," I said standing, "the Matala Leather Shop, known for the finest sandals east of Cape Cod, wishes to honor you on your birthday with a pair of custom-made sandals. We will come to the Mermaid at breakfast, take your foot pattern, and Mark will have them on your feet by this time tomorrow." All our leather shop sales came from referrals and word of mouth, so what could be better than having Dora wear our sandals?

Barbara promised to make Dora a linen blouse with an Afghan embroidered front.

Utah John offered Dora love, undying affection, and sexual favors.

In addition to all tomorrow's flowers, Stefan gifted Dora his own story. His was an angelic, but slightly sinister face. A single blond braid hung over his left shoulder threaded with beads of turquoise, coral, and lapis lazuli.

From his lips drooped a blond Fu Manchu mustache and a pointed Van Dyke beard.

He began, "Utah, at your birthday party in Barbara's cave, you told us that you grew up on a farm. In Poland, my family were farmers, too—urban farmers. We belonged to a commune that squatted in abandoned buildings where people kept chickens and pigeons and rabbits on the roofs. We fed the chickens with chopped up stems and leaves and table scraps. In the spring and summer, we raised vegetables in garden boxes that we built on the roof with scavenged materials from construction sites. Our garden soil was kitchen waste composted with rabbit and bird shit. And our own ... what do they say ... *night soil?*"

Stefan told Dora that he had worked in the art world part time in Poland, taking casual jobs in the art community and at the National Opera. "I was always busy," he said. His principal gig was painting walls of art galleries, and *faux fini* designs on the walls in the town houses of Warsaw opera aficionados. "I did light carpentry on opera sets and helped set up art gallery openings. During the season I worked backstage at the opera doing whatever was required, at times working as a volunteer. When spring returns to Poland, I'll go back. I'll take you home with me, Utah."

As I listened to Stefan's story I reflected on my own life. *Did I have a story to give?* I was happy, most of the time. *Why would I ever consider leaving Matala?* I liked to meet people, like my friends surrounding me. I liked to fall in love, drink, dance. When someone wanted sandals when I was bartending at Delphini, I took a foot pattern and sent it up to the shop. Sale consummated—I toasted the transaction with the customer with shots of raki, just like we were doing here in the Mermaid now. We celebrated Dora, raising glasses of raki, encircling forearms, "*Yassu!*" we saluted one another, clicking glasses and knocking back the fiery, clear moonshine.

One night at Delphini raki got the best of me. I stumbled up the corniche to the Mermaid, drunk. Sliding back the doors, I stepped in the café and fell flat on my face. Rising to hands and knees I steadied myself between the legs of a stocky German girl seated with friends at the table next to the doors. "*Scheibe! Arschfotze!*" she cursed and kicked me away. I fell on my back and hit my head.

I picked myself up again and hurled myself at her, toppling her chair. I grabbed her blond hair and began dragging her out of the taverna, screaming. Her friends, aided by Greeks soldiers, beat me up and threw me outside. I woke up on the floor of my cave at dawn, bruised and bleeding from my mouth, the worst for wear, having no idea how I got back. *What happened?* They told me about what I had done the next day. I was contrite, but Stelios banned me from the Mermaid for a week.

The intensity of my days varied. When business was slow during the week, I might sit outside Delphini and read. No language maven, I was struggling to learn elementary Greek, and not getting very far. The caves had a floating, lending library of all kinds of paperback books, which we cave dwellers shared. At the Mermaid Café books lined a wall bookshelf. Among them were volumes of science fiction, Dickens, poetry of Baudelaire, yoga books, Carlos Castaneda, travel guides, maps, language books and Greek/English dictionaries.

On a slow day I might go hiking with friends or catch up with shepherds who kept little caves or rock huts on the hills past Red Beach south of Matala where they sought shade from the midday heat. When shepherds shared food with me in the hills, it mainly consisted of olives, braided rings of dried figs, dried paximadia bread and krasi, same fare Manoli fed Mark and me when we worked in his fields. If Mark was with me, we talked to shepherds about their animals, crops, fishing, dancing, the attractiveness of German girls versus Swedish girls, and politics. Mark sopped up their conversation in Greek like a sponge and translated for me. We marveled how a shepherd could climb steep hills as if it were no effort at all—long crooked cane in hand, britches tucked into high jackboots, following paths straight up the mountain on animal tracks between the rocks and the shrub bushes and herbs as if the breezes from the Gulf of Messara were lifting him up the mountain.

Not all was so happy-go-lucky for me. I had recurring periods of depression and irritability. Lurking beneath the daily routines of Matala, and the pleasures of the flesh, good food and good company of my companions, my moods swings plagued me. Downswings took me back to the bad LSD trip I had had in Nancy's apartment, and upswings to the extraordinary, sudden awakening event I had experienced in Berkeley. I had episodic flash backs of terror and of the divine, residual from my period of illuminations—and endarkening—a year and half before.

One night, alone, staggering to my cave from a Delphini party, as I stood beside the lapping surf, I stopped to look up in wonder at the brilliant stars bursting forth from a dark, moonless sky. Abruptly ... everything changed! My sense of space and time warped. I felt dizzy as if there were no solid place to stand. *I am looking out from the nosecone of spaceship Earth drifting in infinite cosmos. I am way out in space with no up or down.* And then, a thought-moment happened outside of time ... *"I" am not IN outer space, "I" ... AM the universe!*

Waves of fear rippled through my body in a torrent of terror. My knees buckled, and I collapsed on the wet pebbles and lay in a fetal position, not knowing where my body ended and where the external universe began. Finally, cold damp stones brought me back into my body and my senses. I rose shivering from the beach and climbed up to my cave into my crypt and buried myself in my sleeping bag.

When the light of dawn awoke me, I was hungover and woozy. I thought back to the out-of-body experience last night on the beach. *What is happening to me?* A year ago-Halloween in San Francisco, a period of spiritual awakening had progressed into catastrophic, paranoid insanity. *Was this happening again?*

I rolled out of my burial crypt, pushed back the curtain, folded my sleeping bag, and went out for my morning swim. I figured that whatever was going on would continue to go on and the best I could do was go along for the ride. "This is it," I told myself, here in this place, in this time, in this hard-boiled character role that I successfully faked most of the time. But that was far from a satisfying explanation. From time to time I knew peacefulness and gratitude, but just as frequently, I could turn irritable and belligerent.

Why was I compelled to treat people unkindly here in Matala and put down people and ideas that annoyed me? Couldn't I train myself to act with patience and kindness, which I knew from my experience embodied compassion? Couldn't I manage my relationships in a mature and responsible way, instead of pretending I was a wild rover from the hills, taking shit from no one? I fought with rowdy customers who pissed me off in the taverna, just like I had fought with Frenchie when I came back from Kabul. Frequently in a foul mood, I was a fight getting ready to happen. *There must be a better way to live.*

Returning one night to my cave half-drunk, I hung my clothes on pegs and climbed naked into bed and snuggled under my blankets. As I began to drift off to sleep, in the dim, grey moonlight, something long and skinny twitched from the wooden shelf right above my bed. "Snake!" ... *Really?* ... No, it was not a snake. It was the tail of a cat—a contented gray cat—licking its paws. Having knocked off the lid, it had been feasting from my pot of beans. Enraged, fearing neither fang nor claw, I lunged for the cat. The startled cat sprang from the shelf, upsetting the pot of cold beans that poured onto my head and dropped on the blankets. I leapt up, shouted, and heaved a sandal at the cat as it scratched-off full speed under my reed cave door and sped off into the night. I stripped the top blanket from my crypt, took it out to the edge of the big cave and shook it. I washed myself off down on the beach and crept over into Barbara and Mark's cave to sleep it off in my sleeping bag on their carpet.

In the morning I saw how the cat's antics—and my violent outrage—had knocked books from the overhead shelf onto the bed and cave floor along with the beans. I wiped beans from the cover of *The Collected Poems of William Butler Yeats*. I opened it the way I remembered Mama randomly opened the *King James Bible,* and flipped through the pages. They fell open to a turned-down page and the poem, "The Second Coming." I knew this poem. I had read it in a Modern Poetry class in tandem with T.S. Eliot's "The Wasteland."

The lines struck me as somehow prophetic, if as Yeats were addressing me from the well of his subconscious, as if I were a fellow member of the "Order of the Golden Dawn."

Surely some revelation is at hand;
Surely the Second Coming is at hand ...
And what rough beast, its hour come round at last,
Slouches towards Bethlehem to be born?

Could the "rough beast" represent the violence in mankind, impending doom? My own barely controllable violence? I imagined a rootless sphinx creeping across the Suez Canal and swimming slowly toward Crete, fangs bared.

As I entertained this creepy image from the poem, I noticed a thick, yellow book lying face up among five or six other books that had tumbled off the shelf, the *I Ching: The Book of Changes*. I wiped beans off it. I saw a small envelope taped to the inside of the back cover, opened it, and three brass Chinese coins fell out.

Ah ha! Let's see what we have here. I passed the coins from one hand to another, remembering the first time I had consulted the *I Ching* two years ago in Canyon, east of the Berkeley Hills. *When I had been crazy.*

I turned to the preface, written by Carl Jung. He explained that consulting the *I Ching* required an appropriate question, an existential type of inquiry. Jung wrote that the *I Ching* reveals what already exists, or could exist, not a magical, fortunetelling prescience. He said the more precise the inquirer defined the question in quality, quantity, and time, the more compelling the reading would be. *Ah so. What then would be my inquiry?*

The instructions in the *I Ching* prologue jogged my memory on how to toss the coins, how to construct the hexagram, and how to interpret the divination. I leaned against the wall of my crypt and contemplated the questions I had been struggling with—compassion and ethical conduct, not the easiest thing to do when your bed reeks of beans and cat. The best existential question was what already tormented me:

Can I develop compassion? It needs a timeframe. How about, "Can I develop compassion before the Spring Equinox?" "How" is better than "Can." I copied the inquiry in my notebook, dated it, and I wrote next to it— and then crossed out—"... ~~what beast slouches toward Matala to be born~~?"

On a blank page, I numbered six places from one to six starting at the bottom. I tossed the coins six times on my carpet and drew six solid and broken lines resulting in Hexagram 60: *Chieh / Limitations.* The commentary:

Unlimited possibilities are not suited to man; if they existed, his life would only dissolve into the boundless.

"Wow," I thought. "*Limitations.* Does 'the boundless' relate to my recent astral plane flip-out on the beach? To my other experiences of *Emptiness?*" I continued reading about the moving lines in the first and fourth places that changes the Hexagram 60: *Limitations*" into Hexagram 47: *K'un /Adversity.* The commentary stated:

Often a man who would like to undertake something finds himself confronted by insurmountable limitations. Then he must know where to stop ... He who lets his spirit be broken by exhaustion certainly has no success .... It is true that for the time being outward influence is denied him because his words had no effect.

Literally or figuratively, what was the I Ching compelling me to know? I closed my eyes and dug into this. "Let's see. If I am limited in my will to develop compassion, what stops me? Although I profess to want to become a more compassionate person, my words alone have no effect, because my behavior speaks louder than words, as the old saying goes?"

And then I remembered. In Nancy's apartment a year ago November, I had bargained with God, begging Him to deliver me from the Devil—"*The Beast?*" "Did I not promise that I would thereafter help the needy and oppressed?" Even though I didn't believe in a one God, it was as if I had been reaching out to the totality of all forces—*the ultimate ground of being*—to deliver me from the consequences of my errant behavior, my drift towards criminality. *Was THAT the "Beast?"*

"Ahhh! *Get a grip on yourself, Cary!*" Now, I was talking out loud to myself. "Despite *Limitations* and *Adversity*, despite episodic madness, inner beasts, mythic gods and demons, can't I change my ways? I don't know how that can happen in the next few weeks of winter. Will it be revealed?"

I put the coins back in the envelope, closed the *I Ching*, and shrugged. *Whew! Man that was heavy!* "That's what I get from consulting oracles. Still …."

PART III

Upekkha

There may be in the cup
A spider steep'd, and one may drink, depart,
And yet partake no venom, for his knowledge
Is not infected: but if one present
The abhorr'd ingredient to his eye, make known
How he hath drunk, he cracks his gorge, his sides,
With violent hefts.
I have drunk, and seen the spider.

—Shakespeare
Winters Tale

CHAPTER 13

Our Lady of the Caves

The morning found me washing dishes in Delphini. Finally I was recovering from the rough winter in Kabul that had left me strung out, feeling like someone had thrown me down a flight of stairs. Now I was home. Almost every day, cave dwellers drifted into the taverna to bring latest news and rumors circulating through our little fishing village. Lars, my first customer of the day, walked in Delphini for his morning eye-opener, "A retsina and a potato omelet, Cary. Did you hear Joni Mitchell is in town?"

I wiped soapy hands on my apron and poured Lars a glass of retsina, sliding it across the kitchen counter toward him. He downed it and plunked down twenty drachmas.

Breaking eggs into a bowl, I probed, "Lars, who is this Joni Mitchell person everyone is talking about?" Whipping the eggs with a fork, I poured them into a steel pan swimming with olive oil. As eggs thickened, I spooned in pre-fried onions and potato slices, flipped the omelet over and turned it out on Lar's plate with black olives and a thick slice of bread, *psomi*, to sop up the egg and olive oil.

"Joni Mitchell ... describe her? Well, first off, she's a folk singer, or a singer-songwriter guess you could say. She wrote, 'Both Sides Now' a couple years ago that Judy Collins covered. You'll probably spot her around Matala, surrounded by fans. A real babe."

"In fact, you can't miss her," Lars continued between bites. "Mid-twenties or so but might be younger. Long blond hair. Pretty. Her *Clouds* album blew away my cousins in Stockholm ... they raved about it. *Rolling Stone* reported she got a Grammy award for it."

He pointed out the door, "Hey, Cary, there goes Joni now, walking along the beach with that other chick." I looked out through the open kitchen door and saw two girls walking side by side in the lapping surf, heading toward the caves. *Hmmmm ....*

"I know you Cary ..., you gonna be after her faster than a New York second!"

"That would be *a New York minute*, Lars. Besides, I don't pursue posh chicks like Joni Mitchell who have come to bewitch my pals in Matala ... like you!"

"Sure, you'd say that about any chick who spurns you. What's the children's tale about a fox and bitter grapes?"

"*Sour grapes*, Lars," I muttered, "how can you grow up in Indiana and not know Aesop's fables? And what, me chasing Joni Mitchell? You got to be kidding Lars. You'll be the one drooling about her in your little cave." *Intolerable pain in the ass sometimes, Lars.*

"What's this woman doing in Matala anyway?" I asked, stirring the bean soup.

"Don't know, escaping Hollywood and probing journalists, I guess ...," finishing off his second glass of retsina.

Resuming washing dishes and cups, I remembered hearing Joni Mitchell's song, "Both Sides Now," for the first time at Deward's house in Berkeley two years ago—in the fall of 1968—sitting on a cushion in his living room listening to KSAN radio. This was about the same time the Beatles released the *White Album* and Judy Collins covered "Both Sides Now." Joni Mitchell wrote those incredible lyrics?

Lars approached the counter and interrupted my thoughts. He ordered a Greek coffee, which I prepared in a *briki,* and poured the black, grainy *kafe* into an espresso cup, which I placed on the counter.

I was remembering that fall in Berkeley when I had been struggling with D.T. Suzuki's treatise on Zen, reading it daily in the eucalyptus grove on the Berkeley campus. I was trying to understand esoteric Buddhist concepts of the impermanence of all things, emptiness of illusions, and "non-self"—whatever *that* was.

A few weeks after reading Suzuki, an incredible event woke me up instantly like I had been sleepwalking all my life—a startling moment that suddenly revealed what Suzuki was writing about. After that, I began to understand levels of consciousness I had been reading about but had not previously experienced directly. That awakening experience somehow got conflated with "Both Sides Now" lyrics that I had been hearing on the radio. *Something about knowing directly rather than through concepts, perhaps.*

Sipping his coffee, Lars leaned over to tell me more about Joni Mitchell. "You know she's Graham Nash's girlfriend, right? Graham Nash of Crosby, Stills and Nash?"

"How about that?" I replied, stacking glasses on the shelves, and thinking: *That's interesting. Graham Nash, Huh?* I knew Crosby, Stills and Nash. *How droll.*

Since leaving the States six months ago, I had drifted out of touch with current news except for an occasional out-of-date *Herald Tribune*. I distanced myself from world events, US intervention in the Vietnam war, and changes in popular culture. Food, drink, ladies and good company occupied more of my attention than dismal news of the day.

Lurking in the emptiness between the real and the unreal, dreams of mythical demi-gods invaded my sleep. Divinations from the *I Ching* intimated ideas I felt were true but could not imagine applying to my life. Just days before, I had temporarily fallen unconscious and lost my sense of the physical body while walking on the beach looking at the stars. *All things arise and pass away.* The shifting space between the coming and the going, between the mystic and the mundane, the spiritual and the practical, bewildered and frightened me.

Regardless of my fragile state of sanity, or madness, perhaps, life goes on, I told myself, *Obladi oblada,* as if we were all suspended in a limbo theater of the absurd. In the meantime, Matala was abuzz with Joni Mitchell's comings and goings. Buzz, buzz, buzz, gossip, gossip ... how ridiculous! The idea of celebrities invading Matala repelled me.

Later in the morning, an entourage of fans—some my usual drinking buddies—walked into Delphini surrounding Joni Mitchell who seemed shy and uncomfortable with their attention. *Well, well, the famous Joni Mitchell has come into Delphini, trailing a gaggle of fawning sycophants.*

Before this crowd entered I had begun sweeping up garbage on the dining room floor littered with the remains from last night's bash: food, broken plates, shards of raki glasses, and cigarette butts. Joni Mitchell's companions dragged chairs up to the table, circling her. Her long blond hair flowed down her white blouse. On her neck wrists and fingers, Navaho turquoise jewelry.

The guy I knew as Georgie slithered up to the counter and ordered figs, oranges, and tea. Around the table they were telling her how much they loved her music. On a tray I brought them a tea pot and glasses, oranges and a plate of dried figs.

In the kitchen I finished stacking plates on the shelves and turned down the burner under the bean soup. Eventually they finished their tea and fruit. Georgie paid the bill. I stalked out into the dining room to clear the table. As I advanced, Joni Mitchell stood up, scooped up the trash from the tabletop in her hands—candy wrappers and orange peels smashed in a ball—and handed it to me as if offering a gift. *How charming. Joni Mitchell behaves like a guest tidying up the table for her host. Does she realize how much I resent her being in Matala? Or more precisely, how much I resent cavers kowtowing to her?* Holding out my hands, I accepted her offering of fresh trash, thanked her, and threw it on the floor.

Joni Mitchell and her entourage departed. I resumed my cooking and kitchen chores. *Please, Sweet Jesus, enough celebrity and fame in Matala.*

✳ ✳ ✳

My daily ritual—my early morning eye-opener—continued to be a bracing dip in the sea. I rolled out of bed naked, walked to the ledge outside Big Cave, and dived into the waves rolling on to the cliffs. A shocking plunge into the winter Mediterranean. *Yikes!* I swam back to the beach quickly. Shivering, my dick so cold it was trying to retract into my body like the neck of a turtle, I scrambled up the cliff to my cave, toweled off, massaged olive oil on my limbs, and rubbed it in my hair to keep it from drying out from dust and salt. I pulled on my green Afghan *shalwar kameez*, wrapped my turban, put on my hiking boots, and made off across the beach to town.

My boots crunched across the beach pebbles to the patio at Delphini. The kitchen door was ajar. Standing in the doorway, I watched Mimes, Delphini's co-manager, bend down on one knee fiddling with the regulator on the propane canister. I smelled gas.

An unlit cigarette dangled from Mimes's lips. Why would he smoke near a leaking propane tank? We never knew.

Looking into the kitchen, I was observing an impending disaster getting ready to happen as if viewing it in slow motion. Mimes's right hand dipped into his shirt pocket and flicked open a Zippo lighter. Time froze. Before I could scream "Stop! Mimes!"—BANG!—a bright flash, a wave of heat. A concussion blew me backward onto the stone patio. I was alive! I smelled burned hair. What about Mimes?

I sat up, checked my limbs for damage, picked myself up and went inside. Crouched on his knees, Mimes covered his face and eyes. "Oh my God," I thought. "Mimes!"

I knelt beside him. He removed his hands from his face. His hands, arms and face blushed bright red, and his drooping mustache, singed. "Can you see?" I asked him.

"*Ligo*" (a little), he said, hands over eyes and cheeks. An expat couple dashed up from the beach. We helped Mimes stumble out of the kitchen.

Villagers loaded Mimes into a pickup and drove him to the clinic in Mires where they treated him for severe second degree burns to his face, chest, and arms. Though his eyes were red and puffy, and his eyelashes and eyebrows burned off, it was a miracle the explosion had not blinded him.

The blast had torn apart the kitchen, shattering the glass on the refrigerator counter. Shards of glass, as well as bits of tomatoes, cucumbers, onions, broken eggs, lamb chops, fish, and feta cheese littered the floor of the kitchen. Luckily, this morning, no customers were inside.

The flash of heat had singed my beard. The long shirt of heavy cotton Afghan *shalwar kameez* pajamas had shielded my thighs and male parts from the heat of the blast. Hiking boots and wool socks protected my feet and ankles. The dirty white Afghan turban protected most of my hair. My arms and face flushed beet red.

After seeing Mimes off to Mires, I hobbled back across the beach to my cave. Barbara stripped me and applied olive oil to my reddened skin. I said to her, "We really got off lucky, Mimes and me. I thought we were done for." Mark poured me a glass of ouzo. I vowed to him to stay out of the sun for a few days. After all, Delphini would be closed for the time it took to repair the damage.

The next morning friends stopped by my cave where I was reading to ask how I was doing. "As good as new," I lied. The skin on my face and arms still hurt like a bad sunburn. They invited me to join them on a hike up and over the cliffs to the Roman Baths on the other side of the caves.

"Joni will be there," they said. Without thinking—and breaking my promise to Mark to stay out of the sun—I accepted, slipped on jeans, turban, sandals, put olive oil on my face, and grabbed my cane. As we climbed the rocky, switchback goat path, I knew they hoped to find Joni Mitchell naked at the Roman Baths. So, did I. Morning sun burned my sore face.

On the north side of the cliffs from the caves, a long, smooth sandstone ledge sloped down at an easy angle into the sea. Supposedly, Romans had chiseled rectangular holes in the stone two millennia ago. At high tide, waves crashed up the incline and filled the holes with sea water. As tide receded, sun heated the water and *voila*! warm salty baths.

Topping the cliff, we encountered a dozen or so cave dwellers, half of them naked in the baths, while others basked like seals on the warm sandstone in various degrees of undress. Others hunkered nearby, smoking hashish in a chillum, with a jacket thrown over their heads to shield matches from the wind. Among those clothed stood Joni Mitchell barefoot in a yellow bikini top and a sarong, blond hair rippling in the breeze. She walked up, faced me, and held out a twisted piece of grey driftwood, exclaiming, "Look! A mermaid!"

This chick is probably stoned on hashish.

I hooked the crook of my cane on the belt of my jeans, accepted the driftwood "mermaid" from Joni Mitchell's hand, and assessed it from various angles as if I were an archeologist examining an ancient artifact. I handed it back to her, "Looks like a piece of driftwood to me." She turned away with a downcast expression. I noticed she had a strong lithe body and full, round hips.

No baths, no sunbathing, no hashish for Cary today at the Roman Baths, I decided as I turned away, face stinging, annoyed with all the stoned chitterchatter. With the help of my cane I picked my way down the steep, winding goat path to my cave.

※   ※   ※

Over the years cave dwellers developed an evening ritual of watching the sun set over the sea. The sun would appear to set once, and then seem to reappear beneath a thin cloud hovering on the horizon, only to set again moments later.

"An optical illusion," explained Mark, my partner. "Due to the curvature of the earth, light bends near the horizon causing a viewer to perceive the illusion of the sun setting twice."

Two days after the kitchen explosion, I was crunching across the pebbles on my way to the Mermaid for a drink or two—or three—when I stopped to watch the sunset phenomenon. On the low stone wall next to the closed Delphini, I perched my butt on warm rocks as the sky turned red in the west.

Breaking my reverie, from out of nowhere Joni Mitchell appeared like a blond wraith and sat down on the wall next to me. We greeted each other civilly but exchanged few words as the brilliant double setting of the sun unfolded over the western wave. Together we watched the sunset play out its magic across the horizon. She turned toward me, "That was breathtaking!"

My guard was down. I liked her smile. Lots of teeth. She had an air more relaxed and composed than how I had observed her in Delphini in the company of fans, when she seemed to be trying to hide from others, to hide from herself. Or at the Roman Baths. She smelled of coconut oil, a smell I adore. I was enjoying sitting next to her, admiring her muscular legs and strong, pretty feet. Sandal makers have a thing about pretty feet.

Twilight was replacing the rosy sunset. "Hey Joni, Matala's evening sky always reminds me of Shelly's 'Ode to Night.' Do you know it?" She nodded. Hoping to impress her, I recited the first stanza:

Swiftly walk o'er the western wave,
Spirit of Night!
Out of the misty eastern cave,
Where, all the long and lone daylight,
Thou wovest dreams of joy and fear,
Which make thee terrible and dear,—
Swift be thy flight!

Joni took my arm, "You quoted Shelley by heart. Do you know the whole poem?"

"Sure do. Let's go up to the Mermaid and have a drink," I suggested. "I'll recite you the rest and we can toast the *Spirit of Night*."

Arm in arm we walked past shuttered shops to the Mermaid Café at the end of the corniche and entered the café through open sliding glass doors. Behind the counter, Stelios greeted us as we entered. saluting me, "*Yassu*, Cary!" as the record player played a scratchy, "Sympathy for the Devil." "*Yassu*, Cary," yelled Dora, from the kitchen. Several cave dwellers saluted us with raised glasses, as they ate and drank at tables on the far wall beneath the mural of the Santana Lion album cover Willie Gilbertson-Hart had painted last December.

The Mermaid exuded a mixed aroma of coffee, apple pie, sautéing onions and herbs, and tobacco smoke. Around a table in the far back corner sat a half dozen shepherds and soldiers, smoking and drinking.

Joni and I sat down at a wooden table next to the sliding doors. I ordered raki—perhaps twice the strength of ouzo—for each of us. When Stelios brought over the drinks on a tray, I showed Joni how to toast, Cretan style. Holding up the raki glasses, we entwined arms, and toasted, *Yassu!* saluting each other and tossing off the white alcohol, neat. Eye to eye, we both shuddered. She screwed up her face and her eyes went wide.

"It takes practice to learn to like raki moonshine," I chuckled, remembering how I had choked when drinking it for the first time.

She looked up, "Kind of a ... eau de vie," she said. "Burns but has a distinctive aftertaste like tequila does ...."

As Joni was telling me about her travels, a soldier from the far corner of the room peeled away from his fellows and walked over to our table. He sauntered up, greeted us—*Yassas*—and spun around a chair on which he sat, forearms resting on the curved back, facing Joni from a foot away. From his jacket he withdrew a pack of Benson and Hedges, and grinning, offered the open pack to her. These cigarettes, expensive status-symbols, were probably smuggled into Crete, I reckoned. Joni already had a lit cigarette dangling from the side of her mouth, Jean-Paul Belmondo style. Declining his offer, she dipped her head, saying, "No, no thank you." Curiously, her head tilt in Cretan body-language could be interpreted as either *yes* or *no*. To complicate things further, her "No" could be heard as *née* (ναι)—in Greek, *Yes*. Inadvertently, Joni was throwing the soldier mixed signals.

Despite her protests, the soldier persisted pestering Joni, while she tried to be polite and not offend him, shaking her head affirmatively and saying *yes*. Ah, *la comédie humaine continue*.

Turning to me she looked into my eyes, "He won't go away. How can I get this guy to leave me alone?"

"Knock the fucking pack out of his hand," I told her.

As the soldier pushed the open pack of Benson & Hedges under her nose again, her right hand immediately swept under his and knocked the pack out of his hand into the air. Cigarettes flew about the café like tubular confetti.

In the café, silence; a pause of shock.

Joni shrieked in laughter. Her powerful spontaneous laugh shattered the silence. The soldier broke into a broad grin and the whole room exploded in cheers. Even his fellow soldiers laughed and slapped shoulders. Hers was an irresistible gut laugh that pierced to my heart and caused the hair on my forearms to stand up. At that moment, a fresh Joni Mitchell awoke to me as if I were painting her portrait. "To paint is to see as if for the first time," wrote Henry Miller. It was true. Instantly I stopped perceiving her as a shallow celebrity. Now I saw her as a real woman, mesmerizing, bright, vibrant, alive, laughing, and courageous. Immediately, I sensed her as a friend, someone to drink with and share stories. *I love her laugh; I love this woman!*

Dusk changed to night. We drank raki and danced hoochie koo to Muddy Waters', "I'm a Man," Hank Williams' "Lonesome Blues," and Howling Wolf's, "Smokestack Lightning," Otis Redding's "Pain in my Heart," and Bob Dylan's "Lay, Lady, Lay." The heat of her cheeks burned against mine, still sensitive from the Delphini explosion. The pressure and warmth of her body aroused me.

As a gesture of reconciliation, she asked Stelios to take over a bottle of raki to the soldier she had offended. The table of soldiers raised glasses and saluted us—*Yassas*! Amid laugher and conversation, Joni and I wrapped our arms, faces close, and toasted each other, toasted the sun and moon, the sea and sky, toasted the relative and the absolute, toasted her, and toasted me. Night settled into Matala. Stelios served us moussaka and salad. We were getting sweetly drunk on red wine. We kissed. A warm, wet alcohol kiss. I desired her fiercely.

"Come to my cave."

Arm in arm we staggered drunk down the corniche, along the rocky beach, stopping to kiss as waves sizzled against the pebbles. She was drunk. I was drunk. Climbing the cliff from the beach, she broke off the heel of her shoe on the rocks. She held it up to my face, giggled, "Does that look like a piece of driftwood to you?"

We climbed to Big Cave. At the rear of Big Cave, Mark and Barbara's cave; to the right, my cave. I pushed up the canvas reed door and she entered with me following behind her. With a match I lit the kerosene lantern on the wall and dimmed it.

We embraced, kissed, and fell to the carpets. Like a goat god too excited to unbutton her white linen blouse, I ripped it open, tearing off buttons.

The next morning when we emerged from my cave, Mark and Barbara invited us in for herb tea. They had never done this before when I brought back girls from the taverna. Barbara lent Joni a wrap as she sewed the buttons back on her blouse. After Joni redressed, Barbara accompanied her into town to retrieve her stuff from the cement block house she and her Canadian poet travel companion, Penelope, had rented.

Rumor had it Penelope had absconded in the night with a Greek soldier. Maybe, Joni joked, Penelope's new beau was the impetuous Benson & Hedges soldier from the Mermaid? Joni unpacked her things in my cave and hung her clothes from wall pegs. Barbara showed her how to rearrange reeds in the burial crypt to make it springier and more comfortable. Joni found refuge: No one came to my cave uninvited. I might be short and skinny, but I was mean like a wolverine.

Over the next few days, the hysteria and novelty of Joni's presence in Matala subsided and normality resumed. Joni relaxed and joined in cave life. She did yoga on the beach with bearded Yogi Joe and his faithful followers. Barbara and Joni washed clothes—and my dirty turban—by the standing pipe near Delphini. They bathed and shampooed each other's hair with a cup and a bucket of fresh water. Across the corniche, and up the stone steps from the harbor, I worked in the sandal shop with Mark.

Joni had brought along a sack of drawing pads and art supplies from home. Sitting on the rocks at the lip of Big Cave, Joni drew Matala's beach and seascapes in a large ring-bound watercolor sketchbook with colored felt-tip pens. Lines of poetry annotated her drawings. Bypassing making initial pencil sketches, she drew directly with marker pens. Fine felt-tips outlined beach grass, pebbles, scrub trees, and broader marker-pens, washes of brilliant blue sky. In primary and pastel colors she painted panoramas of the beach, people sunbathing, washing clothes, doing yoga, and swimming. Like Grandma Moses, she populated a beachscape with figures engaged in typical cave activities, depicting the day-to-day life of Matala.

Looking out from Big Cave, she painted the white-washed village of Matala, afternoon shadows framing the grey sandstone of the cliffs. The marker-pens created a visual journal of her life in the Caves, painted in warm emotional colors from perspectives she observed during the days and evenings as the light changed. She chose grey for rocky landscapes, and blues for the sea. Beige fine-point pens illustrated the pebble beach. For sandstone cliffs, grey-pink wash. Happy, bright, sun-lit drawings fit her mood.

Not having to work in the taverna every day, and with little to do in the shop, I had all the time in the world to be with her and watch her activities. When not playing her dulcimer or drawing, she knitted constantly. Unraveling skeins of homespun wool yarn, she knitted a long, knee length sweater.

Her sweater mimicked her drawings. Into it she wove a collage of detritus found on the beaches. To create textures, she incorporated bits of beach grass, tiny shells, twigs, and bleached fish bones found by the water's edge. To represent thorn bushes, she worked tufts of green yarn into the tan background. Joni sang while knitting a wool ecosystem map of Matala. *How splendid, she never stops singing, laughing, making music, drawing, creating things in praise of her friends, her surroundings, her emotions, and feelings. How more relaxed she is now compared to when I met her first in Delphini—when I threw her trash on the floor.*

✳ ✳ ✳

"Joni, when Holly and I first arrived in Matala last fall, Mark taught me how Greek and Cretan customs differ from ours in the States and Canada. A few are hilarious such as how to flag down a ride in Crete. For example, how do you hail a taxi in New York?"

"Like this," she held up her palm high and whistled shrilly.

"You do that in Crete, Joni, and by that gesture you curse the driver, like giving him the finger. Even worse, waving an open palm to somebody with fingers spread means, 'A curse on you and your whole family.'" I went on. "Mark told me he once saw a tourist hold out his open palm, fingers apart and wave it in the face of a Greek merchant and count in English, 'Five! Five! Five!' Can you imagine standing in front of a street merchant in Times Square, giving him the finger vigorously with both hands to signal you want to buy two packs of potato chips? 'Two! Two! Two!'"

Joni threw back her head and howled with laughter.

"Hey, stop laughing. When I arrived in Matala, it took me a while to catch on. Mark taught me Cretan head gestures that mean 'Yes' and 'No.' Joni, do you remember when the Benson & Hedges soldier hounded you in the Mermaid?

"My friends call me *Joan*," she interrupted.

"May I call you *Joan* …?"

"Cary, you may call me any time you want."

"*Joan* … when you shook your head from side to side, trying to tell him 'No, I do not want your cigarettes,' perhaps he thought that you were saying 'Yes' in Cretan body language."

"Oh my," she said, "I *did* do that!" In the following days, she discussed Greek culture and customs with Mark.

✷ ✷ ✷

Joni and I lapsed into deep philosophical conversations. An autodidact, she had been reading extensively for years. She had a mind for philosophy that she absorbed from books and from conversations with people also interested in talking about the nature of existence, ethics, morality, beauty and the divine.

As for me, even though I had touched on philosophy courses of aesthetics and art criticism at UNC, I had the impression she knew more than I did, and I enjoyed learning from her. On top of classical texts, both of us had read popular counterculture books that confronted conventional notions of reality, such as Carlos Castaneda's *Don Juan, A Yaqui Way of Knowledge*, Lao Tzu, and the poems of Gary Snyder. Philosophy became a lens for us to examine our lives, compare values, and to question the nature of being as we perceived it. I struggled to tell her the story of the instant awakening event in Berkeley a year ago, how it shattered and uprooted whatever notions I had held of conventional reality. I tried to detail its aftermath, the fear and trembling, the agonizing darkness, misery, and the dark foreboding still lingering on the periphery of my everyday, ordinary consciousness.

Drinking with her at the Mermaid, I explained how events in my own life had led me to art, dance, poetry, and literature, to seek to understand how artists express ineffable states of being. "Case in point, 'Clouds,'" I asked, "did you write that about a personal awakening experience?"

"By the way, Cary, the name of the album is *Clouds*. 'Both Sides Now' is the name of the song. Now what do you mean by a 'personal awakening experience?' I don't really follow you. What is so unique about the subject of 'Both Sides Now?' Themes dealing with life changes riddle the works of all poets, writers and songwriters I know."

"That may be true, Joan, but these lines, 'It's life's illusions I recall, I really don't know life at all …,'" I groped. "Given all I've said, or haven't said, or … or … floundered around attempting to say …. 'Both Sides Now' speaks to me about a quality of discernment, knowing existence directly, and not through filters of concepts and abstract ideas." I heard myself babbling like a fool. I stood up to collect myself, walked around the table and sat down again facing her, shrugged, and opened my hands as if I were hoping for divine intervention.

"Well, I don't know," said she, "all that is beyond me, I confess. You know, I'm not questioning the veracity of what you are telling me about your experience…. Sure, I have had extraordinary experiences, too—I can't explain very well—experiences that changed the direction of my life." She trailed off, stopped to light a cigarette, tipped her head back and exhaled a long stream of smoke. "Look, Cary, I suppose I can relate to the darkness you talk about, because I fall into periods of funk, sometimes, of … an extremely disturbing—and uncomfortable—nature … How can I say it …? *Blues?*—Not jazzy, deep Delta, Muddy Waters kinda blues, the funky blues, the raunchy blues—I mean *Blues* … like falling into a dark abyss of the soul."

She continued to engage me on the topic of mystical experiences, "Tell me how this *mystical dimension* you talk about differs from LSD experiences? John Lilly, Alan Watts, Aldus Huxley, and Timothy Leary—don't they all attribute opening 'the doors of perception' to hallucinogens?" I could only shrug because I had no answers, only questions. I was tongue-tied. How to describe living in a netherworld, stretched between the so-called "reality" of the mundane world of sandals, wine, and kisses in the moonlight, within an infinite multi-verse of unbounded possibilities—a textbook definition of "crazy?"

She sat on the rocks outside Big Cave, knitting. I came up and sat beside her, and remarked, "Funny, our love affair, friendship, or whatever it can be called?"

She didn't look up but said, "What's so *funny* about it?

"I don't mean '*funny*' like humorous; I mean curious."

"Where are you going with this?"

"I'm thinking about the story, *Arabian Nights*. Aladdin woos the Sultan's daughter, the Princess, by magic, bravado, and luck. The beggar boy runs off with the princess."

"Princess? I ain't no princess. You ought to know that by now," she looked up, grinning.

"Oh, no? In the socio-economic hierarchy of being, differences between the circumstances of my life—vagabond, tramp, troglodyte—and yours span a social chasm as wide and deep as between Aladdin and the princess."

"So what?"

"So, nothing. But wait ... 'Nothing?' Think about it. *Not-a-thing* means devoid of substance, right? Empty of thingness? You know I was struck when I first read Suzuki on 'Emptiness.'"

"Cary, notice how you changed subjects, comparing your self-inflicted poverty and my relative prosperity—but not explaining *why* it matters—and now you're sailing off on a theme of Buddhist philosophy. Here we go ...," she said, cheerfully rolling up the sweater-sleeve she was knitting and placing it in her woven sack along with skeins of wool and knitting needles. She stood up, walked over to our cave and set the sack inside on the floor. "Let's walk down to the Mermaid and get to the bottom of things and *no-things*."

"And whether pigs have wings."

"That, too."

Over wine at the Mermaid we talked about how literature, music, poetry, and philosophy explored ontological domains of reality—terms used by Dr. Shea to refer to existentialism, metaphysics and Zen. "As I was saying, reading Suzuki's *Zen Buddhism*," I remarked, downing the rest of a glass of retsina, "introduced me to the Japanese term *Satori*, meaning a sudden awakening experience. That's why I call what happened to me a *revelation*. *Satori*. Or, more precisely, in the domain of *Emptiness*, what 'didn't happen to me.'"

"'What didn't happen to you?' What in the world are you talking about?" she asked, leaning in across the table.

"Nothing happened to me. It was a subtractive, not additive experience. *No-thing* ... Get it? Dig this mind boggle, Joan. It's a Zen *koan* designed to boggle the mind. Suppose *every-thing* connects to everything else, in a *oneness* which erases all boundaries. Like Paul Tillich's classic definition of 'God' as the 'Ultimate Ground of Being?' Dig it. If *God* is *everything*, and nothing exists outside of *God*, then there could be no outside perspective of God, ... and therefore, no entity, "*God*." The proposition reduces to *Everything* =

Nothing. Ok? Now, suppose you could know *oneness* directly yourself. But how could you?... how could you experience *yourself* if you could not exist outside of the object of your perception? It would be like your eyeball trying to look at your eyeball without a mirror." I was about to run out of steam.

"Sounds straight out of a theology playbook to me, my Dear Cary," she said, pinching my cheek, "Or, is this an example of Russell's paradox? Or, the Empty Set? You can't have it both ways? I don't know. We may have had too little or too much to drink. Let's have dinner." She motioned to Stelios, "What's the Mermaid's special tonight?"

✳ ✳ ✳

In the evenings we usually went across the beach to the tavernas to eat, drink, listen to music, and dance. At Delphini we tried to learn traditional Cretan dances from the shepherds, who danced *pidiktos* and the slower, *sirtaki*, as in *Zorba the Greek*, the one we called the "Goat Dance."

One night during a crazy party, amid shepherds and fishermen and cave dwellers, we toasted *Tipota*! In Greek meaning: "Nothing!" Clearly inspired by out philosophical polemics, with this toast, *Tipota!* eye to eye we vowed to embrace the present moment, undisguised by concepts, attitudes, beliefs or illusions. Eye to eye, we toasted *Tipota*! and *Opa*! drank, and smashed our empty glasses down on the floor. "Joan, breaking glasses reminds me of the final verses of the *Rubaiyat*."

> *Ah Love! could you and I with Him conspire*
> *To grasp this sorry Scheme of Things entire,*
> *Would not we shatter it to bits—and then*
> *Re-mold it nearer to the Heart's Desire!*
> *Yon rising Moon that looks for us again—*
> *How oft hereafter will she wax and wane;*
> *How oft hereafter rising look for us*
> *Through this same Garden—and for one in vain!*
> *And when like her, oh Saki, you shall pass*

> *Among the Guests Star-scatter'd on the Grass,*
> *And in your joyous errand reach the spot*
> *Where I made One—turn down an empty Glass!*

Joni threw her arms around my neck and kissed me hard on the mouth. She laughed a wonderful laugh, that laugh that stirred me with awe and delight, the same laugh I had heard in the Mermaid Café the first night when she knocked the cigarettes out of the soldier's hand. Grabbing her braids I pulled her close and shouted over Cretan music—kithara, aulos and lyre—over the thudding, stomping boots of the dancers: "Joan, I love you!"

I realized I had overlooked something special about her and her poetry, and songwriting. "Joan, whatever it is going on between us is more intense than anything I have ever experienced before with a lover. Now I am beginning to understand why people go gaga over your music. You enchant them. Like a sorceress, you touch their souls."

"Love *is* touching souls, Cary. Love *touches* the heart," she told me, "with an energy beyond words. You *feel* it through your body—it *is* electric!"

"Here...!"

... with that she put her right hand on my heart, and a force like the blow of a hammer shot through my chest, and I nearly fainted.

✳   ✳   ✳

Later I thought about what had happened. *What if she is a sorceress?* I wondered. I had read about scientific experiments studying how inaudibly low frequencies can disturb thinking and sleeping, while higher frequencies, such as certain bells and chimes, may have healing properties. Maybe that was what was going on between me and Joni. Maybe her voice could create healing sounds? *Ode to Joy?* My whole sense of being alive began to shift. I felt myself lighten up.

I loved watching Joni work intently, so focused, her long blonde hair tied back in a ponytail, her posture erect. From the mouth of my cave, I watched her stand up, raise her arms, and stretch from side to side, rising on her toes. She stood with her back to me facing the sea, her stance strong, and her feet planted solidly on the rocks like a statue. When she turned to face me, the silhouette of her breasts showed through her thin white linen blouse against the backdrop of the Gulf of Messara.

Though rarely naked in public, often she sat around in Big Cave barebreasted with Barbara and the other sisters-of-the-caves who came to visit her, to make music, draw, sew and knit. She attributed her slight swayback to having polio when she was a little girl in Saskatoon. The swayback accentuated her bottom. "I love your ass," I told her. She giggled.

※ ※ ※

"The way I see it, you are a soul in conflict, in conflict with your talent and powers. As they say, 'What you want most in life depends on what you just had,' And what you just had, Joan—was Hollywood on the half shell." Sometimes I got annoyed with her indecision.

She: "It is a Faustian deal, and I lose either way. I know my path lies elsewhere. But I don't know where. That's why I fled LA."

I yearned to opine further about this trade off, but wisely decided to keep my stupid mouth shut. Better to be a naive boyfriend than a tedious Polonius. But it did seem like an opportune time to talk about our friendship. "Joan, something puzzles me. Something I've been reluctant to ask you, because frankly, I thought talking about it might break the spell."

"What kind of spell are you talking about, my red bearded rogue?"

"A spell like the one the witch put on Snow White."

"Whoa! I was a Princess. Am I now Snow White? Or did I just get demoted to Witch?"

"Probably both!"

"Well then, if I be Snow White Witch, who be thee?"

"I be Seven Dwarfs, that's who I be, me."

"What?"

"'I be multitudes,'" saith Whitman. "Multitudes bowing before your magnificence."

"Well, be there a collective term for a multitude of dwarfs?"

"Hummm ... a *gaggle* of dwarfs? No? How about a *gargle* of dwarves?"

"Hilarious be thee, my Gargle of Rogue."

The pseudo-Elizabethan repartee allowed me to duck the question about the "spell"—why I was reluctant to talk to her about my feelings—how I puzzled over what I meant to her. *Had she enchanted me? Was I her lover or her protector?* Was I her Aladdin, or her ... what?

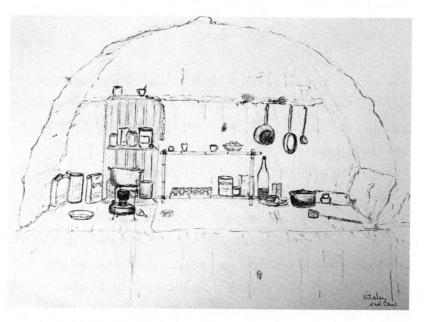

Kitchen in burial crypt in Mark & Barbara's cave. By Barbara Maddux..

CHAPTER 14

The Parting Cup

Ah, love, let us be true
To one another! for the world, which seems
To lie before us like a land of dreams,
So various, so beautiful, so new,
Hath really neither joy, nor love, nor light,
Nor certitude, nor peace, nor help for pain;
And we are here as on a darkling plain
Swept with confused alarms of struggle and flight,
Where ignorant armies clash by night.

—Matthew Arnold,
"Dover Beach"

Lazy days. Joni and I swam, hung around Big Cave working and playing; ate, drank, danced, visited with friends. Escaping from Matala, we took long treks into the hills. One day, alone at Red Beach south of Matala, swimming naked and sunbathing on the rocks, we spotted, way up the mountain, just a moving speck, a shepherd bounding down toward us in big strides over rocks and through sagebrush. He wore traditional garb, baggy britches tucked into jack boots, cummerbund around his waist, a tan military shirt beneath a dark sleeveless sweater vest, and a black, tasseled *kaskol* to control his wild hair. In his right hand he clutched a long, sturdy shepherd's crook. By the time he reached us, we had already hastily dressed and were sitting clothed where we had been naked only a few minutes before. The shepherd was merely curious, it seemed, said his name was Dimitris, and he generously shared with us his wine, olives, and dried *paximadia*. Joni and I were relieved he had not come upon us when we were naked, or even worse.

Late that afternoon bright sun burned us as we squatted together on the front ledge of Big Cave. Joni cursed the sticky black beach tar as we scraped it off the soles of our feet. I retired to our cave, kicked back on Afghan cushions reading *Tropic of Cancer*, and watched her. She set aside her drawing pad and turned to her dulcimer. Laying it across her lap, Joni strummed it with a pic, ending a chord with an upward flourish of the hand, *Strum!* then slapped the soundboard with her hand, *Thunk!* Joni played the dulcimer like a percussion instrument, strumming the soundboard and slapping the strings. It went, *Strum, Strum, Thunk! Thunk! Strum. Thunk.* Decades later, living on Isle de Gorée in the Bay of Dakar, I listened to Wolof *griots* play *koras* with a similar rhythmic structure, thumping the calabash sounding gourd while picking strings with the other hand.

"Checkout the decorative wood motifs Joellen carved into the rosewood. See how the abalone veneer she inset in the scroll sparkles? When I saw this dulcimer for the first time, it was at her booth at the Renaissance Faire. I felt Joellen had made it personally for me.

"I'm learning how to play it. I hope I don't drive you crazy!"

"I'm already crazy."

Joni and Cary on a hike in Crete.

The narrowness of the burial crypt in my cave made it uncomfortable for two people to sleep together. Sex and cuddling may be wonderful, but sleep is necessary for survival. From time to time, we slept together or separately on blankets folded on the carpets covering the stone floor. Looking back now, I suspect sleeping on kilims on stone dulled Joan's enthusiasm for cave life. As swell as my cave was to me, how could it compete with the comfort of her soft bed and goose down pillows in Laurel Canyon?

One morning Joni prepared oatmeal porridge. I felt like a hapless character in a low-comedy farce. The oatmeal reeked of petroleum! Somehow, someway, she had poured kerosene into the pot of cereal thinking it was water. Dipping in a spoon, I took a taste and ... *arrrgh* ... ! I spit it out right on the carpet. "What the fuck is this?" I demanded.

She tasted it, grimaced, and apologized profusely, "Oh God, I probably mixed up the kerosene bottle with the water bottle." It was true the bottles of water, wine and kerosene looked the same and it would have been easy to get confused. Clearly, a mistake, beyond a doubt a freak accident. I dismissed occult hypotheses that might explain transubstantiation of water into kerosene. *But maybe, just maybe in this crazy comedy ... was she out to poison me? Death by oatmeal?*

Not long after Joni took refuge with me, we were sitting outside Mark's cave, drinking Barbara's *tsai tvo vanous*, tea from the mountains, a blend of various herbs, mostly wild thyme. Over tea Barbara decided it was time to induct Joni into the cult of Mickey Mouse chocolate. She brought out a few Mickey Mouse chocolate bars, thin, dark and sweet, and practically tasteless. The bars had become a precious commodity among cave dwellers because each candy bar contained a card, the shape and size of a baseball trading card, printed entirely in Greek. Each card depicted one Disney cartoon character—a picture of Goofy or Scrooge or another Disney character. You unwrapped it hoping to find a rare card, like Dumbo. You ate the chocolate, discarded the wrapper, and added the card to your trading collection. Collections were bought, sold, gifted, and traded. And stolen, too.

The day dawned for community action. The Karate Clan, which lived collectively in a suite of caves below ours, launched a project to redeem caves abandoned to water, wind and sand—or ones that had been used as toilets. Volunteers gathered dead sagebrush and herbs from the mountains to sanitize the caves. They hiked up the hills with sacks to gather brush, which grew profusely on the sun-washed, rocky hills.

Over many years drifting sand had almost completely blocked entrances to caves on the lower beach level. The Karate Clan appointed a team of diggers armed with shovels to clear away cave openings. They shoveled out the sand and swept out vintage human waste and toilet paper and burned the trash and debris.

When sagebrush collectors returned from the hills, diggers went to work smoking out the caves by burning piles of sagebrush inside. Smoking out malodorous caves could take days, until the cave walls and floors dried thoroughly and every hint of stale, shitty air dissipated. When a cave was recovered, the Karate Clan folks got first dibs on it.

Excavating old caves resulted, from time to time, in diggers finding pottery and human bones. In the Mermaid, we queried Christos, the archeologist from nearby Phaistos, about these relics and how cave excavators should treat them.

"The museums of Crete and Greece are crammed full of artifacts from thousands and thousands of years of human habitation," Christos explained. "You have not ignored, I am sure, that shards of pottery and bones litter every path you climb on these hills. For millennia inhabitants broke pots, discarded stuff, and died leaving their bones in the caves. Don't worry," he assured us, "in Crete we have no scarcity of broken pottery and bones."

Wednesday was Market Day in Timbaki, a large village a few kilometers north of Matala. Joni and I and another couple decided to go shopping. Hiking to Timbaki overland involved climbing over the cliffs followed by a trek of about three kilometers or so on goat paths and gravel roads. Joan borrowed my lace-up hiking boots, and because her feet were smaller than mine, chose to wear my thick Afghan, hand-knitted knee-high stockings, patterned red and green, which Melissa in Kandahar had given me in December. I wore sandals.

Trudging up and over rocky hills with our walking sticks and bottles of water, backpacks, and empty bags, we climbed over the north side of the cliffs and picked our way along the mountain goat paths until we hit the wider donkey path that took us to the edge of the ruins of the Palace of Phaistos, not too far from Timbaki. Even at 9 a.m. the sun was strong.

Signposts in several languages stated the village of Phaistos had been inhabited as far back as 4,000 BC—the Bronze Age. Some speculated the Matala caves might be older. Archaeologist, Christos, had told us he was fascinated by how we lived in the caves. Watching us go about our daily lives allowed him to visualize how Minoans might have lived in Matala.

The sun was hot. We took shelter in the shade of conifers growing next to a low wall overlooking the palace ruins where we watched a tour group. In front of us stood a gaggle of British birdwatchers—replete with safari jackets, shorts, white knee socks, sensible walking shoes, and floppy Aussie campaign hats—staring with binoculars in different directions. Their guide, a stern, matronly British lady in tweeds and spectacles—which made her eyes huge like an owl's—lectured them about birds of Crete.

As if on cue, we and all the birdwatchers looked up to see a large, dark bird float in and perch on the top of an olive tree fifty meters away. In synchronous unity all binoculars arose like big guns of a battleship to focus on the black bird. I could not resist. "Magpie!" I blurted loudly. Binoculars dropped and all heads turned in our direction. The matron stared at me.

"Decidedly not," she asserted. "That," pointing at the bird with her walking stick, "… is a Hooded Crow!" Joni burst out laughing.

We hit the road again. The town of Timbaki was nearby. When we arrived at the village, Joni sat down on a stone wall and unlaced the hiking boots. When she peeled off the heavy, Afghan wool socks, her sweaty feet and ankles were patterned red and blue in the same design as the socks, as if they had been tattooed to her feet and calves. Before doing anything else, we went directly to a souvlaki stand and ordered gyro souvlakis rolled in pita bread. The combination of the greasy lamb (or was it really donkey meat as some rumors held?) wrapped in pita bread toasted on the fire of the upright spit, dripping with yogurt and cucumber tzatziki sauce, and the ground red chili sauce … better than best!

We bought fish and other groceries from the open stalls in the covered market area. Joni was practically limping, so we caught a ride with tourists back to Matala in their VW van. Through the window, Joni pointed at a shepherd leading his flock beside an olive grove, dressed traditionally like the shepherd who had disturbed us naked at Red Beach, "Can I buy boots like that?" She asked me.

"The bootmakers in Iraklion who sell Mark and me our leather," I said, "will custom-make boots for you, Joan." We had a plan.

The next day we drove her rented VW up to Iraklion. The bootmakers took our foot patterns and measured our ankles and calves. Instead of the traditional black leather for the boots, Joni chose a tan suede, and I chose smooth brown leather. I pleaded with them to work quickly. For a small premium, they said they would have our boots ready on Orthodox Good Friday, a week away. We checked into a little pension near the port, strolled around Iraklion, drank retsina under sidewalk umbrellas at a taverna, and at night ducked into a jukebox dive near the port with a spinning disco ball. We got drunk and danced the hoochi koo. Next morning after *kafe* and pastries, and fueling the VW, we wound our way back across the mountain roads from Iraklion to Matala.

During the drive, Joni talked about her mother, about growing up in Saskatoon, about polio, about being an art student and playing and singing at clubs to make ends meet, about her marriage to Chuck Mitchell, and about the infant she had put up for adoption. "My career took off after David Crosby found me in Coconut Grove and Elliot Roberts became my manager."

Back at the Caves we uncorked a bottle of wine. After a few glasses Joni said, "Cary, I hate people tagging me as a folksinger. I want to play rock and roll." She gyrated her hips, stuck out her bottom, and played wild air guitar, swinging her hair from side to side.

"Joan, the song you sang the other night sounded a lot like rock and roll to me—'Paved paradise and put up a parking lot?'"

"Yep. It is. 'Big Yellow Taxi' is on the new album, *Ladies of the Canyon*. I finished it before I left LA."

"Ladies of the canyon, huh? From canyons to caves. What's next, ladies of the deep well? If you be lady of the canyon, now you be lady of the caves. Like Sir Walter Scott's *Lady of the Lake*. Or Jean Genet's *Notre Dame des Fleurs*. Nice title—*Our Lady of the Flowers*—until you understand it's an epic poem about a murderer in Paris."

The traditional culture of Crete fascinated Joni and she constantly asked Mark to decode it for her. Mark taught her local Greek sayings such as "the sea is full of sheep," meaning the sea is tumbling with whitecaps. Although we went into the village of Matala daily, her social life mainly revolved around Big Cave with Barbara and a few of her friends, writing, drawing, and practicing her dulcimer. Our Lady of the Caves.

Saturday morning, Orthodox Easter eve, we drove back to Iraklion and took a room with a bath in a pension not far from the port. Joni desperately yearned to immerse herself in a hot bath and shampoo the salt and olive oil out of her hair. How wonderful to sleep on clean cotton sheets instead of coarse woven tapestries and wool blankets. She locked the door, threw her clothes on the floor, and sank into a warm bath. She took a nap, and I went to the post office before it closed at noon. I got an aerogram from Ken Overstreet posted two weeks ago in Paris. He wrote that he and Agate had been married in her parent's home, and despite her being pregnant, they were going to fly down to Athens and join me in Matala. *I had been wondering how Agate's parents and Ken Overstreet would get along…*

Joni and I walked up the street into downtown Iraklion to visit the bootmakers. Hers were light green-grey suede coming up to the knee, ones she later wore on the album cover *For the Roses*. Mine were similar but were more traditional shepherds' boots with smooth, brown leather. I pointed out to Joni how the outer soles were cobbled to the inner soles with little oak pegs. Mark and I keenly admired Cretan shoemaking methods incorporated oak pegs in our sandal making.

When we dressed for the evening, I wore my thread-bare jeans tucked into my new boots, and an olive drab Eisenhower campaign jacket. Joni, however, had style. She wore a white dress, shawl, and a mess of silver, silver earrings, a silver bead necklace and an engraved silver Navaho belt set with turquoise. And beneath her skirt, new boots. As twilight darkened we descended the stairs from our hotel room to the street and set off to find a good restaurant.

Coming towards us from way down the street, a tall man held the hand of a woman in a sari. They came into focus. How crazy and far out! Speak of the devil—Ken Overstreet and Agate Bourguignon! We embraced. I introduced Joni. Kissing cheeks all around.

"We arrived from France in this morning on the ferry. We got the aerogram you sent from Istanbul," said Agate in delightful French accented English, "inviting us to join you in Matala. Did you receive the letter we posted in Paris?"

"Got it today," said I. "Great timing, ya'll!" *What an amazing coincidence, their showing up in Iraklion.* At six months, Agate was totally and unselfconsciously pregnant.

"We got married in France after we parted ways with you in Tehran two months ago," Ken said. "We stayed with Agate's folks in Provins. Cool place. Goes back to the twelfth century. You'd love it."

Agate added, "We booked in at the youth hostel up the street expecting to take the bus down tomorrow to find you in Matala."

After dinner we found a little bar with musicians, and we danced. At midnight, the whole town, children and everyone celebrated Easter in the streets. Elderly women in black widow's weeds chanted and sang and carried silver trays with cookies and shot glasses of raki. They yelled out to us. A passerby translated for us. "She is saying: 'We will raise Christ!'" Superb! *We will raise Christ!* the affirmative, transitive active. Yes! We are in the city of Kazantzakis, of Zorba the Greek. None of this passive, *Christ is risen.*

"This woman commands you: 'come here! Eat these cookies! Drink this raki,'" said our translator.

"Of course, we will! Of course, *we will raise Christ!*" We accepted the sugar cookies from the smiling woman, drank her raki and saluted her, *Yassu, Kyria!*

Easter Morning, we awoke with hangovers. After fruit, yogurt, baklava and coffee in the pension, Joni and I wandered into El Greco Park down the street. We planned to meet Ken and Agate for lunch and drive back to Matala. In the park, paths threaded through a dusty garden of succulents, shrubs, and flowering plants. An old man, in a tunic, Cretan cavalry britches tucked into black jackboots, greeted us beside a fountain in the garden. He spoke no English, but gestured toward his antique camera supported on a heavy wooden tripod. The camera was ancient, a wooden box heavily painted and repainted many times, blue and white. The lens, mounted on the front, was covered with a black lid. Over the back of the camera, a heavy black cloth draped almost to the ground. Next to the camera the photographer had set up his darkroom, a pointed pyramid of a black tent. With hand signals he indicated he would take our portrait.

We were not dressed fancy for an Easter photograph. Joni was wearing the long, knee length sweater she had knitted and a black blouse, a silver Navaho belt, and wore her jeans over her new boots. I had tucked my levis into my boots. I still wore my Eisenhower field jacket and a woolen lumberjack undershirt.

The photographer gestured that we should sit on a park bench in front of the camera. Joni leaned forward, her dulcimer between her knees, and I put my arm around her shoulder. The old man raised his right palm gesturing for us to stay still. He stepped behind the camera, ducked his head under the black drop cloth, resurfaced, adjusted the lens, and replaced the lid. He lifted a glass plate from a leather satchel resting on the ground and slipped it into the camera. To make the exposure, he stood to the left of the camera and removed the lens cap. His lips were moving. He was counting. Then he replaced the lens cap, removed the photo plate from the side of the camera, and disappeared into his dark room tent. He took several exposures. We waited on the bench talking, and in a quarter-hour, he emerged with our portraits.

After lunch Ken and Agate crammed into the VW with us and we drove down to Matala. Along the way they told Joni the story of how we three had come to meet in Mashhad on Christmas Eve three months ago when they were teaching English and how they had tracked me down in Kabul and saved me from death by dysentery—"and by wild women," chipped in Ken.

Arriving in Matala, we sought out Mark, who—always resourceful—found Ken and Agate a decent cave. They swept it out, moved in their bags and immediately changed clothes. Meanwhile, Joni, Mark and I sat under an umbrella drinking retsina on Delphini's patio with Mime's wife, Sofia. Mimes—his burns now healed—came out of the kitchen to serve us a tray of traditional Easter foods, cheese pastries (*kalitsounia*) and little cheese pies (*tyropitakia*), spinach pies (*spanakopita*), stuffed grape-vine leaves (*dolmathakia yialantzi*), and more retsina. I wrote the food names in my journal.

Cary and Joni, Easter morning, Iraklion, Crete, 1970. Credit Cary Raditz

On Easter, Greek families go on excursions. Matala was full of Cretan families from Iraklion, screaming children raising hell, grandmothers dressed in widow's black dresses yelling at them, kids yelling back. Kids ran around challenging each other to Easter egg battles, tapping red dyed eggs together to determine which egg would go the longest without cracking. A wrinkled old lady shouted at a kid horsing around on the beach, who shouted back at her and made obscene gestures. "What are they saying?" I asked Mark.

"Roughly translated, that kid in the green shorts just shouted at his grandmother, 'Go fuck your Virgin Mary!' Sometimes I wish I didn't speak Greek at all."

Agate climbed down to the beach barefoot wearing a tiny black bikini barely covering her breasts. She was round with child, her stomach, and full breasts prominent. She moved deliberately along the beach where the sea lapped up on the pebbles and headed in our direction. Her long, thick dark hair fell to her waist. The gold ring in her left nostril sparkled in the sun. With the complexion of a Gypsy, she could easily have played the title role in Bizet's *Carmen*. Agate had been a dancer and had beautiful, strong legs and delectable feet. Nudity was common on the beach, but this was stretching it on a Greek holiday. Agate had the good sense to wrap up in a towel before venturing up to Delphini.

As Agate walked up to the table, Joni pointed out a man and his wife dressed in a farcical mockery of hippy costumes walking toward the caves. The woman wore clashing flowered scarves and blouse and a floppy hat. The man had an absurd string of pink, plastic hair curlers around his neck. Barbara and Ken had stayed up in Big Cave to stave off invasion by curious holiday tourists like these.

※　※　※

Sunday, 19 April 1970, my twentieth-fourth birthday. Friends treated me to a party in our cave. Attending were Mark, Barbara, Ken and Agate, Joni, me, and several others. Stelios and Dora joined us and brought ouzo, retsina and apple pie. Everyone stuffed into the narrow cave, some kneeling on the carpet, others sitting on cushions, some sitting on each other. In the yellow lamplight, we drank and toasted with ouzo and wine, and feasted on Dora's pie and pastries.

Joni slid her dulcimer out of its carrying bag, sat on the side of the crypt-bed, and put it across her lap. "Here's a birthday song for you, Cary," she said. Then she played the song on the dulcimer. This was the first time I heard it in its entirety. "The wind came in from Africa and the sea was full of sheep .... It sure is hard to leave you, Cary, but it's really not my home." *How endearing!* I tried to think of something to say but I was dumbfounded. I kissed her and everyone clapped.

In the kindest of terms, the song amounted to an affectionate goodbye. Joni was going to leave Matala and me. I had known it for a while and it was only a matter of time. Maybe sleeping on the stone floor didn't help. Although not thrilled about the "Oh You're Mean Old Daddy"—I deserved the epithet for my unsolicited advice, talking down to her, for my bellicose temper and general nastiness ... for a start. Joni borrowed Mark's guitar and played us more of her songs, "Michael from the Mountain," "Chelsea Morning," and "Both Sides Now."

Joni handed Mark back his guitar. He played a Johnny Cash oldie, "I Still Miss Someone."

> *... I wonder if she's sorry*
> *For leavin' what we'd begun*
> *There's someone for me somewhere*
> *And I still miss someone.*

The lyrics struck me as foreboding and sad. *Was Mark singing this because he knew Joni would be leaving?* It was inevitable, wasn't it? Still, I was happy to be among friends, happy to have Joni write me a birthday song, and happy to receive a dozen Mickey Mouse chocolate bars from her. Happy to be alive. Grateful to warm myself in the flame of her affection, creativity, and laughter during the day, and thrilled to have her body next to me at night.

Brer Rabbit—*Greek chocolate trading card, like the cards Joni gave me on my birthday 19 April 1970, in Matala. Credit: from John Flemming as gift from Phil Lawson.*

※ ※ ※

She has so many sides, it strikes me, this Joni Mitchell. She has a curious, critical mind. She plows through philosophy like a hot knife through cold butter and is certainly more learned than I am. We talk about art and aesthetics and about what constitutes the Good, the Beautiful and the Sublime. I share with her what little I remember from Shea's *Philosophy of Art*: Husserl's phenomenology, the art criticism theories of Roger Fry and Clive Bell, Edward Bullough's "Antinomy of Distance," and anything else I can remember about formal theories of art criticism. I dredge up everything I know to further the discussion. Sometimes it even makes sense.

We both tend to be moody. Always attentive and alert, from time-to-time Joni could, nonetheless, slip into dark, self-incriminating spaces: Sorrow. Sadness. Anger. Indecision. What to do? And strangely, independent as she was, she could simultaneously indict the music industry that made her famous, while complaining it was stifling her. *Do not bring up Faustian bargains.*

"Hey, Joan," I insisted, "Stop whining."

She shook her head at my bullying but my reprimand broke her funk, "Stop it, Cary! You're being mean!" She made a face and punched me.

Lazy days went by, and then a riot broke out in Matala. Soldiers seized Stelios, beat him up, and took him away in handcuffs. The pretext for his arrest, Mark said, was that Stelios did not take out a permit to construct a little side building to the Mermaid Café. Did this technicality justify soldiers destroying his new construction with sledgehammers? Dora was distraught.

"The real reason is clearly political," commented Mark. "Authorities consider Stelios a threat to the Junta. A dangerous communist. They hate Stelios for befriending 'long haired undesirables' running around naked on the beaches,' They say, 'He stains the pure fabric of Greek culture. And he lives in sin with an English woman.'"

The military put everyone on edge. This was the tense era of the Junta—the rule of the Generals. What was going to happen next? Would the police close down Matala to cavers? We heard police imprisoned Stelios in the Mires jail where they tortured him, beat his feet—*bastinado*—and burned him with cigarettes.

"Let's do something for Stelios. Let's raise money and get Stelios a lawyer. Let's get Stelios out of jail." People gathered at the harbor below the Mermaid. Travelers and cave dwellers delivered impassioned speeches. They raised fists. Locals hung back; they had more at risk. For them, it was a long crunch, not a momentary skirmish.

Joni borrowed Mark's guitar and walked across the corniche to the harbor. People circled her and stood on the pebble beach or sat on harbor piers as she played and sang old protest songs, Woody Guthrie songs from the 1940s and "We Shall Overcome" from the civil rights movement. Passing-the-hat raised the equivalent of about a $100, which she donated to Dora for Stelios' defense. Whatever transpired after that never became clear to me, but within a week, looking somewhat worse for wear and walking with a limp—but wearing a smile—Stelios returned to the Mermaid.

Ken Overstreet became a Delphini regular. Arm propped around a chair, he laughed and goofed, his broad smile missing several teeth from a prison fight a few years before in a California jail, and his wit filled the taverna with humor.

Always sardonic, at the same time he listened attentively to conversations surrounding him. The poker community welcomed Ken. Like Mark, Ken sported a handlebar mustache. In the pale lamplight of the cave, the two resembled a brace of Wild Bill Hickocks in a Western saloon daguerreotype, cards spread out before them on the red and blue Cretan carpet.

Not long after the Stelios-police confrontation, the grapevine notified Joni and me that our presence was requested in Athens. Phil Lawson, from whom I inherited my cave, sent an invitation inviting us all to the opening of his production of *Hair* in Athens. The musical included a cast of cave dwellers who played roles of hippies and musicians. Joni and I accepted Phil's invitation.

Two days later we dropped the VW at the rental agency in Iraklion and took a small prop plane to Athens. "Joni Mitchell travels deluxe," I taunted her.

"Nothing but first class for me and my mean old daddy," She snickered.

The airport taxi took us at the youth hostel where some of the cave dweller alumni were staying. At least we were not staying at the Athens Hilton, which Joni would have preferred. She humored my low-life, vows-of-poverty attitude by acquiescing to stay in the youth hostel. We checked in with the manager, Speros. I introduced Joni and told him how much we appreciated his kind hospitality. He gave us one of the two single rooms, the one with an adjoining bathtub. Joni asked Speros if she could make a collect call from his phone. It was time for her to check into her "real" life in Hollywood.

While she was on the phone, I met a friendly American-Dutch couple in the kitchen. They knew who Joni was and they stayed cool about it. When she came back, they politely asked how her trip had been, how she had found the caves, but did not press or fawn over her. What a relief.

"A restaurant? A really good restaurant?" Cynthia, the American, suggested a fine, white-tablecloth, Greek restaurant. The *maître d'* led us to the secluded table as I had requested. We ordered from an English menu and dove into a splendid dinner. The restaurant became crowded and suddenly we found ourselves in the presence of journalists, a man and a woman. Apparently, the table was not as secluded as I had surmised. Who had tipped them off? The *maître d'*? Knowing how much Joni had been enjoying her anonymity, I tried to protect her, and brush away intruders. To my surprise, she graciously invited them to join us. She asked the waiter, who spoke English, "Please bring over two chairs and another bottle of wine." They preceded to interview her, questioning her about her trip, about staying in Matala, asking her how the *Ladies of the Canyon* album was being received. Joni was cheerful, and animated, smiling, enjoying the conversation.

"*Ladies of the Canyon*? What do I know? I've been in Matala. I haven't read reviews and I know next to nothing. I should be asking you." They gave her several English language newspapers.

"How long will you be staying in Greece?" they inquired. The question brought into sharp relief how Joni was straddling two worlds. She evaded their question, saying instead how much she enjoyed being in Greece and how kind the Greek people had been to her. They thanked her and left.

"Before leaving the hostel, Cary, I talked to Elliot, my manager. He told me Reprise is happy and the album is moving up on *Billboard*. I intended to tell you all about this over dinner, but then the journalists interrupted us. Finish your brandy, let's get back to the hostel."

I was in the bathtub and Joni sat on the edge of the tub in a robe. "Cary, look. I have decided not to go back to Matala; I'm ready to return to California and go back to work. *Ladies of the Canyon* is out and Elliot needs me back. I need to develop songs I've been writing. But I'll miss you." I slid down and stuck my head under the water. When I surfaced, she hugged me.

"I knew it was coming sooner or later. It was inevitable," I said, "I can't hide that it saddens me." I told her I understood and I wished her all the happiness in the world.

And then I pulled her into the tub.

When we were getting ready to sleep, I discovered my left ear was inflamed again. With my knife, I cut off the thick thread Barbara had put through my earlobe two months ago. She had instructed me to spin the loop in alcohol to keep the hole open and sterile until it healed, which I hadn't done. The next morning, Joni and I went to a jeweler to commission two matching gold heart studs—one for her, one for me. The jeweler promised them the next day.

Phil's funky production of *Hair* took place in a makeshift theatre in the basement of a club with sound system problems. Nonetheless, everyone was excited and energetic. Joni enjoyed the musical and talked to everyone. The journalists from the night before were there—at Joni's invitation—interviewing people and taking notes. The troupe invited Joni and me and the journalists for drinks upstairs in the bar. Her laughter penetrated the surrounding conversations. She was happy; I was annoyed and withdrawn.

Two days later I accompanied her to the airport to see her off to Spain. "Will I ever see you again, Joan?"

"Yes, Cary," she said. "Why don't you come visit me in Los Angeles? Here, take my movie camera. Please make movies of Matala and the caves for me."

I shrugged, "Thanks, Joan, but you know I can't even afford film, much less a ticket to LA. I'll probably end up selling the camera," I told her.

"Okay," she shrugged back, "sell it if you want."

In front of customs and immigration agents, we kissed goodbye. She hurried down the long hall, big woven bag on her shoulder, and swaying around her knees, bristling with seashells, driftwood, and fish bones, the sweater of beach flotsam and jetsam she wore on Easter in the photograph in the park in Iraklion.

She spun around, waved goodbye and—touching her palm to her lips—blew a kiss.

CHAPTER 15

Feast of Ashes

Joni was gone. On the bus ride from the airport into Athens emotions started kicking in. By the time I walked back to the youth hostel, I was feeling rotten and it got worse as the evening wore on. I missed her intensely.

Next afternoon I caught the ferry back to Iraklion, and in the morning, arriving at the embarcadero, boarded the bus to Matala. Back in my cave, back with Mark and Barbara, Ken and Agate, back with my friends and drinking buddies, I put on a happy face. "Raki and ouzo will patch me up," I told my friends. "Bring on the dancing girls."

Mimes invited me back to cook in the newly redecorated Delphini. I told him I needed to think about it. Not that I was still freaked out about the explosion; I lacked the heart to do it. Over at the Mermaid, I chatted up a lovely young New Yorker, Jeannie—who turned out to be an accomplished yogini, with curly red hair, and a strong, freckled, nubile body she could contort like a circus performer in Cirque de Soleil.

Naked on a blanket in Big Cave, she demonstrated yoga poses to Mark, Barbara, and me, and showed how effortlessly she could assume a bound lotus position. Seated on the blanket in a full lotus, she wrapped both arms around her back, her fingers grabbing her toes, and bent forward to rest her forehead on the blanket. Her agility and beauty blew my mind. Within minutes she reappeared in my cave, a few steps away, privately demonstrating other poses. She kept her place in the Hilton cave but began sleeping in mine.

Though exceedingly appealing, Jeannie talked too much hippie dogma and possessed too many hippie traits for my taste—astrology, crystals, tarot, flowers, headbands, paisley designs, psychedelics—though she most willingly played enthusiastic wood nymph to my hungry satyr. *Just what I need to break Joni's spell.*

Matala was giving me claustrophobia; I was getting testy and moody, and slipped down to the low point of my emotional roller coaster. I snapped at Jeannie and everyone around me. People asked me if I had heard anything from Joni. *I have to get out of here.* With nothing more than a general plan in mind, I invited Jeannie to join me on a sixteen-kilometer trek through the Samaria Gorge on the western side of Crete. "There is something strange going on with you, Cary Raditz," said Jeannie with a pinched face. "Please be nice to me." Reluctantly, she accepted my invitation.

The plan was to take the bus to Iraklion, stay in the Youth hostel, then hitchhike west across northern Crete to Xania. From there we could take a bus up the mountain to Omalos and walk the rest of the way over and down the Samaria Gorge to Agia Roumeli, a tiny village by the sea at the mouth of the gorge. A ferry stopped twice a day at Agia Roumeli that would take us east to Agia Galini. From there it was a short bus ride to Timbaki and Phaistos. From Phaistos we could hike over the hills to Matala. Jeannie agreed on the plan.

The first part of the plan worked out fine. We took the bus to Iraklion. Jeannie and I ate lamb and stuffed grapevine leaves at food stands in the bazaar and spent the night in different gender dormitory rooms at the Iraklion youth hostel. Hitchhiking west to Xania the next morning, we got a ride in the back of a pickup truck, and sat on hard sacks of grain. Along the way I had little to say to Jeannie—my mind was tied in knots. She tried to make conversation, but I stayed distant and glum while she put forth an endless stream of nonstop talking. I found her chatter irritating. *Is my lusty wood nymph morphing into a nagging harpy?*

The truck driver dropped us off on the main street in Xania, a block from the harbor. We walked over a couple blocks to a cheap but clean guest house overlooking the sea, which cave dwellers recommended. Once in the hotel room Jeannie stripped off her shorts and t-shirt. She wore no underclothes. She reached over, grabbed my belt buckle, and pulled me to her, "I know how to cheer up my Cary."

Her body exuded pungent, animal scent, the gorgeous aroma of a redhead baked in the sun and full of lust. I couldn't get enough of her and she knew it. Miss Harpy transformed back into Miss Wood Nymph. On the spot, I kneeled before her and inhaled the intoxicating smell of her body from the fine curly red hair under her arms to her round toes. With a foot, she pushed me down to the floor. She pulled off my boots and tugged off my jeans. Climbing on my chest, her moistness commingled with my sweat until we were both covered with it. She wrapped her yogini legs around my waist in a scissor grip and mounted me. We fucked on the carpet until we collapsed, and exhausted, showered and fell into bed.

The next morning at breakfast in the pension, we ate thick yogurt with spoons of delicious wildflower honey, a regional delicacy of Xania and Rethymnon. Over cups of coffee, Jeannie and I argued about insignificant trivia. I snapped at her ideas. "Where is the loving Cary I slept with last night?" she asked. "Where did Cary go?"

I rolled my eyes skyward, "Let's get outta here."

We shouldered backpacks, walked to the sidewalk bus stop, and caught the bus to Omalos as it was boarding. The bus chugged up the switchback gravel road into the White Mountains and discharged passengers in the *plateia* of Omalos beside the few shops, where we bought some bread and cheese to take on the trek. From that point, we did not have much to say to one another.

We began trudging up the steep winding road to Xyloskalo at the head of the gorge. I tramped ahead of her, preoccupied in a dark mood. She quickened her pace and caught up to me at a bend in the road when I stopped to drink from my canteen. She wanted to talk, but I cut her off.

"I am getting sick and tired of your cruel, asshole behavior," she barked.

"I am pissed off with your constant, babbling nonsense," I shot back.

She faced me. "I'm not going to do this anymore, Cary," she snapped. "Except for screwing, you are obviously tired of me and I am fed up with your nastiness. What did I do to you, Cary Raditz, except want to be your friend?"

She went on, "What the fuck is wrong with you?" She stuck her face in mine. "Fuck you, Cary Raditz, and fuck your precious Joni Mitchell. You can go walk the fucking gorge yourself. I am going back down to Xania." She turned on her heels and stalked away on the gravel road. "Fuck you, Cary!" she added over her shoulder, giving me the finger.

"Fuck you," I shouted back at her as she disappeared around the switchback below.

I hiked ahead, turned, stopped, and watched her walking along the gravel road toward Omalos. Immediately, I regretted how mean I had been to her. It was unfair to take out my sadness and anger on her, as if she were somehow to blame for my depression. She was a lovely person, a free spirit. Was this another lesson in refusing a gift from the heart, a lesson I should have learned in Kabul?

My mood improved as I started the path into the Samaria gorge. As down as I had been an hour ago, now I felt elated. I ran into an Irish couple at a resting place beside the path and hiked along with them. It was a switchback, ten-mile hike down. The steep trail descended through mountain forests of pines, following a spring fed creek winding into the gorge, where it narrowed and became rocky. My knees felt like overcooked pasta. When the path began to level out again, high vertical cliffs squeezed the tight passage and stream. At the trail's most constricted point, I could stretch out my arms and almost touch each wall that rose maybe a hundred meters or more up from the stream bed.

At the mouth of the gorge, we emerged from its shadows into brilliant light sparkling off the Mediterranean. I was ravenous. We walked across the strand to Agia Rumelia's one-room taverna and sat down at a table under the grapevine arbor with several other hikers. Lunch was fried fish and salad. We waited for the ferry to come. The ferry took us onboard, churned away from the harbor through a choppy sea, and forty-five minutes later, deposited us at the little ferry harbor at Agia Galini. By evening, after a bus ride from Timbaki to Mires, I hitched a lucky ride and arrived in Matala's square in front of Mama's bakery. *The town's deserted.* Nobody was on the beach, nobody swimming, nor did I see any activity around the caves. *What is going on?*

At the Mermaid few people were eating dinner. Stelios said, "Police closed the caves yesterday. They forbid anyone to stay in them. How long they will stay closed, no one knows," he shrugged. Dora put her hand on my shoulder and pointed down the street to a two-story building, "Your friends, Ken and Agate, are staying there with Mark and Barbara."

I moved in with them. Despite the abrupt eviction, they remained in good spirits, determined to wait out the closure of the caves, which was usually temporary, according to Mark. Having gone through these evictions before, he had the foresight to bring all my stuff over to town.

The following afternoon Dora walked into the Mermaid waving an official looking document. "Cary, this telegram arrived on the bus today."

I read the telegram out loud:

"CARY PLS COME LA STOP WANT YOU HERE STOP CALL ME STOP TICKET WAITING AMERICAN EXPRESS ATHENS STOP LOVE JONI STOP"

Looking around at questioning eyes, "Do you think I should go to LA?" I asked Dora and the others in the room. They cheered, "Yes! Yes! Go! Go!" The cloud darkening my mood parted and I saw sunshine ahead.

Mark and Barbara sitting out cave closing next to rented house in Matala. 1970. By Barbara Maddux.

✳ ✳ ✳

The next morning, sorting through what I owned, I stored everything non-essential in my tomato-can trunk and camel bags, including carpets and tapestries from my cave, books, tools, and Afghan clothing. My trusty kerosene burner, "Uncle Stove," I left in the corner of the kitchen. Into my backpack and hucklebag, I stuffed changes of clothes and toothbrush. Attired in Eisenhower jacket and jackboots, cane on arm, I prepared to go. Mark remarked, "Cary, from a distance, you could pass for a mad Cretan shepherd ... as long as you kept your mouth shut."

The bus driver secured my backpack on top of the bus. Friends came to the *plateia* to say goodbye, "*Adios,* Cary. Come back, your cave will be waiting for you!"

Three hours later the bus arrived at the Iraklion port. I had plenty of time to spare before the ferry embarked. I walked over to the Western Union window at the post office, showed the clerk the telegram from Joni, and composed a reply: YES COMING LA STOP WILL RING COLLECT FROM ATHENS LOVE. Ten words. The charge was 250 drachmas, or about $8.00.

At a taverna across the square, I took a chair at an outside table and ordered *salada* and fried retsina. The salad consisted of chunks of tomato, cucumber, onion, and feta cheese lathered with olive oil. I picked up a *gropez* in my fingers. The head crunched like popcorn as I bit into it. It had sweet, white flesh. With a thick slice of crusty *psomi*, I mopped up the olive oil and vinegar from my plate.

Wearing a black *kaskol* like mine, an old shepherd crossed the other side of the square leading a donkey laden with red sacks made of woven carpets and goods rolled up in reed mats. His khaki riding britches were tucked into black boots, and he carried a shepherd's cane, much longer than mine, which I had hooked over the edge of the table.

Finishing lunch, I paid the waiter and went down the street to say goodbye to the bootmakers. Walking by the shipping office adjacent to El Greco Park where the old photographer had taken our portrait on Easter morning,

I spotted him in the garden next to his wooden-box camera and tripod. He recognized me. We raised our hands saluting each other, "*Yasu! Yasu! Tikanis!* I thanked him, *Efkaristo poli!*"

As evening approached dock workers lowered the gangplank, and I walked up amid the usual throng bearing baskets and sacks. With a few disheveled backpackers, I boarded the all-night ferry. Although it was crowded, below deck I found a vacant upper bunk in the men's dormitory. The cabin stank of smelly socks, mildew, and Turkish tobacco smoke. I greeted my fellow passengers, "*Yassas!*" Trusting fellow Greek passengers, I tossed my backpack on the bunk and climbed up the ladder to the deck for fresh air carrying my sleeping bag and hucklebag.

The ferry chugged out of the harbor into the open Mediterranean Sea. On the deck I spoke to Danish travelers who had come from the eastern side of Crete. They had partied at the notorious "Octopus's Garden" in Agios Nikolaos, the yacht basin crowded jet setters and yachts, and the usual backpackers and travelers. "Irapetra on the south coast is cheaper and much more simpatico." I wanted to converse with other Cretans on deck, but my Greek was limited to counting money, exchanging greetings, toasts, and goodnights, saying my name was Cary, and I was from America, to asking simple directions, and ordering food and drink. From having worked at Delphini, I had learned the names of lots of vegetables, fruit, cheese, meat and menu items, such as *omletta, elia, bamia, pasticcio, moussaka, voutero, biera* and *krasi*. *How can I bear to leave Crete? When I come back, I will buckle down to study Greek.*

As the last shimmers of red sunset reflected over the water and dimmed in the twilight, the ferry rolled gently from port to starboard. Night fell. On deck we marveled at the brilliant swath of the Milky Way overhead. The brightness of the stars and the depth of the heavens filled my heart with joy. Once again, overwhelming wonder and awe soared within me. I imagined this ocean ferry had lifted in flight from the sea and was sailing among the stars like Captain Hook's "Jolly Roger" in *Peter Pan*. No footing anywhere! Vast, infinite space uniting all and dispelling all suffering!

Sunlight crept up from starboard. When I arrive at a port, the first thing I notice is smell. Morning dew held the scent of the harbor of Piraeus—decomposing fish, diesel smoke, petroleum, sewage, and smells I could not recognize by name. I awoke on deck in the morning chill and got a porter to carry my bags down to the pier. I hailed a taxi to go the youth hostel where Joni and I had stayed weeks ago.

I asked Speros to place an international collect call to Joni. The ten-hour time zone difference between Athens and LA meant I had to wait until midnight to reach her at two in the afternoon in Laurel Canyon, when she normally woke up. Joni answered, accepted the collect call and almost immediately, I said urgently, "Quick, call me right back because a collect call to the States from Greece cost a couple dollars a minute."

"Are you serious, Cary? I don't think it will break the bank. You know, I was afraid the telegram would not get to you. Since this call is coming from Athens, does that mean you are coming to visit?"

I said, "Yes! I miss you."

"Good. I already asked my travel agent to book a round trip ticket for you to San Francisco. Claim it at the TWA office Monday, not at American Express as I put in the telegram. I'll meet you at baggage claim in the San Francisco airport."

Joni asked me about Matala, "How are our friends doing, Mark and Barbara, Ken and Agate, Dora and Stelios? How is our cave, your shop?"

"Joan, soldiers closed the caves to cave-dwellers. This time eviction might have been set in motion when Stelios got arrested. You were there. Mark says that police usually lift the ban after about two weeks. Since Matala merchants depend on tourists for their livelihood, they complain to the police commandant when authorities close the caves."

"Oh, no," she said, pausing, "What will our friends do now?"

"It's really not so bad, Joan. They have weathered cave closings before. Some cavers go to Istanbul, Cairo, or Beirut to renew their six-month visas. Others wait it out in Matala, set up tents in the olive groves, or go someplace else in Crete, like Irapetra. Mark and Barbara, Ken and Agate rented a house in Matala where they'll hole-up until they can move back to their cave. The Matala Leather Shop stays open for business, but cave closure means no tourists. No tourists means no customers. Barbara makes leather bags and embroidered vests. Agate knits sweaters. The ladies drink tea, gossip, and tell stories. Ken and Mark smoke hash and play cards. They all send their love."

Although I neglected to tell her about Jeannie, I did describe the hike down the Samaria Gorge. Joan: "Oh, it sounds wonderful, I'd love to hike through the Samaria Gorge with you."

"Let's go back together," I proposed.

Joni told me about her trip to Spain and Paris. "In Ibiza, guess what? I ran into an old friend. One evening, strolling through side streets searching for a restaurant, I heard guitar and singing coming from an alley. 'I know that music,' I am thinking, 'someone is playing Taj Mahal's album, *Giant Step*.' I follow the sound up to a green, wooden plank door. I knock. 'Yes?' I hear. Pushing open the door, there is Taj! He is sitting in a chair in the middle of a bare room with a portable record player on the floor in front of him, listening to *Giant Step*. We had supper together with his girlfriend. Isn't that far out?"

She didn't stop there, "Paris was wonderful! My travel agent booked me into Hotel de Quai Voltaire on the Left Bank next to Pont de Carrousel. Although the hotel was a bit shabby, I have to say, I had the presidential suite or something. It had a bath, which is pretty rare in an old hotel in Paris. I always wanted to stay in Hotel de Quai Voltaire because Picasso and Hemmingway stayed there in the 1920s. Maybe, I imagined, some of their vibes might rub off on me. Even before unpacking, I drew a long hot bath, and soaked in it. I got my hair done at a salon on Rue du Bac, a pedicure and manicure. Do you know the pedicurist scrubbed the last bits of Matala beach tar from my feet? Can you imagine?"

We said goodbye and hung up. I didn't tell her I had never been to Paris. Funny, seventeen years later I resided for months at the Hotel de Nesle, a mere four or five blocks from l'Hotel du Quai Voltaire. *But that is another story.*

Several months later, when Joni and I were in London, events took a bad turn in Crete. Barbara contacted Joni's management office to tell Joni that Mark had been arrested in Iraklion and ask her if she could help. Here was the predicament: police busted travelers at the youth hostel in Iraklion for smuggling hashish. Mark had been buying leather from the bootmakers and they arrested him because he was sleeping in the same dormitory room as the smugglers. This proved the misfortune of being in the wrong place at the wrong time. But the prosecutor eventually dismissed Mark's case and they deported him—a year later. In sadness, Mark and Barbara left Greece, their adopted home, forever.

CHAPTER 16

Perfidy of Desire

In the Athens Youth Hostel Speros served us coffee, *psomi* and jam for breakfast. Afterwards, I walked with two travelers over to the American Express office in Syntagma Square. I needed to cash checks and pick up mail. Funny how my new jackboots increased the length of my stride. *Not many travelers' checks left in my wallet.* Proceeds from the sale of my car, which my father had sent to me in Kabul in January, were beginning to peter out. Although I had rationed my funds for a long time in Matala, quite easy to do, my enormous wealth dwindled day by day.

American Express once again proved its reputation as a rendezvous center extraordinaire. In the vestibule, I ran into Linda Kapeki and her girlfriend, Mona, both Canadians, who had hung with Joni in the caves. Now awaiting the reopening of the caves, they were caretaking an orange grove in Attiki, a rural suburb about a half hour by bus from Athens.

"Come out to Attiki with us, Cary. The farmhouse where we stay sits in the middle of an orange grove, a short bus ride from Athens; I think you'll like it. A café down the road makes great moussaka and rice pudding and has a juke box. As caretakers our sole job is watering the orange trees every day. Cape Town George and his girlfriend, Silvia—you remember them from Matala?—stay with us at the orchard.

"We will be taking the two-o'clock Attiki bus number 732. You catch it there"—she pointed across the square. "If you miss us, here are the directions to the orchard." I copied it in my notebook.

Exiting Amex, I walked down the square to the TWA office. When I showed the lady at the desk my passport, asking if she had a ticket for me, she looked at me askance. *What does that expression signify?* She reached inside her desk drawer and passed me an envelope with my name printed on the front. I opened it and there it was: "A first-class ticket to San Francisco? Is this a mistake?" I asked her, showing her the ticket. "Am I supposed to be flying first-class to San Francisco?"

She confirmed, "Yes, Sir. It *is* a first-class, round-trip ticket from Athens to San Francisco." Judging from her awkwardness, I figured she had not encountered many freaks decked out in the garb of a Cretan shepherd flying first class.

I brought my gear from the youth hostel to the bus stop in Syntagma and got on 732 with Linda and Mona. In thirty minutes, we arrived at the farm. I laid my sleeping bag on a rope bed, put on shorts, and started working right away, filling an endless number of buckets to water orange trees. For a week, I worked in the orchard—getting a good physical workout—ate moussaka and drank retsina at the neighborhood café. Linda fed token after token into the jukebox to play, "Let It Be," over and over again through the evening.

At the end of the week, I stood beside the Attiki bus stop with my bags at my feet to catch the number 1 bus to the airport. I stepped off the bus an hour and a half later. *Adios, goodbye, Greece, see you again soon.*

I checked my backpack and kept my hucklebag as carry-on luggage. In the first-class lounge, I sat apart from the other well-appointed passengers, drank fine wine, ate canapes, and awaited the boarding of my plane. I was dressed the way Joni saw me last, in shepherd's garb, cane cradled over my arm, leather hucklebag slung over my shoulder. To a Greek in Athens, Mark said, my attire represented a romanticized image of a Cretan from the Revolution of 1921.

As I stepped aboard the plane and walked into the first-class cabin, the TWA crew greeted me warmly. The other passengers, with a few exceptions, smiled at me as I walked down the aisle. A steward directed me to my seat in the right front bulkhead. "Did they seat me where I would not cause trouble or be an eyesore to the other passengers?" I wondered. To the contrary, the flight crew treated me graciously. "Maybe this Cretan shepherd provides a welcome relief from snooty, first-class passengers," I speculated.

I put the hucklebag into the overhead baggage compartment and fastened my seatbelt. Shortly, the plane taxied down the runway and we were airborne. When the seatbelt light went off, the steward unfolded a starched tablecloth on my tray, set down a porcelain plate with little thin pancakes and small bowls of sour cream, chopped eggs, and minced onion, along with a dainty bone spoon. He came back with a tin of grey caviar nested in a bed of crushed ice and spooned a large dab on the white saucer next to the condiments. With a flourish, he unwrapped a chilled bottle of Dom Perignon, and poured it slowly while tipping my glass, "I think you will enjoy this." I held up the light, slender flute of champagne and admired its simplicity.

After a bit, the steward presented me with the *Whole Earth Catalog*, a color photo of the Earth on the cover. I had never drunk such splendid champagne before, nor eaten good caviar, nor had I ever heard of the *Whole Earth Catalog*.

The *Whole Earth Catalog*, I was soon to learn, represented Stewart Brand's vision: he thought that seeing a photograph of the earth taken from space would change the mindset of humanity. The *Whole Earth Catalog*, a hippy equivalent of the *Sears Catalog*, targeted the counter-cultural movement in Northern California. It offered practical education—"access to tools"—how to raise chickens, how to build outhouses, how to bookkeep, and offered all manner of sage advice to the back-to-the-earth movement. In this otherwise formal first-class cabin, the TWA steward had grokked the mindset of this crazy freak in a Cretan shepherd's costume.

"May I pour you another glass of champagne, Mr. Raditz?"

With the *Whole Earth Catalogue* open on my tray, espresso, pastries and way too much champagne and cognac, I "took drunk," as they used to say in Savannah. I passed out. When the plane stopped for refueling in New York, I barely took notice.

Finally, awake, somewhat worst for all the booze, I gazed out the window. Mountains rose before me through wispy clouds. *Must be the Rockies.* I am going to LA. Like many San Franciscans, I distrusted the so-called City of Angels. I nodded in and out, head slumping forward and jerking back, like a junkie on his run. Dreams within dreams. The steward folded a warm, soft blanket over my dozing form.

CHAPTER 17

City of Fallen Angels

Hungover and groggy from too many flutes of Dom Perignon and snifters of Chivas Regal, I stirred awake when the plane touched down at SFO. Hucklebag slung over my shoulder, I stumbled down the landing ramp and walked endless corridors, gradually getting my bearings, and ultimately arrived at immigration control. The inspector in the booth peered at my passport, looked up at my bearded face and bloodshot eyes, and asked me where I had been. "Germany and Greece, Turkey, Iran and Afghanistan," I mumbled, slightly nauseous.

He stamped my passport and said, "Welcome back to the United States, Sir." As I stepped away, a surge of bile and cognac rose to my throat. I felt like I was going to puke.

At the baggage carrousel, I piled my backpack and hucklebag onto a luggage cart and pushed the cart through customs. No one checked my baggage or asked me any questions. I imagined how weird this Greek shepherd must have appeared to immigration agents. How could customs inspectors resist the urge to poke into my bags and see what I was bringing back to the States?

"Jesus," I thought, "if they let me through customs the way I look, they'll let anybody through." But there was nothing really to worry about; I was clean and carried no contraband.

Outside customs control Joni stood waiting. Dazzling in turquoise and silver jewelry, she wore the ankle length sweater she had knitted in Matala. I loved that sweater. She stepped forward to embrace me. Wounded by drink and nursing a pounding hangover, I was dumbstruck. "Oh, Joan," was all I could say. *Why had I got so drunk?* Dizziness, headache, and queasy stomach dampened the joy of being back with her. She had gifted me a first-class flight and this is what arrived—a drunk-sick Cretan shepherd. She hugged and kissed me.

I spun her around to look at her and her sweater flared. Poking out from under her long sweater, her green suede Cretan jackboots drew my attention. I was wearing mine, too, plain brown cowhide. We both looked down and touched our boots together, as if our boots, too, were lovers reuniting after separation. At least, thank god, I had brushed my teeth on the plane. All I could do was wrap my arms around her, bury my nose in her blond hair and feel her strength engulf me.

She was not alone. More friends came into focus: Deward, Jennie, Paul and Stan.

What madness had incited me to write Deward telling him my ETA? He in turn had contacted Paul and Stan who invited all of us back to their house in Diamond Heights. "Sure!" I piped up. Another mistake. Joni's face registered displeasure. Outside the airport we slipped into her blue Mercedes convertible and followed Stan's beat-up Ford station wagon into San Francisco with Deward and Jenny tailing us in his vintage pickup truck.

On a corner of a steep street in Diamond Heights, we pulled up in front of a four-story, grey Victorian mansion. Paul and Stan led us into the house through a heavy door inset with stained glass. Joni pulled me close and whispered, "Wouldn't you rather stay at the Fairmont on Nob Hill where I made a reservation?"

"Ah Joan, let's sleep in this great old house and party with my friends." She acquiesced. We retreated into a little lair under the broad wooden stairs with a futon. "This cubby is the nearest thing to our cave, Joan. It even has silk cushions." Joni just wanted to please me and to pamper me, and not share me with a bunch of my friends. I was out of control. Compulsively, it seemed—step by step—I was violating her trust.

Early the next morning before anyone else got up, we cleared out of Diamond Heights. Joni drove the Carolina blue Mercedes sportscar top down, hair streaming in the wind, skirt up around her waist, barefoot. Cruising

Highway 1 to Pescadero we turned off west and drove over the Santa Cruz Mountains to La Honda to visit her friend, Chip Monck. Monck managed event production and lighting and had served as the master of ceremonies at Woodstock two years ago—where Joni had been conspicuously absent—and four months later, master of ceremonies at the disastrous Rolling Stones concert at Altamont.

Joni, the centerpiece, attracted all their attention—and what was wrong with that? Last night we had stayed with my friends; tonight, we stayed with hers. Monck and his roadies lived in a log-lodge in a grove of redwoods beside a clear mountain-fed stream. Nearby a waterfall cascaded from the redwoods above into a deep pool where we swam naked. The pungent scent of the redwood coast, the perfume of bay mixed with eucalyptus, invoked a sense of entering an ancient geological age before Man. This overnight stay with Monck & company initiated me into my new role as sidekick—not a co-principal—in our friendship, a role which would carry forward into Laurel Canyon.

In the morning we loaded our stuff in the car and said goodbye to Chip Monck and gang. The convertible wound along the swerving coastal highway, cliffs rising on our left and dropping off on the right side to the crashing surf of Big Sur below. We drove into the parking lot of the Big Sur Inn. Joni had reserved us a room here under the redwoods. The Inn reminded me of the vernacular architecture of those Beat-hipster settlements I had known in Canyon, east of the Berkeley hills. Pieced together out of salvaged lumber, the Inn maintained the frontier aura Henry Miller wrote about in *Big Sur and the Oranges of Hieronymus Bosch*. Cozy in a room high above the cliffs, Joan and I imagined Henry Miller's outspoken ghost visiting us. As wind whipped through the Monterey cypresses, and waves crashed below, it was as if we were transported back into our Mediterranean cave.

Arriving the next day in Laurel Canyon, Joni parked the car below the steps to her house on Lookout Mountain Avenue. She opened the front door to a two-stage, open living room where windows spread out on several levels looking out on her garden—succulents, shrubs and dryland plants. Her piano sat beside a window in a paneled alcove left and above the living room. Her Lookout Mountain Avenue home was her lair—this house, this alcove and piano—as my cave in Matala had been mine. "Turnabout is fair play," I figured. We unpacked and settled in—or seemed to settle in—for a while.

A stream of visitors began to trickle in to call on Joni and to check out the wild man she brought back from Greece. Joellen Lapidus—who crafted Joni's first dulcimer, the one she took to Greece and on which she had played "Carey" to me on my birthday in Matala—dropped by with her protégée, Laura Allan. Estrella Berosini, *Circus Lady* from "Ladies of the Canyon," came to say hello and introduce herself, further brightening the room.

Several of The "Happy Together" Turtles came to welcome Joni back from her travels. David Blue showed up and I liked him immediately, his cool hip demeanor and wry smile. Messieurs Crosby, Stills and Nash came to visit—a visit probably as unsettling to them as it was to me. They sat together glaring at me, avoiding my eyes as I avoided theirs. *What is there to say?* I felt strangely upset for Graham. Months earlier, it was he who welcomed guests into this house, the home he shared with Joni, as in "Our House," the domestic song they wrote together. It struck me that I might be running interference between Joni and Graham and his buddies. After all, she had told me in Crete that to preserve her identity, she needed distance from these guys—a prime reason why she fled LA. So be it. A bodyguard? I shrugged it off.

David Geffen invited Joni and me up to swim at his post-modern Hollywood estate perched on top of Mulholland Drive, to swim and listen to Jackson Browne's new songs. His pool surveyed Hollywood below through a veil of yellow smog. David waxed with pride about his business deals. He told us he had had this property reappraised and could borrow against its higher value. *Big deal.*

We retired from the bright, hot poolside into the cool dark living room. Jackson gave us a private concert. According to David, Jackson Browne was a twenty-one-year-old prodigy. David sat on the top pinnacle among Hollywood's deal-making moguls. Not only did he enjoy discovering and cultivating talent, as Joni would later sing, "stoking the star maker machinery of the popular song," he enjoyed showing off the talented people he had discovered to his friends. I had no talent, as I could see it. "David is scared of you," Joni whispered to me. I was still in my jackboots. "Maybe it's your knife." I figured she was pulling my leg.

Joni's manager, Elliot Roberts, came over to check on her and to meet me. Elliot appeared friendly, but I distrusted his motives and he must have detected it. But what was there to distrust? Elliot wanted to make Joni happy and if being kind to me served that end, well, that was the order of the day. Elliot told us, "I got us VIP passes to visit Disneyland tomorrow."

The next morning a long black limo pulled up in front. Elliot stepped out in a fringed leather jacket, patched jeans, and cowboy boots. Facing Joni and me in the black seat, he extracted a fat joint from his inside breast pocket. He lit it with a match and passed it to Joni. She took a small toke. This was my first encounter with Hollywood weed, bodacious kick-your-ass weed, far more potent than the black hashish in Kabul. *Why did I take a toke?* Strong weed made me anxious and withdrawn, made me shake as if I had tremors. The last thing I needed here in LA with Joni was to freak out. No. And here I was taking a toke of mega weed ... big mistake.

Skunky ganga smoke clouded the backseat of the limo. *Good Lord, how can the Lords of Entertainment conduct business while smoking this bad-ass marijuana? How can they smoke this shit all day long, when only one toke puts me into a weird, anti-social semi-coma?*

The limo halted in front of the Disneyland gate. The driver opened our door for us. I was so stoned at this point I could barely walk or talk. Paranoia swamped me. Weak in the knees—feeling like I was going to throw up—like a wounded animal I withdrew into my scary inner sanctum. Several very spick-and-span Disney people greeted us and led us around lines of people waiting to enter the Kingdom of Mickey. Donald Duck waddled up to us in white gloves. "Let's do this!" "Let's do that!" suggested Elliot with great enthusiasm. Realizing I was an incoherent drag, I clung to Joni.

VIP status gave us access to everything, bypassing waiting in lines for rides. We went inside a Disneyland clothing store. Elliot picked out a fine Pendleton wool shirt for himself. "Cary, would you like one?" I declined. I felt awkward taking gifts from him, freeloading, perhaps creating obligations I might be unwilling to fulfil. The day went on, the weed wore off, and still I was depressed. The VIP attention embarrassed me. Although, if one were going to Disneyland, I conceded, VIP without a doubt would be the way to go.

Next Friday, July 10, Elliot booked center seats for us to see The Band at the Hollywood Bowl, with Miles Davis opening for them. Although I was a big fan—*Music from Big Pink* had given me solace during a dark, freaked out night in Canyon two years ago—ironically, it was Miles Davis whom I remember most. When I was fifteen, in junior high school, spurred on by Dave Brubeck's *Time Out*, I thought I needed to dig jazz to be cool, like Jack Kerouac-*On-the-Road*-cool. But I didn't get it. I couldn't absorb it or appreciate it then.

The audience was restless. For Miles, the Hollywood Bowl concert must have been disappointing, even insulting, opening to another lesser act instead of headlining. Standing off to the side, on stage right, he lingered at the edge of his band, trumpet by his side, as if he were waiting for a bus that never came. He sulked, barely moving, and only stepped forward to blow a few muted bars now and then as if he couldn't be bothered. Lackluster applause reflected the audience's distain for Miles, an audience that had come this Friday night for The Band. Later in life, as my taste in music shifted, broadened, and deepened, I came to appreciate Miles Davis. But not that night.

✳ ✳ ✳

During July, Joni and I hung out in her cottage. In her alcove by the window, she crouched over the keyboard for hours composing, repeating and repeating sequences of chords as if she were mesmerized, losing herself in a creative trance. I collapsed into my own angst and spent most of the day reading, listening to music, and worrying. During these summer days, Joni and I never discussed philosophy, although philosophical conversations had enthralled us in Matala when we were getting to know each other. Now in the evenings, we went out to movie theaters in shopping centers. Since this was Hollywood, people didn't bat an eye when I wore my Afghan pajamas stuck into my jackboots, dressed in shepherd's attire.

While poking through stacks of Joni's LPs, I came upon James Taylor's album, *Sweet Baby James*. "Country Road" brought to mind the dirt road leading past Jenkin's Farm north on Airport Road where I had lived briefly last summer before going to Germany. I pictured James walking down that same dirt road. As a joke, I pulled the fold-out portrait of James out of the album sleeve and thumb-tacked it to the paneled wall above Joni's piano.

Despite my petulance and her creative trances, Joni and I had our good moments. We were driving down Sunset Boulevard to the Geffen Roberts office in her convertible when she stopped at a stoplight. Kris Kristofferson jumped into the narrow backseat and began talking nonstop about people, events, and random things I couldn't follow. Joni barely had the conversational space to ask, "Well, Hi Kris … how are you?" when he jumped out and was gone. As the light turned green, she and I looked at each other and shrugged, *What was all that about?* and we laughed. *Hollywood.*

Difficult days grew into uncomfortable weeks in Lookout Mountain Avenue. As Mama used to say, "Familiarity breeds contempt." That old saw seemed to sum up the situation. To me, Hollywood represented fast money, dope, fancy cars, and extravagance. Hollywood stood as the antithesis of Matala: nothing seemed right—I saw everything through the glass darkly.

Down and out in Hollywood. Here I was living in Laurel Canyon with a beautiful, famous, exquisitely talented girlfriend, who cared for me, and yet I was ungrateful and unable to fully appreciate the rarity of our intimacy and what she was giving up in her life to bring me home with her, to introduce me to her friends, to expose me to the power brokers of LA, and to try to make me happy.

I failed to grasp how Joni had entered a cycle of creativity that excluded me and everything else. The creative act was absorbing her whole being, transporting her into another realm, an introspective shadow realm populated by emotions, remembrances, regrets and sorrow. While I should have supported her by staying in the background—by shopping, doing laundry, giving her massages, and buffering her from interruptions—providing the solace she needed—instead I acted like a self-centered asshole.

My identity continued to unravel. I questioned who I was and who I wanted to be. In contrast to my devil-may-care vagabond ways, now I found myself ashamed to be poor and untalented, ashamed of living without a plan and living on her good graces. I wasn't caring for the Joan I had professed to love. Here in her house, I was acting fragile and vulnerable, when I should have been uplifting and protective. Where was the compassion I had learned during my episodes of awakening, and the painful Dark Night misery and fear in San Francisco two years ago? Enlightened? *More like endarkened.*

Thus, I bided time in LA, pining to be back in Matala, to be hiking over Crete's sage and thyme brush hills, making sandals in my shop above the harbor, watching the sun set over the Mediterranean. I longed to be cooking, dancing, and throwing back shots of ouzo in the Mermaid. Running my own life—free and independent.

One morning, I threw off the covers, arose and left her in bed, sleeping. All through the night I had thrashed around thinking how our friendship had taken root in Matala and blossomed full of promise in our cave by the sea. She had invited me to LA to be in her world, yet I arrived when her songwriting took over and shut me out. Bad timing. LA had given me a good dose of reality, a slap in the face to shatter delusions of love. *Was the curtain falling on this romantic drama?*

Despondent, I rang Willie Gilbertson-Hart in England, whom I had known in Matala, and told him I was going to quit Hollywood. He laughed, "Get your act together, Old Boy. Come to Jolly England and join me for a wild summer working in the halcyon fields of Albion!" He invited me to stay on his family farm in Laughton, Leicestershire. Speeding off to England gave me an honorable way to save face, to keep my shaky identity intact. Better to retire than get fired.

Joni took my decision in stride. She arranged for her management office to convert my first-class ticket to Athens into an economy fare to London. The difference in ticket prices allowed me to pocket enough cash to cut me breathing room to plan and consider my options. Should I return to Crete, where I can live in a cave in Matala subsisting on olives, dried bread, and fresh fish? Should I buy a seat on the "Magic Bus" to India? *I'll figure out my next steps from Willie's farm in Leicestershire.*

As I packed, fare-thee-wells felt empty. Joni drove me to the airport; we barely spoke. *Was there really any point to talking at all?* Our friendship—our romance—fell apart in the City of Angels, not with a bang, nor a whimper, and certainly not with another love song, but with a *good riddance.*

In front of Departures she put me out by the curb. I watched her convertible pull away. She was heading back home to her piano. Sadly, I turned and entered the airport. There would be no goodbyes at the gate. As the door closed, I sensed my life closing behind me, shutting down a romance I should have known was doomed from the start.

I left the cane behind in her house.

CHAPTER 18

The Isle of Wight Festival

From the window seat I watched the Rockies loom below, appearing and disappearing through the clouds. *What went wrong? Am I a Sisyphus cursed to learn and relearn the Second Noble Truth: expectations sow sorrows, sorrows beget unfulfilled hungers—a feast of ashes?*

The vagabond, having flown first-class to San Francisco, now flies steerage to England. I looked at *myself* as a separate life form, a fictional character in my own absurd Punch & Judy play. Flying east, I comforted myself with snippets of wisdom: Taoism, the *I Ching,* and Ecclesiastes: "That which hath been is now: and that which is to be, hath already been … and there is no new thing under the sun."

For the first time in a long time, I felt truly alone, and realized I had always been alone. I routed my trip from Los Angeles to London, with a stop-off in Chapel Hill to visit friends, Scott, Henry, David, Paul, and especially, my ex-girlfriend, Holly.

When I arrived at the Raleigh Durham Airport, I phoned her.

"When you get to Chapel Hill, Cary, come over to my house. I want to see you and catch up. Right now, I'm in summer school trying to make up credits from the chemistry courses I missed when we were in Munich and Crete last fall."

A ten-minute walk from the intersection of Franklin and Columbia Streets, the epicenter of downtown Chapel Hill, brought me to the address she gave me on the phone, a two-story group house perched on a hill above Airport Road. Would she invite me to stay?

From the sidewalk, I climbed wooden steps to the front porch and knocked on the screen door. Through the screen, I watched as Holly approached. She opened the door and we embraced. Holding my hand, she led me into the living room. *Has something changed about her?* She seemed more beautiful than ever, more mature, more self-assured. Tall and lean, long dark hair down her back, she was physically striking, needing no adornment. I was both happy to see her and confused. She sat on my lap and we kissed.

Her wry smile had always held mystery for me, a smile concealing deep intellect and modest restraint. Her eyes danced with awareness and caution. Her body pressed against me. *Did I love her? Had I ever loved her?* Emphatically yes! but I had blown it. In Greece I had taken her for granted.

Keenly committed to her chemistry curricula, Holly lived in this house with a boyfriend I did not meet, and although I was still strongly attracted to her, and she to me—it seemed—the prospect of returning to a previous status quo was obviously a no-go. We had had our chance in Munich and then in Matala. Just like with Joni, whom I had just left, I knew there was no place for me here. Crawling back over the embers of a smoldering bridge I had burned down.

"Are you in love with your boyfriend," I probed.

She shrugged. "Maybe. He says he loves me."

"Well, that counts."

Holly would succeed on whatever professional path she followed. Hers was a deliberate, purposeful life: she knew who she was and what she wanted to do. Whatever forces drove my life were propelling me to wherever they would lead.

Is she reading my mind? "Do you remember, Cary, when we were hitchhiking south from Munich, you joked: 'Let Destiny be my copilot?' I'll never forget how we put the choice of our destination to chance: 'if the first car to pick us up takes the right fork southeast, we will go to the Spanish Islands and Morocco. However, if the first car to pick us up takes the left fork southwest, we will go to Greece.'

"'Destiny be my copilot!' you declared. Even though I knew you said that flippantly and not with malice, I was wounded, as if your declaration was prophetic. This might sound silly now, but I presumed *I was your copilot—your partner*. Guess it turns out you were right after all. Destiny was."

We kissed goodbye at the front door. I never saw Holly again.

✳ ✳ ✳

I arrived at Heathrow with no plans other than to kip with Willie on his farm until I could plot my next move, most probably to return to my cave life in Crete, cooking at Delphini and making sandals in the Matala Leather Shop.

An airport bus dropped me at St Pancras station. I rang Willie, deciphered the train schedule, and boarded the cheapest train to Leicester, which stopped at every railway station in between. Willie and his girlfriend, Christine, from Athens, met me in Leicester in an open 1930 Lanchester Straight Eight. In the backseat squatted Bonkers, Willie's mongrel dog. Big hugs all around. We puttered directly to a pub that looked like it had never recovered from the Battle of Britain. We quickly set to taking stupidly drunk on whiskey and beer.

Beer was cheap in England in 1970. A pint of bitter cost a shilling, the equivalent of a US quarter. The men's toilet had no door, the sole urinal—a porcelain trough—ran wall to wall. Reeling out of the pub, we chugged across the county to the cattle-gated hamlet of Laughton, and to Willie's family home, the Croft. Sturdy wooden gates swung open to a gravel yard in front of a two-story brick house of indeterminate age. It stood within a large compound of garages, gardens, a greenhouse, and an apple orchard, all enclosed by an eight-foot brick wall.

My first night in The Croft, we dined with Mr. and Mrs. Hart, and Fred, their dairy farm manager. After supper Willie and Chris retired to their room above the garage. I rolled out my sleeping bag on a pallet on the floor of the den, a room with a TV between the kitchen and the stairs to the bedrooms above where Mr. and Mrs. Hart slept. Willie's parents were polite and kind to me. Apparently, they took in stride putting up homeless vagabonds Willie dragged in from God knows where. I became a volunteer farmhand.

The den where I was to sleep every night served as a center of activity where everyone gathered in the evenings to watch television. I had to wait to go to sleep until Mr. and Mrs. Hart and Auntie Vi, Willie's maternal aunt, turned off the telly and went up to bed. Fred would bid me a "goodnight, Cary," and go to his house at the dairy farm down the road to Gumley. *Cosy* was what Mr. Hart, Willie's father called me, after he saw the return address on an aerogram I had sent Willie from Hollywood. "Who is this *Cosy Radish,* Worm" (*Worm*: Mr. Hart's affectionate nickname for his son).

Farm work began early after breakfast. Mrs. Hart served thick fried bacon and ham, fried tomatoes, fried mushrooms, cold toast, jam, butter, and pots of tea. I found working with Willie Hart on his dad's farm and on neighboring farmers around Laughton and Gumley was no holiday; it was hard work. But it was late summer in England and Jolly England in midsummer is the stuff of dreams. Long days punctuated with heavy farm work devolved into short evenings of pub crawling and heavy drinking. It was a kindness pubs closed at 10 p.m.

Mid-morning, Chris drove out to the fields in a little English Ford station wagon to deliver us tea and cakes. At noon we came into the house to sit down for dinner around the dining room table with roast beef or chicken, Yorkshire pudding and gravy, and many potatoes, followed by yellow custard dressed in a glob of red Jell-O. At 4 p.m., Mrs. Hart brought tea and cakes and scones to us in the fields. Supper in the evening was an informal affair around the dining room table. More potatoes. More gravy. Then out to the local country pubs where we snacked on pickled sausages, Scotch eggs, crisps, beer, and whiskey.

I started gaining weight like crazy, up to 150 pounds. When I left Matala, I must have weighed about 130. Farm work was like basic training; it made me stronger than I had ever been, throwing bales of hay up on trucks and in hay lofts. I evaluated my strength, astonishing myself by doing popup pushups. Lying face down, arms straight out over the head, I could pop up the torso between fingers and toes. In a handstand near a brick wall, I could shoulder press my weight up from arms fully bent to arms fully extended. Eight months earlier in Afghanistan I had been dying, or at least could have died, had Agate and Ken not rescued me. In Kabul, I would have been lucky to tip the scales at 120.

In the evenings after work in Laughton's fields and barns, we puttered around country roads to pubs in the Midlands. The Lanchester's soft top barely worked and usually stayed down except in heavy rain. The spare tire was mounted on the right side of the car. Willie, Chris, and I stuffed ourselves into the Lanchester along with Bonkers, stopping at every open pub on the road between Leicester and Melton Mowbray, drinking a pint at each. At the humped bridge over the canal near Gumley everyone had to hop out to push the Lanchester over the crest of the little bridge, Willie jumping over the door into the seat to steer once we had made it over the top.

One weekend, Willie, Chris, and I hitch-hiked to Scotland to attend Pope Barrow's nuptials in Edinburgh. Pope, Henry's older brother, whom I had known for years in the States, was getting married. In a clearing in the woods, we stabbed potatoes on sticks and cooked them black over a fire and ate them seated on a blanket in the woods. That night we found a barn and slept cozy and dry on hay. On the way up to Edinburgh, it started to rain. Willie and Chris decided to give up on Scotland and return to Laughton. I on the other hand caught a ride in a lorry to Newcastle, and walking and hitch hiking, got into Edinburgh in the evening.

I rang Pope from a pub, and at the bar, I ordered, "A pint of bitter, please."

"Where are you from, my son? Here in Edinburgh, we call it a 'heavy,' not a 'bitter,'" chided the publican. Shortly, Pope walked in the pub, sidled up to my stool, and pretended to strangle me. We ordered pints of heavy. In a couple days, he was to marry Pippa, whom I knew only from Pope's lurid, self-referencing stories.

"Cary, I can't believe you made it here. Where are your friends?" he shouted over the music and pub commotion.

"Willie and Chris threw in the towel when it started raining this morning."

I slept on Pippa's couch. I don't remember much about the next day except I was dressed wrong and surprised at how everyone was nice to me, as if I was family, and asked how I was related to Pope, who lied I was his cousin from Savannah, Georgia. He invented stories of how we shrimped in the creeks and shot ducks in the Sea Islands. Champagne flowed, a buffet feast with roast beef, beer and whiskey, and brandy ... and ... I woke up on the floor beside the couch never having undressed or even taken off my boots. A faint memory that I fell down dancing .... I felt like a muddy tractor had run over me and then parked in my mouth. When I brushed my teeth, red-shot eyeballs looked back at me.

After coffee, cold toast and jam with the bride and groom, I kissed them on both cheeks three times, bid them goodbye, and wished them happiness. Shouldering my pack and hucklebag, with a worrisome hangover, I walked to the edge of Edinburgh and began hitchhiking. A lorry hauling sugar beets picked me up and deposited me outside Glasgow. In a pub I had a heavy and a meat pie, walked out to the edge of a highway entrance and stuck out my thumb.

A sergeant on leave picked me up in a military lorry and dropped me off near a tube station in north London. I took a train into Chelsea, found the cheap youth hostel, showered, and slept under clean sheets. In the morning I went cross-town to American Express to check on my mail and catchup on scuttlebutt with travelers.

Elliot Roberts had left a note for me with his business card two days before on which he had written a London phone number with instructions to ring him. From a red phone booth on the sidewalk, I called him. "Cary, you just now got the message at American Express? We've been trying to get hold of you for days. Can you come over right now? Joan is here in London. We're all going down to the Isle of Wight Festival this afternoon; Joan wants you to come with us."

"Okay, Elliot. Tell her I'll be right there," I said, hanging up and flagging a cab, giving the driver the Knightsbridge address. The elegant building stood around the corner from Harrods. Buzzed in, I took the lift up to the

Warner Brothers apartment. At the door Joni met me with a big kiss. *Well! This is a happy surprise!* Behind her, lugging suitcases and guitar cases, were Elliot and Neil Young.

No time to talk. Within minutes we were chauffeured away in two vintage automobiles, a classic Rolls-Royce carrying Elliot and Neil, and a Bentley carrying Joni and me in pursuit. We set off through rural Surrey to Portsmouth to catch a ferry to our destination, the Isle of Wight. With my arm around her shoulder, it was as if we had returned to the familiarity of Crete. "Joan, I'm happy to be here with you. I hated the way things ended in LA."

"I am truly sorry about that, Cary. I was unreachable. That's what happens when I am composing. I drive everyone around me crazy. But … here we are." She kissed me.

Both cars embarked on the ferry and we retired to the ferry pub bar. I coaxed Joni into chasing a whiskey with a Guinness Stout. She knocked off the whiskey and downed the Guinness. "Oh! You're the girl after my own heart!" I hugged her. The ferry passage went dandy until we debarked in the harbor and the police arrested Elliot.

The charge was carrying controlled substances. With hordes of rockstars debarking the ferry for the festival, why would the police have suspected Elliot? How could they divine that a longhaired, mustached freak wearing a leather fringed Buffalo Bill jacket and cowboy boots—carrying a silver Zero Halliburton briefcase—chauffeured to the Isle of Wight in a vintage Rolls-Royce—might have been carrying controlled substances?

Curiously, the police did not inspect our Bentley, nor did they pat us down. Except for the Halliburton briefcase, Joni and I must have appeared equally culpable as Elliot. "Go ahead to the hotel," Elliot whispered in a low voice. "I'll be along to join you as soon as I get this squared away." The police booked Elliot, impounding his Rolls-Royce. His chauffeur sat down on a bench, lit a cigarette, pulled out the *Daily Racing Form*, and settled in to wait. Our chauffeur drove Joni, Neil, and me to the bed and breakfast where we had reservations.

Joni and I unpacked and joined Neil in his room, to await the outcome of Elliot's arrest. About an hour later, Elliot knocked on the door and entered, noticeably frazzled, and told us the story of his bust. When the police opened his briefcase, they found a film cannister containing controlled substances, and another cannister packed with Panama Red. Elliot told us he paid a thousand pound fine and the police freed him, minus the cannisters. "I'll get more from The Who," he said, smiling. By now, twilight was coming on. Time to investigate the festival.

Festival grounds were ten minutes from our guesthouse. We joined Elliot and Neil in their Rolls. As it passed through a security gate, a guard checked Elliot's VIP pass, and waved us on. At the fenced off performers' area behind the stage, gatekeepers scanned a clipboard and issued us backstage badges.

The festival lineup included Joni, Jimi Hendrix, The Doors, Miles Davis, The Who, The Moody Blues, Jethro Tull, Sly and the Family Stone, Ten Years After, Emerson, Lake & Palmer, and other bands I didn't recognize. Leonard Cohen was supposed to be here, as well as Donovan, and Joan Baez. As we looked around in the performers' parking area, we encountered a fleet of vehicles including vans, motorcycles, and equipment trucks, as well as other Rolls-Royces and Bentleys.

On a hill overlooking fields and hills beyond, a bank of spotlights illuminated the stage against the evening sky. Across from the stage tents in all shapes and colors formed a vast, motley collage. People were camping both inside and outside the corrugated metal perimeter fences. Crowds moved through firelight and shadows, many congregating close to the stage. Summer twilight made campfires and crowds resemble a military field bivouac.

In the first century AD, a Roman centurion might have stood where I was now standing, surveying the armies encamped on these hills just as it was now. Would Aulus Plautius himself have viewed his soldiers circled around campfires, singing and dancing and drinking like these folks here? Would he have felt their *esprit de corps* as he walked among them encouraging their valor as the impending hour of the invasion of Britannia drew near?

At this point, festival managers could have benefited from Aulus Plautius's leadership and discipline. A core of disgruntled freaks demanded free entry. They complained the entrance fee of a few quid was prohibitive, arguing that the artists and promoters were rank capitalists and that entry to the music festival should be free to everyone. They slammed their bodies against the sheet metal fences from outside, trying to invade the campgrounds as they felt entitled to do. Barechested freak revolutionaries attacked fences with lengths of building lumber as battering rams, while police, some with dogs, futilely commanded them to stop. Although we could not know this, promotors verged on losing control of the event. Angry vigilante groups stridently derided the festival, cursed greedy promoters and performers, and spoke out strongly against the state of the rudimentary toilets. They protested everything except protesting itself.

Uniformed festival guards warned us not to venture out into the crowd, saying it was dangerous and they could not provide security. This news shocked Joni who had hoped for the legendary love and peace sentiment that had flowed at Woodstock a year before. Although she had not attended Woodstock personally, because of scheduling conflicts and security issues; nonetheless, she had composed the "Woodstock" anthem. This 1970 Isle of Wight Festival was different from Woodstock. This was not Yasgur's farm's flowerchildren, but Isle of Wight's vicious, freak revolutionaries.

In the year since Woodstock, what social malaise had changed the temper of festival crowds? Was it the Kent State shootings? Student movements in Europe? Manson family cult murders? Vietnam war protests?

Joni and I remained in the performers' stockade where road managers mingled with artists, sound and electrical engineers, groupies and hangers-on like me. I tagged along next to Joni and Elliot as she joked with friends, very few of whom I could identify. Occasionally she introduced me to someone or another, but obviously they couldn't care less. As midnight approached, we saw a few performances and then Elliot decided we should leave. The chauffeur delivered us back to our hotel. Joni was due to play tomorrow, Saturday, the third festival day.

For breakfast, we ordered soft boiled eggs, toast and jam and tea from room service. Elliot took charge of Joni's guitars. Neil was keen to explore the event grounds among the attendees as he was not on the bill, would not be performing, and feared not the ire of the crowd. When we got through the gates in the Rolls and Bentley, it was mid-morning, and the vigilante revolutionaries were becoming increasingly cantankerous and nasty.

The festival promoters were frantic. They sought ways to quell the riot. Although Joni had been scheduled to perform that night, the promoters, wishing to pacify the crowds, asked Elliot if Joni could move up her performance and go on now in the afternoon. She retreated to Donovan's gypsy caravan to dress, to gather herself, and tune several guitars. The caravan, paneled in dark wood like a small private library, had window seats covered in sumptuous purple velvet and red Moroccan pillows propped up against the stained-glass windows. At the far end of the room sat a small antique steel and brass wood stove. *Very mellow. Very mellow.*

A roadie came to the caravan and notified Joni that she was up. Given the hostile crowd, she was understandably apprehensive. Up the ramp onto the stage, we walked alongside her, Elliot on one side, and I on the other. There she was, bright yellow dress, guitar, and mikes, out front of the drunken, drugged, pissed-off legions of Aulus Plautius. I watched from upstage left.

Joni started—or rather false started—on guitar with the "Song About the Midway" and "Chelsea Morning" during which she ran out of steam and broke off mid-song to request more volume to override the noise from the crowd and drown out shouts from a band of persistent photographers who were harrying her. For amplitude mainly, she put down her guitar and moved over to the piano, from where she played "For Free" and "Woodstock."

Wait a minute? Who is the bearded guy sitting in a lotus position next to the piano playing a drum? Holy shit, it's Yogi Joe from Matala! Bizarre! How did he get here? When Joni and I lived in the caves, Yogi Joe served as the self-appointed guru who gave yoga classes on the beach, which Joni used to attend. I had pegged Yogi Joe as a windbag. And here at the edge of the stage, he sat drumming, same beard, shaggy hair, and the same righteous pomposity. He stood up, and with wild LSD eyes, approached Joni, grabbed a pedestal microphone, and started ranting something about Desolation Row. Although I readied myself to throw him off the stage, burly roadies stepped in first to tear the mike out of his hands and were forcibly escorting him offstage, when Elliot intervened to manage his ejection more humanely. The crowd howled in uproar. Joni sat on the piano bench, momentarily stolid, but clearly shaken.

Taking up the mike, Joni turned from her piano, faced the audience, and speaking from her heart, chastised them for their bad behavior. She accused them of acting like callus tourists she had witnessed at a sacred Hopi Indian dance in New Mexico the week before. She begged the audience to behave with respect. The crowd received her speech well. Things quieted down some and she resumed her performance.

Concluding her set with "California," "Both Sides Now, and "Big Yellow Taxi," Joni, Elliot and I left the stage down the backstage ramp to the performers' area while applause rose in volume. Holding Elliot's hand, she walked back up the ramp to the stage and took her encore.

After Joni's performance, I descended into the photographers' pit to watch The Who's set. Their thunderous energy drowned out the rancor of the Barbarians, and the tornado of sound from The Who's colossal bank of speakers came close to bursting my eardrums.

Back in the performers' area, I noted a rambunctious crowd milling around a long moving van parked in the middle of the lot. Who else but The Who were operating a walk-in bar installed in a full-size moving van? Sliding inside The Who Bar Van, elbow to elbow with a well-lubricated crew and performers, I ordered whiskey and beer from the bartender, drummer Keith Moon himself. I drank long and deeply.

Stepping out of the Who van, I felt demon alcohol beginning to do its devilish thing. I saw a shimmering, double image of Joni standing in a circle talking to Elliot and a few of their friends. A grinning John Sebastian stumbled up, greeting everyone, obviously whacked out on controlled substances, rambling on incoherently about who knows what. Looking at him next to me, I was remembering his sweet vocals on "Nashville Cats." Beside him, a large, bearded road manager passed a fat joint to Sebastian who took a toke and passed it to Elliot. Elliot took a long drag, coughed, and passed it to Joni, who without taking a hit, passed it to me. This proved to be the toke that took me over the line. I inhaled. *Mistake!—Man, this shit is powerful!*

Who Bar whiskey coursing through my guts made its insidious way into my bloodstream and into my brain where it combined with the road manager high octane cannabis. Dizzy and nauseous, I needed relief, a mellow place to sit down and get my bearings. *Maybe I need speed and more drink to balance out the weed?*

A short distance away stood Donovan's Gypsy caravan radiating ultimate mellowness. I lunged up the stairs and entered, holding the doorknob to stay upright. Way more than fully drunk, rowdy and half-sick, I demanded beer and coke from Donovan, and explicit sexual favors from a long skirted hippy woman with flowers in her hair seated on the window seat playing a recorder. Horrified, she looked to Donovan for protection. Donovan politely took my arm, drew me off to the side, and speaking to me in a mellow voice, kindly asked me to leave, which I did, falling down the caravan steps prostrate into the parking lot dust.

Joni located me wild-eyed, covered in dirt, reeling around, bouncing off the sides of trailers. She rescued me from further nonsense and ridicule and crammed me in the back seat of the Bentley, returning us to our quaint Isle of Wight guesthouse. Holding my hand over my mouth, I stumbled into our bathroom and puked. I went back into Neil's room, feeling better but still drunk as a loon. He and Joni were playing guitars. Despite his earlier predicament, Elliot was once more armed with an ample quantity of cannabis he rolled into fat joints. I took a toke. *Mistake!* Holding my head by the hair as I retched violently again in Neil's toilet, Joni helped me into the bedroom, stripped off my clothes and left me in bed to sleep it off.

The next morning, I woke up in bed alone feeling like I'd died and had been reborn in hell. *No Joan.* I tidied up a little, brushed my teeth with her toothbrush, washed up with a washcloth, and ran my fingers through my unruly hair like a comb. The shirt I wore last night had vestiges of caked vomit soiling the front, so I put on one of her sweaters. A bit shaky—*dicky on the pins*—holding the banister, I walked down the stairs into the breakfast room. Joni sat alone having tea and scones. She greeted me warmly and kissed me on the cheek. "Did I misbehave?" I inquired. She nodded affirmatively, rolling her eyes.

After a hearty English breakfast ... and a Guiness ... we packed up, hopped in the Bentley and drove to the ferry. On the way back to London, cruising through the South Downs roads and hedged lanes of Sussex, she told me how upset she had been with the whole festival. "Cary, this was a total disaster, from beginning to end. How did I ever get talked into this? Somehow, I suspected things would go wrong." She stopped, turned her head, and looked directly in my face, "But I always think things will go wrong, don't I?"

I raised my eyebrows hesitating to affirm or deny what she said. After a pause, I replied vaguely, "Sometimes you do and sometimes you don't." The rest of our conversation is lost to memory.

When we arrived at the apartment in Knightsbridge, Joni verified that her instrument cases were in the Bentley while her chauffeur retrieved her traveling bags from the concierge. We kissed at the curb and said goodbye. She smiled and waved as her Bentley pulled away from the curb to take her to Heathrow and to a first-class flight back to LA. A flashback: how very different from our cold breakup at LA International weeks ago. I walked over to the Knightsbridge tube station by Harrods and caught a train towards Shepherds Bush to crash on my friends' couch. I intended to hitch hike up the M1, hitch to Laughton, and join Willie at the Croft. I had no idea that the next episode in the Joni Saga was about to begin.

CHAPTER 19

Antinomy of Distance

Les chiens aboient, la caravane passe

The next morning I took the tube over to American Express to check on mail. My plans remained to head back to Laughton, work with Willie on the farm, and figure out what to do next. Exiting American Express, I ran into three South African friends I had known in Greece, Alan, Marie, and Sarah, who had been living in the caves in Matala at the same time as Joni and I. We ducked into a coffee shop to catch up. 'What about Joni?' Asked Marie. "What is she doing? And what are you doing in the UK?" I brought them up to date. They too, had been at the Isle of Wight Festival and said they had a great time. From their point of view, it had been crazy wild and not all that barbaric. *How about that?*

"We are going down to Kent to pick hops. Why don't you join us? Picking hops at Smugley Farm in Goudhurst, can make you a hundred quid in a month."

"Hey! That's a great idea," I affirmed, jotting down the address of Smugley Farm. I noted what trains went to Tunbridge Wells, twelve miles west of Goudhurst. From a public phone booth, I rang Willie in Laughton, leaving a message with Mrs. Hart that I was going to pick hops, and headed down to London Bridge Station to find a train. An hour later I disembarked at the Tunbridge Wells station and asked directions to Goudhurst from the station master, who was reclining in a chair smoking a pipe in his stuffy, smoky office.

"How are you getting there, Young Man," he inquired.

"Walking, Sir," I replied.

"Noooo, Young Man. Walking will take you all day," he said. "Better to flag down a lorry ... or better still ...." He got up, stalked outside the station to shout at a man smoking a cigar slouching on a grey Rover, "Gerry, you are going past Goudhurst, right? Can you take this young man and drop him at The Vine?"

About a half-hour later, Gerry dropped me off at The Vine. All was going according to plan. I asked the publican directions to Smugley Farm. He took me over to the county map on the grimy side wall and drew his finger along the roads that would get me to Smugley's Farm. He told me to walk down Bedgebury Road and I'd run into it. Walking out the door, I got a ride with two Irish freaks in a VW bus who were going to Smugley's. What luck!

Together, we three went into the farmhouse office. A pleasant, middle-aged woman at a desk greeted us and signed us up to work. No problem at all. She gave us an overview of what the farm expected of us and what they offered as pay, meals and a bunk bed. She turned us over to a no-nonsense farm manager who took us out to the yard and pointed out the bunkhouses where we would be living for the month.

"Bunkhouse on the right is for gents," he said, "and the one on the left for ladies." During the month, as we discovered, gender cards got reshuffled, and lots more. In the men's bunkhouse I found a bottom bunk, unrolled my sleeping bag and plopped down my pack. In the mess hall below the bunkhouse, I found my friends from Matala—Marie, Sarah and Alan.

Other travelers arrived during the afternoon. Among a group walking into the mess hall strode an older, tall, and cheerful man with a grey ponytail, confidently greeting everyone. Introducing himself as Wesley Knapp, he confided without pretense he was a veteran hop picker. Wesley carried a regal bearing with a warm informality that made me like him immediately. At 6 p.m., we all gathered in the mess hall to enjoy our first supper together in Smugley Farm—beans, bangers, and mash. Then half of us walked into Goudhurst to The Vine and drank a couple pints of bitter and got to know one another.

Mess hall windows surveyed acre upon wide acre of green vines and hop buds blanketing a network of cables suspended between telephone poles. This was a typical hop farm layout, I was to learn. Also working at Smugley Farm were family members, employees and seasonal workers, mainly several families of Gypsies who lived in caravans on the edge of a wood hidden from view by barns and the conical oast houses, where green hops slowly cured over peat fires. We travelers, about thirty altogether, half men, half women, did the field work while family members, mechanics and Gypsies did the technical work in the sheds, engineering in the machine shop, and managed quality control in the oast houses.

A typical day dawned wet, and wet it stayed during the month even on days when the sun shone through clouds highlighting glistening hop fields and the high black-thorn hedges and wild roses which enclosed them. Finishing breakfast of oatmeal porridge, fried eggs and tomato slices, bacon, bangers, butter, jam, and cold toast, we buttoned into yellow rubber rain suits and knee-high Wellington boots, men and women alike. Yellow storm hats turned up in front, poked out back in a duck's tail, reminded me of whalers in *Moby Dick* illustrations.

Breakfast over, we went to work. Harvesting hops involved a sequence of activities starting with cutting hop vines from the wire grid above the fields and transporting them to the barns. In the barns another crew of workers took over the unloading and stripping operations, conveying hop flowers to the oast houses, where they dried slowly on grates above smoldering peat fires.

When daily work started, tractors hauled trailers out to fields along with two cutters and two men that we called *loaders*. Management informed us that only women drove tractors because men made unreliable drivers, driving recklessly—sometimes intoxicated—whereas women were careful, trustworthy, and sober.

In the spring, farm engineers laid out hop fields with every step of the harvesting process in mind. Horticulturalists cultivated hop vines in raised mounds of four vines, each vine trained onto a string of hemp twine tautly stretched to hooks attached to wire gridworks. As plants matured, growing vines snaked up the twine, producing clusters of maturing sticky hop flowers that dangled down from the gridwork like chandeliers strung up and down long rows across the fields.

The way harvesting hops worked in those days, two cutters ran ahead of the tractor that pulled a special trailer manned by two workers who collected and stacked cut vines in the trailer. Walking ahead of tractor and trailer, cutters severed the vines from their hills and separated them to hang freely like dangling ropes. As a cutter, my job was just that—slicing the vines at knee level with one slash of a hand scythe and with second and third slashes—swoosh, swoosh, swoosh—cutting the twine tying together four vines above the mound until each vine swung independently from the wire grid.

I carried a sharp, curved hand scythe in my right hand and held a tapered rolling pin-size whet stone in the left. That was the cutter's job: approach one hill at a time, three slashes of the scythe, walk ahead five paces to the next cluster of vines, repeating the inveterate procedure again and again frequently in light rain and fog, which made cutting appear like a dreamy scene from a Hiroshige painting. Our rubber boots went squish, squish, slogging through wet grass under the vines.

Directly behind us, the tractor and attached trailer crept through the swinging vines. Loading vines, which I did on alternative days, meant cooperating with your fellow loader. A loader stood on each side at the front of the moving trailer. He seized a vine by the butt end as it draped slowly across his shoulders and jammed it down between two upright steel posts attached to the trailer floor. He held the end of the vine against the upright post until the momentum of the tractor broke the twine from the grid, freeing the vines to fall into the trailer bed one after another until it was filled like a heap of green spaghetti.

"Okay! Done! Full!" loaders shouted at the tractor driver and jumped off the back. The driver drove the tractor and loaded trailer across the fields to the processing barn. Harvesting continued through morning and afternoon. A very efficient operation—and it had to be—because the hop season was short, all hops had to be harvested, processed, and dried before they fully matured and flowered.

I walked down to the barns to observe next steps in the process, stripping, sorting, and drying. As a tractor drew a loaded trailer of hop vines into the barn, it pulled up under the stripping station, unhitched the trailer, and drove through to the other end of the barn where it stopped to hitch up an empty trailer and haul it back to the field. Above the stripping station, a running train of hooks and cables whirred overhead. Two men—one was usually Wesley—climbed on the trailer full of vines and alternatively lifted each vine out from between the steel poles and raised it to gangs of hooks running above, which peeled the vine off the trailer. After unloaders emptied the trailer, another tractor immediately pulled in with a full trailer to repeat the process.

Meanwhile, the train of hooks fed the line of swinging vines into the mouth of a machine that stripped the vines of their leaves and hop buds and dropped them onto a vibrating conveyor belt, which shook the loose leaves from the belt leaving only the heavier hop buds. Workers bagged and carted green hops over to the oast houses to be dried and cured. And so it went on, hop harvesting day after day in August and September in the hop fields, barns, and oast houses of Smugley Farm, Goudhurst, Kent, and all the other hop farms in the county.

We seasonal workers got to know one another. Wesley became our unappointed leader. He possessed a senior air of confidence and his constant cheerfulness drew us to him. In evenings when we did not go to The Vine in Goudhurst to join crowds of pickers from other nearby farms to drink beer in the streets, we gathered in Smugley Farm bunkhouses.

The publican at The Vine said the cider from nearby Frogs Hole Farm was the best around. He said we could buy it in casks from the proprietor, Bob Luck. The next rainy afternoon, several of us went to buy cider at Frog's Hole Farm. Following the publican's hand-drawn map, we drove in drizzling rain a dozen miles east on Sissinghurst Road toward Biddenden. At a signpost, we took a right turn down an unpaved lane, and ran right into our target, Frogs Hole Farm. We could tell we had arrived because wooden cider barrels of all sizes lay strewn haphazardly in fields surrounding the cider works. When we pulled up our van in front of the farmhouse, a stout older man in overalls with a black umbrella shuffled out to greet us, Bob Luck, proprietor of Frogs Hole Farm. Old Bob had a ruddy complexion and a red bulbous nose straight out of Charles Dickens illustrations. A jovial man, he welcomed us into the barn and sold us a ten-gallon wooden barrel of cider with a tap. "You should try some of my special vintage," he chuckled, motioning with his thumb to shelves of gallon bottles. "It's very good," he giggled, "and very strong."

We thanked Bob Luck and drove back to Smugley Farm with our treasure. In the mudroom outside the dormitory, we installed the barrel of cider on two sawhorses, screwed in the tap and offered it to all. It was a *rough* cider, very dry and more potent than commercial, semi-sweet, bottled cider.

Clustered in the bunkhouse, downing tumblers of Frogs Hole Farm cider, we circled Wesley and plotted ways to introduce social changes to Smugley Farm—fair labor practices and healthier food. Yes, there must be equal pay for women. Yes, we want brown rice at lunch to supplement potatoes. These were the tough policies we advocated. Wesley and two women on our team took our grievances up to the farmhouse. Without hesitation, Smugley management agreed to our demands on the spot. Collective bargaining at its best.

Wesley urged us to consider hop picking as a sport, and to master it, he pitched, we needed to practice the art of teamwork. And it worked. The harder and smarter we worked, the more fun we had. Smugley management told us we were doing a great job. At the end of the harvest season, we were like a family, or a football team. Disbanding our closely knit team and parting ways was sad.

Each of us had earned a hundred pounds sterling for a month's work. A few of the crew were crossing the channel to France to harvest grapes in the *vendange*, the wine harvest. A hundred quid was plenty, I figured, to fund overland passage to India and back over the next year if I lived the frugal life of a sadhu, ate chapattis, curry and fresh fruit, wore gauze pajamas, and slept on the floors of temples.

Immediate plans to head East got postponed when Wesley invited Charles and me to join him at a farm in Worcestershire to finish the hop season there. Wesley, through his network of contacts, had already lined up a job with a mandate to recruit more casual workers. On the train, we learned that the farm where we were going grew Guinness hops, which had a later season than Fuggles, which Smugley Farm grew. Fuggles were a smaller and more delicate hop than the hearty, sticky, late-maturing Guinness hops.

A far smaller enterprise than Smugley Farm, the Worcester farm was organized differently. Instead of bunkhouses, Wesley, Charlie, and I slept on cots in an upstairs room in the main farmhouse. The three of us worked alongside the farm family and several families of Gypsies, and this time, we had no jolly teamwork as at Smugley Farm, and no female co-workers, although everyone was kind and happy to have us aboard.

During the first week, Wesley and I cut and loaded hops to trailers in the fields, similar to the operations we had mastered at Smugley Farm. We then took on other jobs on the farm, mostly working around the oast house—called in Worcester, *the kilns*—moving heavy hemp bags of fresh hops from a conveyor belt over to the kiln station. Although I missed being out in the fields, cutting and loading hops, here in the Worcester farm I got to learn more about hop farming, and got to be part of a close family operation. We dined at the family table at lunch and dinner. Beef, Yorkshire pudding, potatoes, and gravy. No brown rice.

After three weeks, the Worcester farm earned us eighty pounds apiece and we returned to London. Now I felt financially secure. Wesley bid me farewell and broke off to join his sons on a farm near Oxford. I took a train up to Market Harborough where I resumed work at the Croft, which I had left when I went to Isle of Wight Festival and then to Smugley Farm.

Besides working around sheep and cows on Willie's dad's farm in Laughton—cleaning stables, washing out the milking rooms, digging a garden, laying out a concrete driveway—Willie and I hauled hay for a neighboring farmer whom Willie affectionately called Squid. Squid, or "Squiddy," resembled another stock image of an avuncular Mr. Pickwick. From the field, we walked behind a creeping truck to toss heavy hay bales up on the truck bed, where two farm employees grabbed them and stacked them to be restacked in Squiddy's barns. I swore these Leicestershire bales of hay seemed twice as heavy as the hay bales I had hauled in North Carolina as a boy.

In chilly, foggy mornings, we walked out to the fields dressed in woolens and coats, and by noon we would be unloading the truck in the barn and stacking bales in the loft, stripped to the waist, sweating, skin coated with the itching powder of dried hay. At 4 p.m., Mrs. Hart brought tea to the field. In the evening, after a quick sponge bath and supper, Willie, Chris and I drove over to local pubs where Willie was well known.

Off and on we went round to the dairy to help Fred clean up stalls after milking. We roamed around the pasture and cast sheep—flipping over those that had fallen on their backs and were too heavy to stand up. We always ended up having a smoke in the tool room, a great place to dry out on wet days. The low-ceiling tool room had walls stained dark by smoke and it stank of cattle feed and sour milk.

Some of Willie's wild tales I had heard before in pubs, yet he kept modifying stories, or characters, or locales, as if he were practicing lines for a play. Which he was, of course, because whether in a pub, or in a barn, or in a drawing room, or in the tool room of the dairy, Willie was always on stage. He continuously fiddled with a corncob pipe, filling, tamping, lighting, knocking out ashes on his boot in a rhythm to punctuate his stories—the pipe, a theatrical prop.

Shortly after arriving in England in August, I took up rolling my own cigarettes. Cheaper than Marlboroughs, rolling cigarettes was a skill. I kept rolling papers inside my tobacco tin. Between pipe smoke and cigarette smoke, and smoke from the woodstove, the tool room could become as claustrophobic as a smokehouse filled with hams. Fred didn't smoke but he never complained about our smoking.

Willie Gilbertson Hart and Cary Raditz in the Laughton Dairy, October 1970. Photo by Frankie Bingley.

Willie Gilbertson-Hart, Bonkers, Cary, Laughton, Leicestershire, October 1970.

Fred's nephew, Frankie, regularly helped us haul Squiddy's hay. An educated photographer, Frankie found it hard to find enough photography work around Market Harborough to keep him busy although he took commercial commissions in London photographing real estate properties. One day while taking snapshots of Willie and me horsing around with Bonkers outside the milking room, Frankie mentioned he had a gig in London tomorrow and would not be here to help with the hay. I asked if I could ride with him. It was an opportunity to visit my friends, see a play in the West End, and pick up mail at American Express. I could easily hitchhike back to Market Harborough. Ready for any eventuality—I thought about how unexpectedly the Isle of Wight festival and hop picking had popped out of the existential woodwork—I carried my hucklebag and backpack along with me.

Frankie dropped me off by a tube station in a light industrial zone of warehouses in north London. At American Express, I picked up two pieces of mail, a letter from my parents, and another handwritten note from Elliot Roberts, dated the previous day. Elliot wrote, "I am at the Warner Brothers apartment in Knightsbridge. Call this number when you pick this up. Joni is here, too, and she wants to see you. I want to talk to you about managing my farm."

Exiting the phone booth, I hailed a cab and went right to the apartment. Elliot opened the door, dressed in a plaid checked shirt and jeans, worn out at the knees. Inside the vestibule sat a brown leather suitcase and the same Halliburton briefcase we had come to know so well. Elliot shook my hand, pulling me into a surprise hug and led me into the giant kitchen. "Here's the thing, Joan wants you to join her at the London Palladium theater this evening. Here's ten pounds for a taxi. Show starts at 7 p.m. Show up at the ticket window at about 6 p.m. Your name will be on the guest list, along with a note from Joan."

"Oh, yeah, the other thing I mentioned, Cary, involves helping me manage my farm in the Santa Cruz mountains. I fly up about every other weekend, and I would like you to take care of the place while I am gone. By the way, it is adjacent to Neil's farm."

He glanced at his watch, "I got to split. Go meet Joan at the Palladium. I'll talk to you more about the farm when you get back to the States." I helped him with his bag into the hall. The elevator opened and closed. We descended to the vestibule and the doorman opened the front door to a waiting taxicab. Elliot was gone.

Outside on the sidewalk, I stopped. *What does he mean about "when you get back to the States?" I have no plans to return to the states for a long time. If ever.*

From Knightsbridge, I took the tube over to my friends' house in Shepherds Bush to drop my pack with them, figuring I'd be back there in the evening. Katie and John were in the parlor watching television. *Why squander ten quid on a taxi?* Instead of taking a cab to the Palladium, I decided to pocket the ten pounds, and for a few pence, take the tube to Oxford Circus Station, and walk over two blocks to the Palladium. It was almost 5 p.m.

The marquee read, "James Taylor: Tonight, Sunday 25 October." *A James Taylor concert? Why did Joan ask me to meet her here?* Since I was early, I ducked into the closest pub and ordered barley wine and a shot of whiskey. Realizing the peril of drinking on an empty stomach, I bought a cone of cockles and whelks from a girl hawking them on the sidewalk and ate them at the pub bar with a Scotch egg. *Have to be careful, especially given my drunken debacle at the Isle of Wight Festival.*

At 6 p.m., as Elliot had instructed me, I walked back over to the Palladium. It was almost dark. *Must be early. No queue, no crowd, no one around but me.* Sure enough, the ticket booth guy found my name on the guest list, and handed me a folded piece of paper marked, "Carey."

The note read: "When you arrive, tell them to ring me backstage. I'll meet you in the lobby. Joni."

The ticket guy picked up his phone, and within minutes Joni walked into the lobby. She looked great. She wore a long sweater like the one she had knitted in Matala. We kissed.

"Cary, I have something to tell you that may upset you."

"What is it, Joan?"

"I've fallen for James Taylor. I wanted to tell you face to face, otherwise I feared you would avoid me and not come down. Are you okay with this?"

"Sure. It seems you finally came to your senses, displaying good taste in boyfriends, Joan." She laughed and hugged me.

"I was hoping you wouldn't freak out. How about we see his concert? Cool venue, The London Palladium," she said, taking my hand, leading me into the empty auditorium to the orchestra, a few rows back from the stage.

"Joan, you know I knew James from Chapel Hill, which is only a small town. Remember last summer when I tacked his photograph from the *Sweet Baby James* album on the wall above your piano?"

"Yep, that was a little cheeky."

"Yeah, cheeky maybe, but prescient, too, as it turns out. When I had the Other Ear Gallery, I knew lots of artists in Chapel Hill—painters, sculptors, writers, musicians ... James was just another local musician at the time. When his first album came out with the song, 'Carolina In My Mind,' Chapel Hill went bananas. And then, *Sweet Baby James*. Wow."

In singles, couples and groups, people began filing in and taking seats. Joni brought me up to date on what she had been doing since the Isle of Wight Festival, working on a new album. She spoke of meeting James again, getting up with him on his movie set in New Mexico. I told her about picking hops in Kent and Wooster. The house was now full.

Lights dimmed, curtains opened, the band was set up on stage, and James walked into the spotlight, armed with his guitar. He sang "Fire and Rain" and "Carolina in My Mind." I turned to Joni, "He's really good." She squeezed my arm.

At the end of the set, Joni stood up and said, "Let's go backstage." We brushed past the security guard at the stairs on stage left.

In the green room, James sat on a chair tuning several guitars, chatting with the drummer. He stood up and greeted Joni with a warm hug, and shook my hand, "Hi Cary. I'm happy to see you again. Thanks for coming. Will you be sticking around after the show?" he asked, looking over his shoulder at Joni, who nodded *yes*. We chatted about Chapel Hill, mutual friends, familiar places, trying to figure out where we had first met (not sure), the Tempo Room? Harry's? The Carolina Coffee Shop? The Other Ear Gallery? Had we met at parties on farms?

While Joni was talking to other people, I told James about picking hops. "That is fascinating." I told him briefly about Matala where I met Joni and the caves in Crete. "That is so cool," he said. "Joni told me a lot, but I want to know more." From the wings, Joni and I drank wine as we watched his second set, equally impressive as the first. After he took his second encore, the curtains closed and as the audience stood up and were leaving the theater, James handed his guitar to a roadie, and said, "Let's get outta here, while the getting is good!"

We went out through the stage door, where a plain black limousine waited. Joni said, "Cary, come over and stay with us at the apartment. The place is enormous as you know and no one else will be there except the roadies, the cook, the maid, and us.

"Will you come?" she asked me again, as James opened the door to the limo, and practically threw me inside. *Well, this is pretty weird, but what the hell, looks like I've been kidnapped.*

In light traffic, we arrived shortly in Knightsbridge. Although I had been here before, I hadn't had a chance to roam around the flat. *This place is enormous.* We congregated in the kitchen. The stove area was unique; I loved it immediately. Six large chem-lab burners on flexible cables occupied the top of a heavy oaken table, about three by six feet, with enamel gas cocks on the side and a deep exhaust hood above it all. A large stock pot of chicken soup was simmering on top of three burners, which the cook had pushed together. Ingenious. James opened the door to the walk-in refrigerator and asked us, "What's your pleasure? Wine, beer, or cider?"

Joni said, "Wine. White, please."

I said, "Cider."

James came out with a bottle of Muscadet, and a liter bottle of Woodpecker cider. "I'll join you on the cider," he said, opening the wine with a corkscrew. He poured Joni a glass. He popped open the cider and poured each of us a glass. "Skol!" we three clicked glasses and toasted the Palladium show.

Roadies were drinking beer and smoking weed, which they offered but we declined. I rolled a cigarette with Golden Virginia. James asked if I would please roll one for him. What a polite Southern gentleman. Joni pulled out her guitar and sat down on a chair, tuning it. The bass player unpacked his standing bass.

And so began a late evening of music and drinking until James said, "I'm exhausted. And drunk, too." He and Joni bid me *goodnight* and told me to stay here with them while they were in London. *I don't know where all this is leading, but I'm on for the ride.* James led Joni down a hall. I went to the bedroom they had shown me, stripped off my clothes, and took a shower in the adjoining bathroom, which felt wonderful, as I had not fully bathed in days. In the cabinet were razors and toothbrushes like in a hotel. The bed was soft, the down comforter, warm.

The next morning, I awoke to Mozart and the smell of coffee. I took another hot shower and washed my hair—a luxury. *Ah, yes. This is the way to live!* In Laughton, to bathe, Willie, Chris and I went to a public bathhouse in Market Harborough, where bathtubs had small water heaters you had to feed with one-shilling coins.

In the kitchen, the cook, a young lady with a long, dark pigtail, was preparing pancakes. The roadies asked me to join them at the breakfast table. After pancakes and coffee, I rang Willie at the Croft, told him the story of Elliot's offer, about Joni and James's concert at the Palladium, how I was kidnapped and explained to Willie the unusual circumstances that detained me. "I am not sure when I will get back to The Croft."

He said, "Sounds good, Cosy. Congratulations on the job. Hay is practically done here. Frankie is back and we won't miss your strong back," he joked. "See you in the sweet by and by."

Finishing coffee and pancakes, I left James and Joni sleeping late, and took a train over to Shepherds Bush to retrieve my backpack from my friends' place. "Where have you been?" demanded Katie, opening the door. "We were expecting you last night. Why didn't you ring? We thought you might have fallen off the end of the earth or been kidnapped."

"I was kidnapped."

I laid out the whole story: Elliot, Joni at James's concert at the Palladium, and my surprise guest status at Warner Brother's apartment in Knightsbridge. "Sorry for not ringing you. It's all sort of weird? Incredible, yeah?"

"I'll say," said Katie. "Weird, good."

"I'll just go with the flow. Better by a long shot than mucking out stables and hauling hay and fixing fences in the rain in Leicestershire."

Days ahead seemed to blur into one: moving around London in limos, record company offices, drunken music business lunches and social dinners. On 29 October, the BBC filmed Joni at the Paris Theater singing and playing guitar, dulcimer and piano. I sat on a back row and enjoyed the show as James accompanied her on a long set. Before playing "Carey," she introduced me as a friend "... from Matala, London, Los Angeles, and North Carolina ...." She described Matala—more or less accurately—calling out to me in the audience asking if I knew how many people lived there.

Joni and James invited me to join them at Peter Asher's wedding, a civil ceremony with bride, groom, bride's maids and ushers in fancy morning dress, black coats, white ascots, pin striped trousers. As we arrived at the wedding on the steps of a grand municipal building with fluted, white Corinthian columns, who comes striding up the steps behind us but Manfred Mann in a black leather jacket and sunglasses as if he had just stepped off of the cover of his record album. He hugged Joni and James and nodded politely to me. *Wow, Mr. "Do Wah Diddy" hisself.*

Peter Asher played a central role in the London music scene and in James's career, producing at Apple Studios James's first album in 1968. *Is Peter still James's manager ... ?* I didn't ask many questions in this swirling London of record executives and strangers. In this flux, I surrendered to the flow of activities, well lubricated with Woodpecker Cider and Calvados. Often Joni would bow out before midnight and go to bed, leaving James and me to visit late-night pubs and hotel bars.

Complicated regulations governed opening and closing times of pubs in various London neighborhoods, but if you knew where you were going— cab drivers always knew—you could find someplace to drink any time of the day or night. James introduced me to Strega, a great, late-night digestive. Among all the folks he could hang out with in London, among friends and colleagues in the music business, why he chose me as company was a question I never posed. *Do you ask friends why you are their friend?*

James and I got along well as if we had known each other a long time. In a way, I was more at ease with him than with Joni, whose moods seemed less predictable, more mercurial. *Does Carolina bond us somehow?* In another surprise—as I prepared to return to Laughton—Joni and James asked me to fly to New York with them. It was all a puzzle. Had Elliot already prearranged this sojourn with Joni and James when I met with him in London? I figured the management company was most likely picking up the tab. *What do I have to lose? If I work on Elliot's ranch, I will have income when I get there. What's the risk?* After all, I could always go back to Crete or head to

India where I could live for next to nothing. Therefore, to avoid courting indigence, I responded affirmatively: "Sure!"

※ ※ ※

We flew business class to New York. We settled into two rooms in the Albert Hotel on the corner of 10th Street and University Place, a few blocks uptown from Washington Square Park, and a block south of Cedar Tavern, an old hangout for artists and communists. Like the Cedar Tavern, the Albert had its fill of musicians, secrets, writers, animosities and artists of all sorts.

The next morning, I dressed, threw my hucklebag over my shoulder, knocked on their door and told them I was going out for a while. "Where?" they asked.

"To visit my grandmother, Henrietta Raditz. She lives several blocks away on the corner of 8th Street and 6th Avenue. MomMom was a concert pianist before she gave up her career to marry my grandfather, Lazar Raditz, a portrait painter."

"Really!" they said. "May we come with you?"

"Well, I'm sure she'd enjoy the company of young musicians."

I rang MomMom to ask if I could bring along my friends. She said, "By all means." Joni and James followed me out the door and into the elevator, carrying guitar cases, and we walked three long blocks over. At her door, MomMom, gracious as always, and elegant in a silk Japanese kimono, which she wore on special occasions, greeted us and invited us in. Joni and James surveyed her walls covered with paintings, landscapes and portraits—many by my grandfather—19th century Japanese Utamaro prints, along with fine furniture, Chinese vases, and porcelains. MomMom served us tea and ramekins of flan, my lifelong favorite. They asked her about her life, and why she had given up the piano.

"Two artists under the same roof makes for an uncomfortable home," she said. Joni glanced at James. They smiled at each other, raising their eyebrows. "One of us had to compromise," she continued, "and it was me. Of course, Lazar was famous among Philadelphia and New York portrait patrons, and earned far more in a month than I ever could in a lifetime. Lazar liked to be the center of attention and that was fine for me, as I am by nature rather shy, and I didn't mind playing second fiddle as his wife. And then there was the matter of children, Violetta first, and then Albert, Cary's father. I became a mother."

James asked, "Would it please you if we played a few of our songs for you?"

"Oh yes, it would please me very much."

They removed their guitars from cases, tuned them by ear, and sitting across from one another, faced MomMom and me, and played, "You've got a friend," and "Chelsea Morning."

"Here's a song I wrote for Cary in Crete on his birthday," said Joni. "I composed it on a mountain dulcimer, so I may mangle it on the guitar," she giggled. She adjusted the tuning. "James, you know the melody?" He nodded. As they played it, MomMom turned her head and smiled at me. I could do nothing but grin.

They played a few more songs. MomMom and I clapped. As they began putting their guitars away, they told her how much they enjoyed meeting her. MomMom rose, and said, "Excuse me a moment, please, I have something for you." She returned with several sheets of music and a manila envelope. "When I was a young woman, before Lazar and I got engaged, I composed this piece. The lyrics come from a poem by William Blake, whom I was very fond of. I'd like you two to have this, and may I dedicate it to you?" They nodded. She went over to a desk and signed it, "To Joni and James from Henrietta Herman Raditz. Thank you for my private concert." I kissed MomMom goodbye, and she kissed the cheeks of James and Joni.

We left. It turned out that this afternoon with Joni and James at MomMom's apartment would be the last time I saw my grandmother alive. MomMom died a few months later when I was in California, overseeing Elliot's ranch.

※ ※ ※

From the Albert Hotel, we embarked on a tour of college campuses, concluding with a concert at Princeton on November 7, where James performed together with Joni. The next day, we moved to the Plaza Hotel facing Central Park South, a giant step up from the Albert. After a late dinner following the Princeton concert, Joni told us she wished to turn in. James and I took a taxi up to a bar around 80th Street and 3rd Avenue, which James described as one of his favorite hangouts in Manhattan. Apparently, this bar, whose name I forget, was a favorite of other musicians, too.

As we walked in from the street, Al Kooper came up to James, gave him a hug, and escorted us back to his table. They discussed people, music business, light gossip. I couldn't resist: "Not to flatter you, Al, but your penny flute on 'Highway 61 Revisited' flips me out every time I hear it." Al took a shallow bow. James was now rolling his own cigarettes, too—Golden Virginia in a tin that he had brought back from London. We did not stay long and wished Al goodnight.

Under the Plaza's sumptuous sheets, I fell asleep almost at once. As dawn came through my window, I awoke from a bizarre, fading dream: I split off from a group of people with whom I am living communally, to conduct an important secret mission of some sort. To fund this portentous mission, my dream-self opens a large file drawer in a heavy oak desk, a file drawer filled with bank notes. The observer watches the dream-me distractedly withdrawing handfuls of $100 bills and stuffing them in his pocket as if it were no big deal, the mind intently focused on my single purpose: to track down an item that curiously looked like a silver Dr. Scholl's foot pad inscribed with Chinese characters.

How utterly weird! The dream faded as I became awake and lucid. First, the nature of the mission—*what could that silver footpad mean*? All that money, and how I handled it so nonchalantly, as if it meant nothing at all? *What was that all about?* In the real, non-dreamworld, I was a poor tramp.

Far more ironic indeed would have been a dream of my looking through a crystal ball, seeing myself fifteen years down the road, ten blocks south and two blocks east of the Plaza, stepping out of a limousine in front of the Waldorf Astoria, dressed in a dark suit befitting a Park Avenue banker—which I was to become—managing hundreds of millions of dollars, which I would eventually do. Such is the stuff of bizarre dreams and fruits of a bizarre, unplanned life.

From the Plaza, Joni, James, and I flew to Boston and from there took a commuter plane out to Martha's Vineyard, where James had been going all his life with his family, and where he was now building himself a house in the woods. We took rooms in a modest motel. James's new house had a roof, plywood floors, no walls but studs. In what was designated the living room, sat a table saw and boxes of tools. Heavy duty electrical cords and junction boxes threaded through doorways and walls like orange snakes.

We had supper with James's older brother, Alex, his wife, Brent, and his son, James, of the eponymous song, "Sweet Baby James." James's sister, Kate, dropped by Alex's to have dinner with us. Hearing James was back, neighbors began dropping by to say hello. One close neighbor, who was building his own house, had a sixteen-year-old wife with an infant son in her arms. James led Joni and me into the woods where another friend had constructed a simple, one-room framed cabin, about 12 x 16 feet, in a forest clearing. Most of James's friends seemed to be local contractors, tradesmen, and craftsmen, people who lived in Martha's Vineyard all year long. This was no gated community, just a bunch of friends building their homes close to one another in the woods. I gathered that this community of family, aspiring artists and craftsmen kept James grounded. Celebrity is a tough row to hoe, as some in Carolina might say.

Then Elliot arrived. We picked him up at the little Martha's Vineyard airport and he took a room at the motel where we were staying. As Joni's manager, it was no surprise he would check in on her, but he seemed more distant and less amicable now compared to our last meeting in London a few weeks earlier. *Was Elliot uncomfortable with my close friendship with James and Joni?*

A little while later, Elliot took me aside. "Cary, I have to tell you, Joni and James feel crowded by your constant presence. Your being here all the time is awkward for them."

"Is that so, Elliot?" I responded, taken aback, since Joni and James had invited me to be with them each step of the way. "Is that the way they feel? Did they tell you to tell me that?" I asked. *Am I deluded?*

He shook his head, "Just look at the situation, Cary."

Returning to my room ... I looked at the situation. Should I take what Elliot said at face value? Joni was perfectly capable and willing to say, "Cary get out of here, you are in the way!" She had already kicked me out of her house months ago in Los Angeles. But, yes, it could look odd—three of us traveling around together—two popular musicians along with Joni's ex-boyfriend-vagabond-tramp. *What do I care what people think?* Then I had a revelation.

Had they invited me to hang out with them because my presence might divert attention from their budding, celebrity romance, which Elliot seemed so intent to foster? My suspicions fixed on the question, *Why did they invite me to hang out with them in London, New York and now here in Martha's Vineyard? Huh?* Did I provide a buffer to deflect public curiosity when their relationship was far from settled? "Or maybe," I thought, "they simply liked my company and considered me a mutual friend?" I didn't feel all that attractive.

Although I was skeptical of Elliot's idea, that I was somehow upsetting the apple cart, getting in the way of a celebrity relationship of grand proportions; nonetheless, I had to admit that he might be right. I could not deny that Elliot, who certainly had known Joni long before I showed up, might have a point. I made up my mind. No need to discuss it further; it was time for me to pack up and move along.

I joined Joni and James in the motel coffee shop for breakfast. I told them I was leaving.

After breakfast, Elliot inquired, "Cary, where are you having Thanksgiving?"

"In Chapel Hill," I said. "I have friends there and will probably go from Chapel Hill to your ranch."

"How are you traveling to California?"

"Overland."

Elliot handed me two crisp $100 bills. "An advance against your salary," he said. "Meet me at my ranch. Here's my address and phone numbers." I pocketed the bills.

A bit later, when Elliot was in his room, I asked James if he and Joni would be celebrating Thanksgiving in the Vineyard. "Nope. In Chapel Hill," he said. "As usual, it will be a big family affair."

This is weird. We are all heading to Chapel Hill. Wouldn't you just know it? Here I was ready to abandon our fellowship, and ironically, it turns out we will all be passing holidays in Chapel Hill.

"Where are you going for Thanksgiving?" James asked.

"I'll probably be in Chapel Hill, too," I said awkwardly.

"Call us when you get there," said James, writing down a phone number and an address. "This is the home phone. My mom likes to be called *Trudy*; my dad is *Ike*."

"Sure," I said, sticking the note in my wallet. "Look forward to seeing you two down there." James's invitation made me feel like a legitimate friend again, not just a peripatetic bum. I would call them in Chapel Hill, I decided; nevertheless, I would give them a wide berth at Thanksgiving.

After lunch I took Elliot aside and told him about their invitation, affirming, "Elliot, I did not cook this up. As you suggested, I do intend to keep my distance from them during the holidays."

He said, "I think that's best."

Elliot ordered my airline tickets from Martha's Vineyard to Boston, from there to the Raleigh Durham airport. The brief saga of Joni, James and Cary dissolved. We broke up. The next day I flew south.

※ ※ ※

At the Raleigh Durham Airport, Scott Bradley picked me up and drove me to his farmhouse—Jenkin's Farm—near Chapel Hill. On the eve of Thanksgiving, I dialed James at his parents' home. The home phone must have rung ten times. A woman's voice answered and I introduced myself. "Hi. Is this Mrs. Taylor? This is Cary Raditz, a friend of James and Joni."

"Hi Cary, I know who you are. Please call me *Trudy*, everyone else does. James said you might call. He just flew in from California, and Joni is expected tonight. Unfortunately, James's friends have dragged him away to a party. It never stops. Are you coming over?"

I replied, reluctantly, "Thank you, Mrs. Taylor ... I mean *Trudy* ... but no. I don't want to disturb them; I spent weeks this fall with James and Joni in England, New York and Martha's Vineyard. They've probably had enough of me in one serving," I joked. "I just called today to wish them a Happy Thanksgiving."

"How thoughtful of you, Cary. Too much of you in one serving? Ha! I'm sure that's not true at all. They told me lots about you and I know they would love to see you. Will you reconsider and join us for Thanksgiving dinner tomorrow?"

"That's a kind invitation, Trudy, but I sincerely wish to give them a break to relax at home with family and old friends. At any rate, Mrs. Taylor ... *Trudy* ... I'll be in California soon and I'm sure we will get together there. Have an excellent family Thanksgiving. Please give them my love."

"Yes, I will, Cary. How can James reach you?" I gave her Scott's telephone number at Jenkin's Farm. "I will let James and Joni know you called." We rang off.

On Thanksgiving Day Scott and I drove through campus on Cameron Avenue. Most students had gone home for the holiday. Only a few people could be seen walking in McCorkle Place near the Old Well. While I adored the campus robed in autumn's pallet of red and gold, most of all I loved the old campus by South Building in the springtime. As we drove past Coker Arboretum, thinking of spring, I remembered a special ceremony in the lower Arboretum in May 1969 when flowers and sweet-smelling blossoms blanketed the campus. The administration was commemorating officially Dick Kinnaird's relief sculpture created in tribute to Thomas Wolfe's novel, *Look Homeward Angel*. As officials untied the cords, drapes shrouding the sculpture fell away to reveal an angelic figure emerging from stone, its head cocked back looking behind as stylized wings bore the stone spirit forward.

Today on Thanksgiving, I reflected, "How does my own life resemble this stone figure, looking back while moving ahead?" Like the Thomas Wolfe angel, I had returned to the Old Well where this journey began three years ago in summer of 1967, the "Summer of Love," when the Other Ear was conceived.

CHAPTER 20

The Empty Cup

After thanksgiving Scott and I put Chapel Hill in the rear-view mirror. As we drove west on Interstate 40 to Nashville, the car radio picked up the perfect John Loudermilk tune:

But that's just my life out on Interstate 40 but I'm a happy son of a gun,
The governments givin' me Interstate 40 and the good Lord's give me a thumb

Loudermilk might be happy hitchhiking Interstate 40, but thinking back to when I hitchhiked across Germany, I was grateful to be driving it with Scott. In Nashville we kipped with fraternity brother Joe Ledbetter for a night, and the next day pushed across the Midwest to stay with Scott's friends in Boulder who worked in the notorious restaurant, Magnolia Thunder Pussy. Five years later, Scott and these Thunder Pussy reprobates would appear on Broadway in *Diamond Studs, The Life of Jesse James*.

On day three, Interstate 80 took us straight up to Rawlins, Wyoming, where we crossed the Great Divide. We turned north on US 287 and drove a couple of hours until we entered the Wind River Range. Our destination was Lander, Wyoming, and NOLS—the National Outdoor Leadership School—where Scott had taught wilderness survival training. We took a room in a simple motel. It was cold.

Two days later when we arrived in the East Bay, we went directly to Deward's in Essex Street to shower and crash. Deward was in good form. Over oatmeal the next morning, he made me spit out, step-by-step, the history of my comings and goings since June, when he and Jenny had waved Joni and me *Godspeed* as we left San Francisco driving south.

We had crossed the Bay Bridge and were driving down the Peninsula toward the Santa Cruz mountains when Scott turned his head and smiled at me, "Let's make a slight detour. I have a treat for you." In Redwood City he pulled up directly in front of the Whole Earth Catalog store, the Bay Area counterculture equivalent of F.A.O. Swartz. I remembered the kind airline steward who lent me his Whole Earth Catalog when I was flying from Athens to California last summer. Scott bought me a Christmas present, a hand tool gizmo to remove the tops of glass bottles and wine jugs to make drinking glasses.

Leaving Redwood City, we drove up Route 35, the two-laned Skyline Boulevard into the Santa Cruz Mountains above Mountain View. Following a road map and Elliot's instructions, we turned onto his unmarked driveway as dusk began to fall. The road took us through majestic groves of mature redwoods interrupted by fenced-in pastureland, and further down, foggy ravines of bay laurel and eucalyptus. On the horizon red rays reflected over the Pacific coastal range. Sitting high on a raised foundation of redwood blocks, Elliot's farmhouse looked out over pastures on one side and deep eucalyptus canyons on the other.

Walking up to the front porch we pulled a thumbtacked note off the door—

Cary if you get here before we do, please come in, help yourself to food in cupboard. Beer in the fridge. Sleep on a cot in the living room. Elliot.

We opened the front door and saw the bedroom door ajar, surprising Elliot in a state of undress with an equally unclad blond lady. He closed the bedroom door and yelled, "Cary, please wait a moment while we get dressed, I'll be right out!" In a minute, he emerged with the lady. They wore matching striped bathrobes.

I stuck out my hand to Elliot and he pulled me into an awkward hug. I apologized for intruding. Elliot returned the apology, "I completely forgot to remove the note from the front door. Gloria, meet Cary, and ... "

Whereupon I introduced Scott: "Elliot, Gloria ... my good friend, Scott. We drove out together from North Carolina." Elliot shook Scott's hand. Gloria shook our hands too, then stood off to the side, smiling and quiet.

Elliot took my arm and pulled me aside. We talked about Joni, "She's fine. And James, too. They are at her place in Laurel Canyon. Give her a call, Cary."

"You guys take the cots here in the living room," he said, pointing to camp cots stacked against the wall. He opened a cedar trunk and showed us folded blankets and patchwork quilts. "Please excuse the mess," pointing at stacked lumber and tools. "We're gonna start remodeling as soon as we get all the building permits approved. Tomorrow I'll introduce you to Brian Benson who manages Neil's ranch next door. The bathroom is just off the kitchen," he pointed. "Now, please excuse us. Gloria and I are beat, and we are going back to bed. Let's talk in the morning." They retreated into the bedroom and closed the door. Ignoring the chest of blankets, Scott and I unrolled our sleeping bags on the canvas cots, threw our clothes on chairs, and although it was still early fell right asleep.

Next morning Elliot greeted us in jeans and a plaid cowboy shirt. Gloria followed him into the living room dressed in Hollywood casual fashion *du jour*: a fringed leather jacket over a tie-died t-shirt, and torn, embroidered jeans that clung to her like a second skin. Like Elliot, she wore fancy snakeskin boots.

After a less-than-hearty breakfast of Frosted Flakes and skim milk, Scott and I followed Elliot's rental car over the hill to Neil's ranch where he introduced us to Brian. That done, Scott said goodbye and drove off, saying that I could contact him at John Whisnant's in Berkeley.

I drove Elliot and Gloria to the airport and returned to Neil's ranch in the rental car. Brian and I kicked back, shot the shit, and got to know each other better. "Brian, it's pretty isolated here in the pastures among cows, redwoods and eucalyptus ravines. What do you do for amusement around the ranch?"

"Amusement around the ranch? I read a lot. Watch TV. Listen to music," he said, turning to the long shelf of LPs lining the wall and a bank of professional stereo equipment and speakers. "There are cowboy bars nearby in Mountain View and Redwood City, and around Palo Alto, bars chock full of college girls from Stanford. I like old bars with pool tables and pinball machines, the ones with old ranchers, drunk cowboys and other locals. There's a good taqueria in La Honda."

"Sounds promising. Hey man, I'm driving a rental car. What do you do for wheels?"

"Wheels? Follow me."

Brian led me around the side of the house, and low and behold, a long, white Cadillac limousine. "My wheels. Check this out." He popped open the truck and removed a long cardboard drycleaner's box, from which he unfolded a double-breasted, khaki-colored, chauffeur livery with a matching billed hat. I smoothed my hand across the tan worsted lapels and down the dark satin strip running from waist to cuff. Catching my eye, he said, "Guess what we're gonna do today, Cary?"

We flipped a coin to decide who would be rock star and who would be chauffeur in this masquerade. I ended up driving, wearing the chauffeur's livery, while Brian lounged in the back in a white sport coat over a Grateful Dead t-shirt, playing rock star. In the rearview mirror I looked funny, hair exploding out in curls under the cap. I tied it back in a ponytail with a rubber band. By mid-afternoon the white limousine had crossed the Golden Gate Bridge into Sausalito and parked at The Trident on Bridgeway beside the San Francisco Bay.

At the Trident bar I ordered Brian a tequila and took it over to his table, standing behind him with chauffeur cap in hand as he sipped it. No one paid us a lick of attention. After a while, Brian told me to knock off the chauffeur act and drink a Dos Equis with him. Looking around one last time, he said, "No talent here today. Let's split. Guess it's too early." *Or maybe, The Trident gets so inundated by celebrities it's become desensitized to rock stars and their nonsense.*

We ended up in San Francisco south of Market in a beat, scuzzy pool room bar near Howard and Fifth, way downscale from The Trident. In the Michelin Guidebook, this joint would have rated zero stars—or minus stars. The sign on the sidewalk door spelled it out, "*7 a.m. Eye-Openers.*" I was still wearing the chauffeur livery minus the cap. More Dos Equis. Brian met Rosie, a tipsy woman of indeterminant age playing eight ball, bending over the table, jeans stretched tight across her more-than ample rear end. "Oh, you gotta do what you gotta do," remarked Brian. With Brian making out with her in the back, we blasted off to the Santa Cruz redwoods. Rockstar &

Chauffeur might be a ship of fools, but we were all too willing to sail it into parts unknown.

Next day, Brian chauffeuring and me playing rock star, we cruised into San Francisco, parked on the corner of Van Ness and Geary Street and kissed sweet Rosie goodbye. At Tommy's Joynt we gorged on buffalo stew and drank $1 Irish coffees. Crossing the Golden Gate Bridge, we crept through Sausalito traffic past The Trident, past the houseboats, and turned up Miller Avenue into downtown Mill Valley. Brian was looking for a bar where Grateful Dead road-managers hung out—guys Brian knew.

On Throckmorton Avenue I spotted a blond girl in baggy jeans walking a German Shepherd down the sidewalk. "Wait a minute! Pull over here, Brian! I recognize that girl!" He immediately pulled the limo over to the side of the curb and parked.

I jumped out of the limo and ran right up to her, "MaryEllen? It's Cary from Matala. Remember me?"

"Oh, Cary! How can I ever forget you?" she kissed me, grabbing my sleeves and holding me out at arm's length distance to look me over. "You haven't changed much. Beard and hair longer. Hey, nice wheels," gesturing with her thumb at the conspicuous white limo. "You going to the prom?"

I introduced them: "MaryEllen, Brian; Brian, MaryEllen."

Turning to face Brian, "You're his chauffeur, right?" she enquired facetiously, still holding on to my sleeves. "Cary here woke me up on the morning of my nineteenth birthday in a cave in Matala, Crete. There I am sleeping then suddenly, 'Here Comes The Sun' blasts out from a portable record player he put at the entrance of my cave. His way of serenading me. I was impressed."

"Did it work?" asked a grinning Brian.

"Are you asking if this birthday wake-up song led to ... intimacy? No. It did not ...." pausing as if she were trying to recall *why it did not*. "Oh yeah. You had a girlfriend. And then you left Matala with some other guys to go to Afghanistan or India ...."

I interrupted her reverie, "MaryEllen, we came to Mill Valley to kidnap you and drag you down to our ranch in the Santa Cruz mountains."

"What? You came to Mill Valley to kidnap me? Give me a break. I rarely come to Mill Valley except to see my parents and babysit for friends. I live with Connie, my sister, in San Rafael. You remember Connie?"

"Of course, I remember Connie very well."

"Joking aside, tell me, Cary, what really brings you into Mill Valley?"

"No shit, MaryEllen, we drove up from the Santa Cruz Mountains today. Brian and I oversee a pair of ranches near Skylonda off Skyline Drive. The limo belongs to Brian. We're just playing around. I work for Elliot Roberts, who manages Joni Mitchell. He lives in Hollywood but comes up to the ranch on weekends. We've gone AWOL."

"You two manage rockstar ranches? No way!" she stepped back, feigning disbelief.

"Oh yes. But let's get real. Brian basically house-sits for Neil, as I do for Elliot on his adjoining ranch. Not a real job for either of us. We are both biding time. I'll tell you the whole story, but not on the street. It's too long and too complicated. Where's the nearest bar?"

"Cary, I can't go into a bar, I just turned twenty. But hey, where are you and Brian crashing tonight? Going back to your rockstar ranches? Hey look … Connie and I rent a house behind Ali Akbar's School of Music in San Rafael. Why don't you and Brian come up and stay at our place tonight? We have plenty of room, you know," she gushed.

"Well, that sounds like a fine invitation." I looked over at Brian. "Are you sure Connie won't mind?"

"No way! I know she'd really like to see you and hear your stories. She talks all the time about us going back to Europe to bum around." She pulled a piece of paper out of her purse and wrote down her address and handed it to me. "It's off West End Avenue in San Rafael. Give me an hour to grocery shop and I'll be there to welcome you. Hope you like brown rice."

Brian parked the limo next to the house, a dark, shingled bungalow nestled in the shade of eucalyptus and second growth redwoods on a side street directly behind the famous music school. Connie came out on the porch with MaryEllen to greet Brian and me. She looked exactly like she had looked a year ago in Matala, slightly taller and more angular than MaryEllen, with an air more serious. Although thin, Connie's large breasts pushed out her blouse like the grill of an armored vehicle. She obviously liked the cut of Brian's jib and complimented him on his official chauffeur attire, as she welcomed us through the screened door into their home.

We four dined that night on brown rice, adzuki beans, miso soup and seaweed, a nutritious macrobiotic meal popular with freaks subsisting on food stamps. "What a great dinner, I absolutely loved it," I complimented the cooks. Brian nodded in agreement. Connie and MaryEllen beamed and bowed to us. We drank green tea and talked late into the night while Indian ragas drifted through the redwoods. I told them about my adventures after I left Matala in December, crazy times in Kabul, my affair with Joni, Hollywood and Laurel Canyon, England—Isle of Wight Festival, farm work, picking hops and the London music scene—and what happened when I came back to the States with Joni and James—New York, concerts, Martha's Vineyard, Chapel Hill, and now here.

"Time for bed," whispered Brian as he disappeared into a bedroom holding hands with Connie. MaryEllen laid out quilts for me on a spacious futon-couch in the living room.

When I was tucked in, she stood beside me and said, "Can I make you some chamomile tea?" In lamplight, she wore a silk slip with nothing underneath to hide the contours of her torso, her breasts, her buns and a shaded area below her abdomen. "What a fine-looking girl," I thought to myself.

She brought me a cup of tea and sat down on the side of the couch, her legs nudging mine. In a soft and husky voice, she told stories about adventures she and Connie had hitchhiking around Europe, and the time they got arrested in Amsterdam traveling in a van with guys that got busted with hashish. She smelled like patchouli oil, the pungent scent I associated with runaway hippy chicks. MaryEllen was like a gift some mischievous demi-god was bestowing on me by mistake, way too good to be true, and yet, for reasons unknown, I didn't grab her and drag her under the covers, nor did she invite me to sleep in her bed. I desired her, but felt oddly protective of her or something, as if she had been a little sister. That night, Cupid's arrow missed its mark.

The next day, Brian and I recrossed the Golden Gate Bridge and drove back down the Peninsula and up Skyline Boulevard with MaryEllen sitting in the back seat next to me. As we descended the long gravel driveway through the redwoods to Elliot's and Neil's ranches, we looked west. The Pacific stretched out to the ocean horizon, and in the foreground, the coastal range floated above a white pillow of fog.

When we passed through the gate to Elliot's farmhouse, we found Scott sitting on the porch in a rocking chair reading. Brian let us out and returned to Neil's ranch a few hundred yards away. I retrieved the key from its hiding spot and let us in. Scott had just returned from Berkeley where he had been staying with Whisnant. We heated some Chef Boyardee ravioli from cans we discovered in the pantry. I took blankets and quilts out of the chest and I gave them to MaryEllen, offering her the cot. Scott and I undressed, crawled into our sleeping bags, and turned over to sleep. But MaryEllen had other ideas.

"Cary? Cary?" I opened my eyes to see her in her silk slip looking down on me. She spoke softly, "Cary, can I get in your sleeping bag with you."

"Yes." I unzipped the bag and she slipped beside me and kissed me full on the mouth. That was it. I slid her slip above her breasts and ran my tongue over her nipples. She grabbed my hand and shoved it between her legs. Her pussy was wet and slick. We slept that night on the floor, in the December chill, sleeping bag below us, quilts bunched up on top. The aroma of bay and eucalyptus mingled with her patchouli and the musk of sex that covered us. Scott slept through it all ... or else he was being very discrete.

In the morning we walked over to Neil's ranch to call on Brian.

"Howdy, MaryEllen and Scott, welcome back to the palace of rock and roll," said Brian, obviously happy to have company. "Did you have breakfast?"

"We ate what we found in Elliot's pantry, Kellogg's Frosted Flakes."

"Frosted Flakes? Jesus, that's not breakfast; that's dessert. Come on in and I'll fry us up bacon and eggs and hash browns. And brew some coffee." I looked around the spacious one-floor ranch house. The furniture appeared to be Mission, and the long dining room table and chairs, Stickley. Nice. Brian brought out plates of fried eggs, bacon and potatoes, and MaryEllen laid out the knives and forks and napkins. We had coffee and dug into a real breakfast.

Brian looked across the table at MaryEllen and cocked his head to the side, "*MaryEllen* is a fine name, but it's too long. Too many syllables. We need to give you a nickname," he teased. "What do your family call you?"

"Just plain *MaryEllen*. My great aunt's name. Mamma loved her and named me after her. I hated the name *MaryEllen* when I was a kid. I sounded so … prissy. When Mom would call my name when I was around other kids, I would cringe. I wanted to be named something normal, like *Susan*."

"What if we call you *Maggie*?"

"Oh, I can't stand "*Maggie*" either. Everyone wants to call me Maggie. No way. Reminds me of magpie."

"How about '*Marlene*?' Like a German spy. Mysterious. *Marlene* Dietrich?" MaryEllen raised her eyebrows.

"So be it!" Brian and I raised our coffee cups, and toasted—"*Marlene!*"

What is driving this name conversation?" It seemed like Brian wanted to *name* her and *claim* her like an explorer planting a flag in newly discovered territory. *Why not? She is delectable.* MaryEllen rose and curtsied, "Okay if it pleases you, it pleases me. *Marlene*, it is." And so, what started as a joke, took root. MaryEllen would remain *Marlene,* a name she adopted and by which friends and strangers alike would call her for the next fifty years.

✳ ✳ ✳

I drove MaryEllen … *Marlene,* that is … back to San Rafael in the rental car. Later that afternoon Dana showed up from Palm Springs with his buddy, George. Connie had met Dana traveling in Europe last year and they had hit it off. Dana and George let on they had been in Palm Springs, dealing heroin in weight. They generously laid a two-gram vial on me, just enough to get me in serious trouble if I didn't take care—or kill me if I got reckless. "It's pure, uncut China white, Cary. Lethal if you get greedy. Don't fix more than a matchhead."

Always equipped for battlefield drug maneuvers, I had assembled a set of works from Deward's lab back when Scott and I crashed with him. Since then, I had carried the outfit in an eyeglasses case in my leather hucklebag, for exactly a fortuitous occasion like this. The two-gram vial fit perfectly into the glasses case next to a small 1cc syringe and a set of points. I couldn't wait. In the evening while Marlene was still in Mill Valley, I went into the bathroom, sat on the edge of the bathtub, and cooked up only a smidgen of the pure white, way less than an eighth of a teaspoon, as Dana had recommended. I tied off and fixed. Dropping the syringe in a glass of water, I felt the smack hit me like a soft freight train and I went into my run. I threw up in the toilet and nodded out. China White was, as Dana described—superlative!

Decades later, when I had put my opiate hungers behind me—mostly, at least—I realized I was fortunate to have survived chipping junk episodically the way I did and not end up with a full-blown jones. Or dead. I liked shooting junk. I liked the satiating way it made me feel—the combination of a full-body orgasm, with the satisfaction of drinking cool water when you are parched. I had a stupid, romantic sentiment that I belonged to an exclusive clan of desperados, hip Beats, in cahoots with John Coltrane, Charlie Parker, Lenny Bruce, with William Burroughs, and my pal Paul Davis. Junkie delusions. Without much difficulty, I could pick up smack and I could put it down. It was the same with alcohol. I could take it or leave it. Why me and not others? Did I lack the addictive gene that compelled others to turn into degenerate junkies, leading them to rob family and steal from friends to feed the beast? Or more likely, was it because I detested getting junk-sick more, and feared developing the uncontrollable craving to get high?—I feared getting addicted more than I craved getting down.

A day or so later, Neil rang Brian asking him to deliver a box of tape reels to Graham Nash in Haight Ashbury. At that time, Graham was remodeling a house on the edge of Buena Vista Park above Haight Street. Graham, quite animated and pleasant, chatted amicably with Brian and me for a few minutes. Neither of us mentioned Joni, nor how he and I had met at her house in Laurel Canyon with Stephen and David last summer. It was all civilized. All smiles.

※ ※ ※

All good things must come to an end, they say. Elliot fired me.

Neither dope nor drink had seriously interfered with my work at the ranch, if you could call what I did work. Mostly, I fetched hay or cattle feed, and did other menial tasks. Except for hanging out with Brian, I read or hiked around in the redwoods and eucalyptus ravines. I sat around and watched local cowboys put up a fence for Elliot. I thought about building a treehouse in the bay and laurel ravine behind Elliot's farmhouse. Mainly, I was bored.

Maybe it *was* drink after all, because one afternoon, a Dos Equis wedged between my legs, I skidded off a wet mountain road with a bale of hay sticking out of the open trunk, smashing into the dirt bank on the right, knocking out the headlight and leaving a muddy gash in the front fender. Man! had I gone off the other side of the road, I would have rolled the car down a deep forested redwood canyon, and then I would have been royally fucked. *Whew, death averted once again, thank you Jesus!*

Although badly banged-up, the car seemed to run well enough to get back to the ranch with the hay, but it was ugly. When I picked up Elliot at the airport, he blew up. What really irked him was not that the car was banged up—insurance would cover that, but that I had been keeping the rental car for weeks, running up a large bill, instead of turning it in to Hertz. *Well, what was I going to do, Elliot?* I explained that I had no money to buy my own truck or a car. "How was I going to work without a vehicle?" I argued. But no, that didn't fly.

I guess in the end, Elliot figured that he had had enough—enough was enough! —and that he had done enough for this thankless ingrate on behalf of Joni. No hard feelings—I was next to useless at his ranch anyway. "Cary, this isn't working out well for either of us." Which was true. Elliot gave me two $100 bills and a few lines of coke folded in aluminum foil. He bid me farewell and asked me to stay in touch. Instead of feeling bent out of shape, I felt like I had just escaped exile.

Just escaped from exile? On the bus heading to Deward's I thought about my history with Elliot. *Why don't I trust Elliot? Why had I handled my job at the ranch so ... lackadaisically?* I narrowed down the root cause of my resentment to three incidents. The first was meeting Elliot in Los Angeles when I came from Crete to visit Joni. The second was the Isle of Wight Festival and his job offer in London. The third incident was Elliot crashing our party on Martha's Vineyard—Joni, James, and me.

In the first instance, I pictured Elliot picking up Joni and me at her house in a limo to go to Disneyland ... embarrassingly stoned ... offering to buy me a Pendleton shirt ...? *Why?* Had Elliot simply wanted to give me a gift because he was a generous person? Kabul came to mind ... when I declined Ghulam Dastagir's gold Lapis Lazuli ring. I had been wrong to refuse the gift of the ring from the kind goldsmith; was I wrong to have turned down the Pendleton shirt—had it been Elliot's *Gift from the Heart?*

And what about the Isle of Wight Festival? Elliot had watched me get hideously drunk. Did Donovan tell Elliot about my barging into his caravan demanding drugs and sex from his bevy of groupies? Did Elliot see my drunken belligerency as a threat to Joni's reputation? Doubtless Elliot was inured to rock & roll delinquency—used to bad behavior—it came with the territory of a talent agent. But could he have thought, "*Cary has gone berserk. How reckless could his behavior become? Is he going to publicly embarrass Joni?*" But ... Elliot had offered me a job at his ranch *after* we went to the Isle of Wight Festival.

What else? Martha's Vineyard? Joni, James and I had been together since James's London Palladium show in October. Elliot had showed up on the Vineyard and convinced me to leave ... and paid for me to go to his ranch. *I resented him breaking us up.*

However, to be fair, was I giving Elliot a fair break? Was there another side to this I had not been considering? Was he simply looking out for Joni's welfare? *That makes sense.* Elliot, a highly competent Hollywood talent agent and Joni's friend, must have been sensitive to how the press could react to our three-way ensemble. Joni and James hanging out with an indigent ... dressed like a Greek freedom fighter. *How would that look to the public?* Sure, Elliot was most likely shielding Joni and James from getting carved up by the press. *Why wasn't I giving him a break?* Why didn't I talk with him directly about how I felt? I realized I had been acting blindly, irrationally, and above all, not acting in good faith. Maybe *that* was it.

✳ ✳ ✳

It was a lonely Christmas Eve in Berkeley. Deward and Jenny had gone camping to remote hot springs deep in the Sierra Nevada. Marlene and Connie were spending Christmas in Mill Valley with their parents. A year ago today, I had been celebrating Christmas with Ken and Agate in Mashhad under the shadow of Goharshad Mosque.

At Deward's dinner table I sat, beer bottle in hand, alone in this silent house except for a friend of Jenny's, a sullen, unattractive woman, sequestered in the spare bedroom. She wouldn't talk to me. That annoyed me. I thought she could have passed for the illustration of the witch in Grimm's *Hansel and Gretel*.

I was in a rotten state of mind. I envisioned myself as a model for Caravaggio, kneeling on stone in tattered robes, hands open, eyes cast up: the pose of contrition. Blah. Blah. Blah ... my mind stream spun on and on like a broken record.

Before I left Martha's Vineyard, James had said they were going to spend Christmas in Chapel Hill. Since I had no luck connecting with them on Thanksgiving, I decided to ring them now during this Season of Joy. When we were together, sometimes I suspected I knew James and Joan better than some of my cousins.

Mrs. Taylor answered the phone. "James said you might call. He and Joni are out caroling in the neighborhood with friends. By the way, Cary, James tried to call you on Thanksgiving. He said he left a message with somebody named Scott asking you to call back. Did you get that message?"

"No, Ma'am. But here I am, returning his call belatedly a month later. Today, I am in Berkeley. Please tell them I'll talk with them when I see them. Here's my number." I gave her Deward's. *Why didn't Scott tell me James had called?*

"Merry Christmas, Cary."

"Merry Christmas Mrs. Taylor."

"Please Cary ... *Trudy*," she corrected me.

✳   ✳   ✳

What a miserable excuse for Christmas. How to celebrate? Certainly not with the unpleasant woman holed up in the bedroom. What next? *I'll call Jonathan.* First cousin, Jonathan Flaccus, lived in Diamond Heights in San Francisco with his wife, Linda, head of a private school in the East Bay. Jonathan answered. I proposed, "Let's go to Canyon for a sauna."

"Brilliant idea! Linda went to Philadelphia to spend Christmas with her folks," explained Jonathan. "So, I'm alone, too. Canyon is a great idea! Hold on, Cary, I'm on the way."

About an hour later Jonathan pulled up in front of Deward's house in Essex Street. I hopped in his Volvo, and we chugged up through the Berkeley Hills to Snake Road, which led down into the twisty switch-back Pinehurst Road taking us into the depths of Canyon. Canyon was unique even by the eccentric standards of Berkeley counter-culture weirdness.

Several dozen families of Beats, artists, musicians and freaks squatted in homemade dwellings throughout Canyon's hills and redwood ravines. Some lived in the simplest of tents and lean-tos with plastic walls and roofs, others in rather fantastic dwellings such as Catherine and Williams's abode, a magnificent redwood-shingled treehouse perched securely on telephone pole pilings that had been driven into the hillside with a pile-driver. You reached their house on foot on a steep, wooded path along this same bay laurel ravine. I knew it well. I had gone crazy at their place two years ago. We parked near the sauna at the bottom of this ravine.

Canyon children, dressed in the finest fashions from the Salvation Army store in Walnut Creek, bounded up and down Canyon's almost vertical trails in motley, barefooted gangs resembling the feral boys in *Lord of the Flies*. Within the Canyon community, a group of classical Indian music devotees studied sarod, sitar, and tabla at Ali Akbar Khan's School of Music in San Rafael, located, coincidentally, next to Connie and Marlene's place.

The sauna was about six by ten constructed of roughhewn redwood boards with a heavy planked, sloping roof. A local metal worker had converted a fifty-five-gallon oil drum into a wood stove that pumped out an enormous amount of BTU's burning lumber scraps. From the top of the oil-drum a stove pipe wrapped in asbestos insulation jutted out through the plank roof.

Fog began to roll in. Two women and a man were taking showers naked under a standing six-foot pipe with a shower head, which stuck out of a wide concrete slab. Another three people lay on the roof steaming like lobsters lifted from boiling water. Jonathan and I disrobed, hung up our clothes on wall hooks outside, and stepped into the extremely hot, dripping interior and shut the door. Light glowed from a dim yellow bulb ensconced in a marine glass case on the wall. Two young women sprawling naked on the wooden shelf seats sat up to make room for us. A note tacked to the door stated: "Abide in silence." Another rule: "Outside—speak softly. *Om Shanti.*"

One of the women unlatched the stove door and heaved hunks of wood onto glowing coals. The exterior of the stove was so hot that the barrel showed pink in places and it quivered with the intense heat. She dipped a metal cup into a galvanized bucket and splashed water over the stove. A cloud of steam burst forth, driving the temperature way up. Soon the women exited, leaving Jonathan and me alone. We heard them climbing the ladder to the roof. Jonathan gestured with his thumb *let's get outta here.* Outside the temperature was about forty-five degrees. We climbed up on the roof and lay on our backs on warm redwood planks next to the two women. Steam rose off their bodies, making them appear in golden twilight like pre-Raphaelite figures in a Maxfield Parrish painting. We stared at the sky through the feathery branches of surrounding redwood trees looming above. *What a magical place, Canyon, where heaven and earth become one.*

✳   ✳   ✳

Now unemployed—*freed from exile!*—I hung out for days at Jonathan's. We went down to the Grateful Dead's New Years Eve bash at Winterland, which was a wild affair. Friends of the Dead threw handfuls of pills into the dancing audience. Hot Tuna played between sets of the Dead. At midnight, a burly Hells Angel in diapers slid down a static wire from the gallery across the dance floor to the stage. *Unbelievable.* Before leaving the ranch, Brian had given me a hunk of hashish for Christmas that Jonathan and I smoked in a little soapstone pipe.

Two days later, Jonathan got a call from his mother—my aunt Violetta—delivering the sad news that MomMom had died, and that her funeral would take place three days hence. Jonathan packed on the spot and took the next flight he could find to New York. I couldn't afford to buy an airline ticket, but I did not regret missing her funeral because the last time I had seen MomMom alive was in November, when Joni and James walked with me from the Albert Hotel to her apartment to serenade her. Better for me to have had that private concert as the final memory of my dear grandmother than to see her laid out in a casket.

✳   ✳   ✳

Down and out in Diamond Heights. With Jonathan gone and Linda in Philly, I had no one to keep me company but Jonathan's stereo, his extensive library, and his collection of jazz LPs. One of Linda's friends, Susan, came by. She made out with me on the floor but wouldn't fuck me and left in a huff. *That stung.* I needed to go somewhere to kick back and digest what had been going on during the past few weeks. I shot up the last vestiges of Dana's heroin; I might as well have swallowed an aspirin. I decided to take refuge with Marlene in San Rafael.

I took the bus across the Golden Gate Bridge to Larkspur where I caught a ride to San Raphael and walked over to Marlene's and Connie's. It was comforting to have Marlene snuggle up to me at night under fragrant redwoods and eucalyptus. Ah, the perfume of eucalyptus and bay—an exotic fragrance that permeated the Bay Area. Marlene had strung eucalyptus seeds on a cord and tied them around her dog Sweetie's neck to keep fleas away. The unique eucalyptus smell reminded me of arriving in Berkeley with Deward in his Morris Minor in fall of 1968 and feeling like I had come home. The smell revived the memory of sitting on a huge, half log seat in the middle of the Berkeley campus eucalyptus grove reading D.T. Suzuki's *Zen Buddhism*.

I found Joellen and Laura Allan's address in my notebook. How could I forget Laura Allan, whom had I met at Joni's house during the summer with Joellen? I rang, Laura answered and said, "Joellen and I are living in Forest Knolls at our friend Carolina's house. Why don't you come out and visit us? Have supper?" I heard her saying aside in the background, "Joellen, guess what? Its Joni's friend, Cary. He's in San Rafael and I invited him to visit us."

"Marlene, I'm thinking of going out to Forest Knolls to visit Joellen and Laura."

"Good timing. I'll be in Mill Valley with Mom, Dad, and Connie. I'll put the key under the side mat in case you come back before I do."

I hitchhiked out Sir Francis Drake through San Anselmo and Fairfax to Forest Knolls. When my ride let me out beside the road, I looked up to the left and recognized Carolina's house on the hill surrounded by redwoods exactly as Laura had described it. Laura showed me all around the old, shingled house. It had rustic redwood plank walls and heavy workbenches where she and the others crafted stringed instruments. Hanging on wall hooks were woodworking tools—chisels, saws, rasps, clamps, and more equipment. "I live here with Joellen, Carolina, Earl and Robbie who also study with Joellen. In a way, you could say that it's Joellen's domain."

The house itself was a Marin County gallery of sorts, riddled with nooks and sleeping lofts, shelves with brass Buddhas and Hindu statuettes, walk-in closets, bedrooms, and a bathroom that Laura had meticulously tiled with unusual junkyard objects such as segments of plastic doll arms, pieces of driftwood, bottle caps, beach glass, and tiny bric-a-brac rescued from beaches, trash dumpsters and yard sales. Curious, I unscrewed the cap of a tin container glued on the bathroom wall. Inside was a white pill. I had never seen anything like this extraordinary house before. "We are the *Glue Artists*," said Laura. "*Brothers and sisters of Bondo.*"

Laura, Joellen and I had supper—brown rice, beans, and miso soup—and listened to mountain dulcimer recordings until about ten when Laura asked me, "Will you spend the night with us, Cary?"

"Yes," I declared emphatically. *This could be interesting.*

"Great I'm so, so happy. I am gonna make you the best pancakes for breakfast you ever had! Knock your socks off! Earl's up in Portland, you can sleep in his loft," she said, as she climbed an installed wooden ladder to show me Earl's sleeping berth half-way to the rafters of the cathedral ceiling. *This was not what I wanted to hear. Oh, well,* I thought, *I hope I don't roll out; it's a long way down.*

Laura Allan's pancakes hit the spot. After washing dishes, she walked over to her workbench and brought over to the dining table a piece of latigo strap about two inches long. With a ballpoint pen she drew two tiny stick figures holding hands and printed in tiny letters: "Good for a dance or two, and when we're through, we'll kiss the moon," and she slipped it in my back pocket. I hitched back to San Rafael and I kept that piece of leather in my wallet for fifteen years, waiting to dance.

✳   ✳   ✳

Usually waking up among the eucalyptus at Marlene's place gave me joy; however, today the familiar smell occasioned discomforting physical and emotional memories, memories of the bad trip in San Francisco and Berkeley, memories of visions and dreams in Matala, memories of days of wonder and fear that changed my life forever. These memories lodged in my body—ponderous, mixed-up, tangled logjams of images, visions, thoughts, and sensory residues that weighed as heavy on me as a cheap wine hangover.

In this melancholic state, I began to get an inkling how cycles of my life worked. Good times followed bad times, grief followed joy, and all arose and passed, disappeared and reappeared as if anew. I perceived how senses, emotions and thoughts—even visual images— reduced to vibrations. I put Beethoven's Ninth Symphony on Connie's record player and lay back on the couch. I couldn't describe what I was hearing in musical terms, but it began moving me deeply, stimulating a whole spectrum of perceptions. Though I couldn't begin to explain it, I detected sensory waves emerging and receding, somatic themes where *meaning*—intangible, ineffable *meanings*—superseded language. I literally *felt* the genius of Beethoven flow through me.

Such was my state of reverie when Scott's automobile pulled into the parking area next to the house and parked under the eucalyptus. He was returning from his Christmas adventures out in the wilds of Napa, Sonoma, and Portland, Oregon. My first question was, "Hey, Scott, why didn't you tell me James Taylor called me at Jenkin's farm at Thanksgiving?"

"Oh. Sorry about that. It was Jake who answered. I was in Chapel Hill with you. He told me later and it slipped my mind."

Scott had come back to San Rafael to get his bearings, to regroup with Marlene and me for our next sortie. I told him all about getting fired by Elliot, to which he replied, "Yeah, I agree. It never made much sense to me at all, that so-called *job*. Yeah, I can see how you might feel you had been shuttled off in exile to Mountain View ... your Elba."

Scott reported that our dear fraternity brother, Alex Porter, was now stationed—("you might call it a *military exile*") at the marine base near Long Beach, California—and obviously required our company. "I can feel it in my bones. He needs our spiritual support," joked Scott. "Let's go down to Long Beach and check on Brother Porter and make sure he is not getting into any trouble without us."

"Super! While we're there, let's check on Joni and James and see how they're doing."

Marlene said, "Can I come too? I got nothing going on around here. I like hanging out with you guys."

"Marlene, we wouldn't think of leaving you behind. Pack your bag 'cause you're coming with us." Within an hour we were driving up and down through San Francisco, only to stop at a Doggy Diner for chili dogs, French fries, and milkshakes. Cruising down Highway 101, Marlene and I were screwing under a blanket in the back of the Scout, when Scott, bless his soul!—possessing an unfathomably deep well of practical-joke humor—picked up a young student hitchhiking back from Christmas vacation to the University of California at Santa Cruz. Marlene and I, still coupled under the blanket, kept still, or close to it. Scott dropped the guy out on the highway near an exit to Santa Cruz and we continued south.

Scott chuckled, "You guys should have seen his face—it was priceless!—when he glanced down and saw your feet intertwined next to the gear shift lever between the seats. His jaw literally dropped when Marlene's pink toenailed feet twitched! He actually blushed!" Scott was having a good time.

We stopped later for a burger in San Luis Obispo where Highway 1 merged with Highway 101 again. By nightfall, we were drinking beer with Marine Captain John Alexander Porter and his girlfriend, Kay, in Newport Beach. Alex and Kay lived in a nondescript apartment building along a nondescript strip of almost identical apartments. A suitable Marine-type exile habitat.

An easygoing guy in his mid-20s, Alex had led several lives before getting here. I hadn't seen him in four years since he dropped out of UNC Chapel Hill to enlist in the marines. When he came back from finishing a tour, he attended NC State to complete his forestry and economics degree, during which he played rugby and worked as a private detective. Then he reenlisted in the Marines as an officer. With an arm around Kay's shoulders, Alex spun stories of his days as a private detective, repossessing cars and following adulterous husbands. He related the time he fired .25 caliber rounds into the house of an errant deadbeat he was tracking down … "to make a point," he chuckled.

Lapsing into his military misadventures, he told us the "Tale of the Toasted Toad," recounting a survival training course he had led in the Mojave Desert for young marines in basic training. How exactly did a survival training in the desert translate into war in Vietnam jungles? Alex couldn't explain that. "A team bonding thing, I guess."

"So, I send them off, the new recruits, to scrounge up food and fuel to make a meal off the land. One young marine comes up to me holding a twitching desert toad by the hind leg. He asks, 'Captain Porter, Sir, can we eat this?'

"'Yes, Private Johnson,' I lie to him, 'it looks edible to me.' I'm thinking, *this does* not *look edible to me!*

"An hour later he reports back, waving a stick impaling the nasty, charred carcass of the toad, withered black legs sticking out like shriveled twigs. 'I cooked it, Captain Porter, Sir. Would you like to sample it?'

"The remnant of the burned toad looked hideous—really, *really* hideous—but what could I do? I was their leader, after all, and I had to set an example. 'Yes, of course, Private Johnson!' Whereupon Johnson tears the rear leg off—which appeared more charcoal than flesh—and hands it to me. I take a tiny bite and before I chew it, I realize I had just bitten into the worst fucking thing I had ever had in my mouth in my life! 'How the fuck did you cook this toad, Private Johnson?'

"'I cooked it on that fire yonder,' says the private. I walked over to his fire. Have you ever smelled burning creosote? Greasewood bush? No wonder the toad tasted so bad—he barbecued it over creosote!"

We spent the night with Alex and Kay and drove back up to LA. Scott parked in front of Joni's house in Lookout Mountain Avenue. I entered the front door as if I still lived there, Scott and Marlene trailing behind me. In the bedroom, Joni and James were sitting on the floor nursing a large, half-empty bottle of wine, watching a vintage black and white movie. "Hi!" they greeted me as if I had just come back from a walk around the block. I introduced Marlene and Scott.

In the living room I noticed a profusion of instruments, more than were here last summer. By the doorway into her small kitchen, Joni had hung a chalk board, on it written in her unmistakable cursive script: *Phenomenology = Subjectivity of individual experience.* She tried to learn a new word every day. *Back to philosophy it appears.*

Joni and James invited us to their favorite burger stand on Sunset Strip. "Joan, Elliot fired me. Guess I didn't make a very good ranch hand."

"Elliot told me. I was surprised when you accepted the job." This didn't seem like the right time to dig into this sensitive conversation. *I'll bring it up with her later.*

When we returned to her house, James said, "May I borrow Cary for a while? I want to take him by A&M studios to listen to what you are recording."

Joni nodded, "Yeah. Please do, James. I'll call Henry."

As we left, Joni was playing studio tapes of her new songs to Marlene and Scott, asking them what they thought of the horns on a song. I jumped in James's rented car next to him and we set out across Hollywood. Along the way, James said, "Cary, the music business is not what it's cracked up to be. I think I should open a chain of restaurants—*James's Chicken Burgers.*" James has the most delightful sense of humor—a dry humor, but that makes it all the more hilarious.

When James and I got to A&M, Henry Lewy, the studio sound engineer, said, "Joni asked me to play a few songs for you." Henry sat me down on a chair in a soundproof room not much bigger than a coat closet and clamped earphones on me. He played me tapes from the new album Joni was working on. First, I heard my song, "Carey," which I knew, of course, but had never heard with full orchestration. *Oh that is fantastic!* Nice! How sweet of her!

And then Henry played me "A Case of You." I got its magnificence!—when she hit the high notes, "... I could drink a case of youooooo"—it just about blew off the top of my head. So fantastic! The song embodies the power she revealed to me in Matala—during her self-proclaimed "shamanic period"—when the touch of her hand on my heart knocked me over like a bolt of lightning.

As James and I were heading out the door of A&M, Henry Lewy pulled me over to share an afterthought. "Cary, millions love Joni's music, but few realize the scope of her talent. Collaborating with her, I've learned she is beyond a competent studio engineer—she could run this studio without me … if she wanted to. And more than that, she masters everything that can affect her music, everything that can compromise her integrity, including the inscrutable, greedy machinations of the music business." *Everything else and everyone else, including me,* I felt impelled to add. But didn't.

"Let's go, Cary." James said, glancing at his watch. "I'm late to a meeting that started a half-hour ago. "Shall I drop you at Joni's on the way?" We said goodbye to Henry and jumped back in the rental car.

"Sure, James," I replied, quoting Frost,

The woods are lovely, dark and deep,
But I have promises to keep,
And miles to go before I sleep,
And miles to go before I sleep.

❋   ❋   ❋

Fast-forwarding fifteen years later, to my New York flat, 21 East 21st Street, apartment BB. Betsy and I are setting the table for a dinner party. Joni is coming to dinner tonight along with other friends: Nick Wolfson, Dick and Gaby Duane, and my nephew, Greg Broom.

We spread a starched, white linen tablecloth over the rough plank, Mission-style table that Dick Duane and I had built from heavy framing timbers we pinched at night from a construction site in Gramercy Park. On the table, I place candles into gothic silver candelabra Mamma gave me, now tarnished almost black. Uncorked bottles of Beaujolais breathe on a silver tray atop the upright piano. On the record player, Johnny Hartman and John Coltrane, "… you are too beautiful my dear to be true, and I am a fool for beauty …."

I take Hartman-Coltrane off the turntable and put on *Blue*. For years I've been ruminating about songs on the *Blue* album, songs I have wanted to ask Joni about. Tonight's the night. I had heard her play several of the songs in Matala. Some songs I had heard at the BBC Paris Theater in October 1970, with James accompanying her on guitar. Still others I heard at A&M for the first time. And a few songs I didn't hear until the album came out. It dawns on me the *Blue album* frames a year-in-the-life romance and close friendship with Joan. *Maybe tonight, Joan and I can talk about it.*

I sit down on the couch, close my eyes, relax, and let my mind range over the memories and emotions the songs on *Blue* provoke. *What do these songs mean to me, personally?*

I think of "Blue"—what a great song and an album title. The lyrics broadly capture the zeitgeist of Hollywood in 1970: "Acid, booze and ass, needles, guns and grass, lots of laughs, lots of laughs ...." I suspect Joan wrote the song for David Blue. Not sure if David represented all those deadly vices, but he could have laid claim to several. To me, David was more than a portrait of cool—he had a good heart. When I used to come down from San Francisco to visit Joni, he invited me to stay on the couch in his apartment. One time when I crashed at his place, he gave me his briefcase as a gift—what did I need with a briefcase in 1973? I took it with me to Africa a year later.

Three weeks before Christmas 1982—by then I was an Assistant Manager, a junior international banking officer, at a Park Avenue bank—David dropped dead of a heart attack jogging around Washington Square Park. A week later, Elliot, Joni, Leonard, and I arrived together in a limousine for David's memorial service in an East Village synagogue chapel. David would have liked riding in that limo with us, cracking cynical jokes. David Blue was sorely missed by those who knew him, but at the time of Joni's writing the song "Blue," he had been very much alive. I remember feeling uncomfortable when I saw sadness set in David's eyes. It was fitting that David took "Blue" as his last name, replacing Cohen. Success came to others, but forever eluded him. When he died, Joni was soaring in her career, and he was not.

What about "This Flight Tonight?" In fall of 1970, before Joni, James, and I met in London—when Monte Hellman was directing James in Rudy Wurlitzer's *Two-Lane Blacktop* in Tucumcari, New Mexico—Joni is flying in to visit him on the set. On the plane she broods that the visit is ill-timed, worrying that the relationship is unsteady. She hopes things will work out, but worries that they won't.

I first heard about the movie from Joni at The London Palladium when we attended James' concert. At the Isle of Wight Festival, confronting a disrespectful audience, she had tried to calm the rowdy crowd by talking about attending a Hopi ceremonial dance in New Mexico. Therefore, she had been at the movie set before we went to Isle of Wight together. In London James asked me if I would be interested in playing a minor role in a prospective screenplay that Wurlitzer had written, a film set in India—"You play this guy on a train who shares a car with me. About all you have to do is smoke dope."

"Sure thing," I replied, "I can handle that." The film never happened. But that is how I relate emotionally to "This Flight Tonight" when I hear it—*quashed expectations*. Recurrent themes of thwarted expectations run through *Blue* album songs, like the disappointment I used to see in David Blue's eyes.

In Matala Joni had told me the heartbreaking story behind "Little Green," how anguished she was at putting her infant child up for adoption. "At the 1968 Mariposa Folk Festival," said Joni, "a woman came up to the fence surrounding the performers' area and beckoned me over. 'This is my daughter, *Joanie*. I wanted her to meet you,' the woman said. A little later, in a flash, it occurred to me that this child at the fence might have been my child. I went out of the fenced compound to search among the audience for them, but to no avail."

In those days, I didn't comprehend how much losing a child in this way was agonizing to women, agonizing to Joni. I was callused: broken romances and children born out of wedlock were part of the 1960's cultural landscape. Joni had given up the chance *to be a mother*—a tragic choice, which she never forgot.

People ask how I relate to "All I Want," and "My Old Man," songs that refer to Graham, which express her deep, enduring affection for him. The way I see it, Joni can love and leave, but she never forgets her family, friends and ex-lovers; they remain stars in her constellation. If these songs to Graham and "Little Green" were part of the "before-Carey saga," then "River" and "The Last Time I Saw Richard" express a "post-Carey" aftermath. In "Richard," I imagine Joni confronting the heartbreak of encountering an old friend, an ex-lover who chose a course in life that bleeds him of his aliveness, his dreams and ambition. I couldn't help hearing "Richard" without imagining that I could be a potential model for the song character, Richard. *It gives me shivers.*

In her on-stage patter tuning her dulcimer at the London Paris Theater, Joni had mentioned she wrote "River" the year before—Christmas 1969. Did she ever play it in Matala?—but then again, my cave lacked a piano. "River" evokes tumultuous images of salvation, as if she is calling for a natural force—a *river*— "to skate away on"—to uplift her with the strength, inspiration and determination to propel her past sorrow and regret.

Although I had heard Joni play "A Case of You" on the piano in London that October when she and James and I were hanging out together, when Henry Lewi played me the fully produced version four months later at A&M, "A Case of You" shocked me to my core. The song is fine and chilling. I have never recovered from hearing it at A&M. As profound as it is, when I hear it, I am reminded of a funny event. When we were staying in Martha's Vineyard, as a joke, I brought a couple of bottles of Taylor wine back to the motel. It was a weak, corny attempt at humor—a play of words—conflating James "Taylor" with a case of Taylor wine.

Ahhh. "California." I heard it first in London with James's guitar backing her dulcimer. And then Henry Lewy played it for me at A&M. It's a great song, although I'm not flattered with "Redneck on a Grecian Isle ... ," and " ... he kept my camera to sell." That goddamn camera. People are always asking me about it. She gave me the camera to film Matala, to film its fragile presence like Brassaï had captured an essence of Paris in 1930—but that would be a flattering comparison—it was about recording a point in time and space. Joni had witnessed the fragility of Matala, how the police had closed down the caves while she was there. She knew Matala and its cultural lifestyle were bound to change and disappear, not unlike Paradise in "Big Yellow Taxi."

I look at my wristwatch. Guests will arrive soon. I need to dress .... The buzzing doorbell startles me out of my reverie. I walk down the long narrow hall in 21 East 21 to open the door, passing the theater poster of Robin Moyer as *Dionysus Wants You!* on the left and Joni's signed prints from *Mingus* on the right ....

... and what about my own song, "Carey?" Hadn't it already come to follow me around like a specter? No, not a specter—too grim—more like the six-foot tall *pooka*, the invisible giant rabbit in the play, *Harvey*. A year ago in Abu Dhabi, while staying at the Hilton on business, I was in the hotel bar after dinner and the band began playing "Carey." Here in New York I've heard "Carey" played in taxis, in restaurants, in department stores. No, I haven't entirely disassociated with the song. I'm not unmoved. I keep it in my heart—a present from Joni on my birthday in a cave in Crete. In Matala, Joni was always leaving but never left. And she never left my life, nor I, hers.

... and Joni took the hammer. New York, 1982. Credit: Dick Duane

EPILOGUE

Date: October 2022. This desk overflows with memorabilia, yet few notes, journals, notebooks, and friends survive to help fill in memory gaps of late 1970–early 1971. Who can help triangulate anchors of remembrance, when written records fail? I stand grateful to those individuals and many others for helping me recall events of those days, even though their recollections do not all reconcile. After a while, stories arise, free themselves from the teller and take on their own lives. In the end, leave it to me to reweave connective threads between their factual warp and woof in the narrative tapestry between leaving the Other Ear Gallery in 1968, and walking into A&M records in early 1971, when Joni was recording *Blue*. The ending of *Carey: Genesis of the Song*, like Anthony Powell's *A Dance to the Music of Time*, branches out into other long, interconnected tales—where the same characters appear and disappear—and dissolves into sinuous mycelia of memory, where dreams and reality coincide:

And, tired of aimless circling in one place,
Steer straight off after something into space
—Robert Frost
"On A Tree Fallen Across The Road"

May joy be with you all! Credit: Dick Duane

REFERENCES

1. "'I didn't want anyone to know it was me: On being Joni Mitchell's 'Carey,'" Kate Mossman, *The New Statesman*, 19 December 2021.

2. "Touching Souls, *Joni Mitchell's lessons in love,*" book review by Dan Chiasson, *The New Yorker*, 02 October 2017.

3. "Motoring to a hippie reunion with college friends in Chapel Hill, North Carolina." *Voyager: Travel Writings*, Russell Banks, (Ecco, 2016)

4. "Broadcast interview with Cary Raditz," Art Silverman, "All Things Considered," *National Public Radio*," 09 December 2014

5. "Joni Mitchell on the Muse Behind 'Carey,'" Marc Myers, *The Wall Street Journal*, 11 November 2014.

6. "When Joni Mitchell Met Cary Raditz, Her 'Mean Old Daddy,'" Marc Myers, *The Wall Street Journal*, 11 November 2014.

7. *Girls Like Us*, Sheila Weller (Atria Books, 2008)

8. Variously mentioned or described in magazine articles, interviews and on stage over the years. *Rolling Stone, Vanity Fair*, & others.

Made in the USA
Columbia, SC
13 November 2023